Praise for *The RevOps Advantage*

"This is the playbook we've needed. *The RevOps Advantage* simplifies complexity, unifies teams, and transforms operational chaos into a competitive edge. If you're serious about growth, start here."
— **Mike Rizzo, CEO of MarketingOps.com**

"Finally a book that understands what RevOps really is. Reading this felt like grabbing coffee with the smartest ops person you know."
— **Matt Volm, CEO of RevOps Co-op**

"[*The RevOps Advantage*] is powerful, contextualized for the RevOps community, and crafted beautifully. This book demystifies RevOps and showcases how it is a powerful value differentiator in business. It's the definitive guide on how to unlock success and deliver sustainable transformation in the ever-evolving landscape of business operations."
— **Christi Lopez, EVP of Sales Operations and Strategy at TRADEBE**

"Since its debut, RevOps has puzzled many companies. Now the fastest-growing US business function, this handbook shows how to make it truly strategic."
— **Erik Charles, fractional CMO, CRO, and expert in sales enablement and performance**

"I am not much of a 'sit down and read a book' person, but this book was so captivating and informative, I couldn't put it down. Just when you thought you knew everything about RevOps, this book comes along and you learn so much more!"
— **Jim Sbarra, former VP of Global Sales at Domo and AVP of Sales Financial Services at Salesforce**

"Whether you are a beginner to RevOps or a chief revenue officer, this book has everything for you to become the most insightful person in the room. Step up your game in one easy read."

— Rob Levey, RevOps leader and former executive at Nokia

"This book is more than strategy—it's a recipe for building world class organizations."

— Oscar Armas-Luy, VP of Revenue Operations at Garner Health

"A must-read for every department. Gain insights from top-performing RevOps professionals and discover how Revenue Operations drives cross-functional impact and fuels business growth."

— Mari Manglaras, VP of Business Ops and Analytics

"Finally, a book that understands the real work of RevOps. It's full of practical playbooks, hard-earned lessons, and the kind of clarity you wish you had on day one. If you're building a RevOps function from scratch, or trying to fix one, start here. This book will save you months of trial and error and help you make better decisions faster."

— Jared Barol, GTM leader and RevOps advisor

"AI is changing how we work, but structure still determines whether we scale or stall. *The RevOps Advantage* shows how to build a future-ready RevOps function that thrives on agility, automation, and strategic insight. This is essential reading for every modern GTM leader."

— Louis Poulin, former VP of Revenue Operations at Amazon, Google, PayPal, and Cisco

"*The RevOps Advantage* is a must-read for any CEO looking to compete in today's world of light-speed maneuvering with AI technology. Having RevOps at your leadership table is the secret-weapon of today."

— Whitney Merrill, VP of Sales & Revenue Operations

"With so many ways to operate and automate, it's easy to feel overwhelmed about where to start or how to scale. *The RevOps Advantage* cuts through the noise with practical tools you can use right away, revealing the engine behind revenue growth and offering a clear framework you can implement."

— Laura Hayes, revenue leader and former Head of Ops at SurveyMonkey

"The FACTOR framework isn't just a model—it's a mindset shift. *The RevOps Advantage* redefines how we think about operational excellence and revenue acceleration."

— Sara Colton, VP of Revenue Operations at Labster

"We've all felt the pain of misaligned teams, messy data, and tech overload. The FACTOR Framework helps you bring it all together so people, process, and performance finally click."

— Cody Guymon, President of Zonos

"A must-read for every operator, seasoned or new. This book distills the history, proven strategies and real-world insights that have powered the success of some of today's most thoughtful GTM leaders."

— Lonny Sternberg, VP of Revenue Operations

"RevOps is getting the spotlight it deserves, and not a moment too soon. This book gives voice to the function as a driver of growth built on data, smart processes, financial know-how, and real cross-functional teamwork."

— Katerina Ostrovsky, Revenue Operations executive

"Many people ask me 'what is Revenue Operations?' This book not only answers that question but is the standard bearer for how to setup and operate a world class organization designed for efficient growth."

— Tom Germack, SVP of Revenue Operations at Oracle

"*The RevOps Advantage* shows how RevOps helps companies stay grounded and adaptable, even as everything around them changes. It reveals the secrets that will help a business keep growing no matter what."

— **Ben Davis, President and CRO of Lendio**

THE
REVOPS
ADVANTAGE

THE REVOPS ADVANTAGE

HOW TO

MAXIMIZE

YOUR

REVENUE

TEAMS' POTENTIAL

Amy Osmond Cook, PhD
Ryan Westwood
Bala Balabaskaran

PEAKPOINT
— PRESS —

Peakpoint Press books may be purchased in bulk at special discounts for sales promotion, corporate gifts, fund-raising, or educational purposes. Special editions can also be created to specifications. For details, contact the Special Sales Department, Skyhorse Publishing, 307 West 36th Street, 11th Floor, New York, NY 10018 or info@skyhorsepublishing.com.

Peakpoint® and Peakpoint Press® are registered trademarks of Skyhorse Publishing, Inc.®, a Delaware corporation.

Visit our website at www.skyhorsepublishing.com.

10 9 8 7 6 5 4 3 2 1

Library of Congress Cataloging-in-Publication Data is available on file.

Cover design by David Ter-Avanesyan

ISBN: 978-1-5107-8368-3
Ebook ISBN: 978-1-5107-8369-0

Printed in the United States of America

Contents

Part 3: Performance for Sustainable Growth

Introduction

The roar of engines at the Indianapolis Motor Speedway was deafening on May 31, 1965, but it wasn't just the cars on the track making history. Jim Clark, a driver from Scotland with a Lotus-Ford, started the Indy 500 in the middle of the pack against two-time champion A. J. Foyt. Clark's team had a secret card up their sleeve—Glen and Leonard Wood and their Wood Brothers Racing team.

The race kicked off with the iconic cannon blast, and the thirty-three cars were off. Clark's Lotus-Ford took the lead by lap 3, where it stayed until lap 65, when he handed over the lead to Foyt for a pit stop. This is where the real race was won.

According to a historical account from the Indianapolis Motor Speedway, the Wood Brothers Racing team was famous for pioneering choreographed pit stops in the NASCAR Grand National circuit, a stark contrast to the more improvisational approach typical in open-wheel racing at the time. With careful preparation and new innovations, including using a new gravity-flow refueling system that put fifty-eight gallons of fuel in the car under fifteen seconds, the Wood Brothers redefined what it meant to be part of a pit crew.[1]

Clark only needed to make two stops during the entire two-hundred-lap race. At the time, each pit stop was expected to last up to a full minute. Clark's pit crew got the Lotus-Ford back on the track within a groundbreaking seventeen seconds on the first stop and twenty-five seconds during the second, adding up to less time than most other cars would spend in the pit for the entire race.[2]

The Wood Brothers' approach gave Clark the edge he needed to win, according to an official historical account from Wood Brothers Racing. His Lotus-Ford became the first car with a Ford engine to win the Indy 500.

Clive Chapman, owner of Team Lotus, "jumped over the wall and congratulated us right there on pit road, hugging our necks and everything," Leonard Wood was recorded saying. Later, he said his brother and himself "got the most publicity in the least amount of time that we ever got in our lives."

"We hit a home run for sure," he said.

Every millisecond saved on that pit road was a strategic advantage, perfectly executed. At the time of this publishing, the world record for a pit crew change is now 1.8 seconds—made by the McLaren Racing Limited pit crew in 2023, according to *USA Today* reporting[3]—but it was the revolutionizing Woods Brothers who are remembered for kicking off the race for ultimate efficiency and coordination.

Today, Revenue Operations (RevOps) is the business equivalent of the Woods Brothers' pit crew. Just as their precision and innovation transformed pit stops into a fine-tuned, choreographed dance that wins races, RevOps unites sales, marketing, finance, and customer success into a synchronized engine of growth. RevOps wins the revenue race.

Defining the RevOps Advantage

Like the Woods Brothers, every race car driver has a pit crew. But not every driver has a perfectly choreographed pit crew and a powerful refueling system in their back pocket.

Every business has developed its own approaches to enabling and supporting sales and revenue-related functions, but not every business has figured out how to use these core operational processes to its strategic advantage.

Consider a start-up company that is entering its growth phase. During the first few years, the company is able to rely on a tight-knit, cross-functional group of leaders to establish a Go-to-Market strategy and then to support the organization in consistently meeting its revenue goals. In the initial phases, you're really working alongside one person sitting within the sales operations team and one person in the marketing operations team. It's a much smaller environment, so you're always talking to each other.

But as this company keeps expanding, core operational processes can no longer be managed by a single, internally aligned group. Sales, marketing, and customer success all become their own fully formed divisions with defined workflows and articulated quality-control processes. Bureaucratic principles take over. Seamless, effortless communication gives way to much more limited and formal interaction—and possibly to silos and distrust.

In an organization like this, it's not uncommon for:

- The marketing team to never have received a comprehensive description of the target ICP.
- The sales team to be in the dark about a new marketing campaign even after it's already rolled out.
- Customer success teams to be handed a new customer without knowing anything about what motivated them to buy.

Most businesses don't have good solutions to these challenges as they scale. As a result, businesses often resign themselves to inefficiencies, lack of coordination, and communication breakdowns.

But when a business has a strategic RevOps core, it isn't forced to give up on efficiency, coordination, and cross-functional planning to achieve growth. To the contrary, the business learns how to lean into these practices while scaling to transcend beyond bureaucracy and achieve a new interconnectedness among complexity.

That's the essence of the RevOps advantage. It's about fundamentally altering our paradigms about what it means to go to market and how it should be achieved.

In this book, we'll show you how to become the RevOps pit crew your business needs to win.

Our version of the Wood Brothers' gravity refueling system is AI-enabled RevOps software and processes—tools that eliminate inefficiencies, speed up decision-making, and empower teams to focus on what really matters. But how and where to implement that system is key. RevOps leaders deserve a strategic seat at the table because they can see everything from a bird's-eye view; they can know things that other executives don't.

When seamless coordination and split-second precision define success, RevOps is the ultimate advantage for getting ahead and staying ahead of the pack.

Who We Are

If you're reading this, chances are you've felt the challenges of aligning your company's Go-to-Market efforts, from sales to marketing to customer success. Your Go-to-Market plan may look like a work of art on paper, but in execution, it's a little chaotic. Maybe you've struggled to scale efficiently, or perhaps you've wrestled with how to move from a great strategy on paper to execution that actually works. This book is your road map to unlocking the full power of RevOps—not just as a function, but as the strategic seat at the table for scaling smarter, faster, and more efficiently.

We know what works because we've been there. The three of us (Ryan Westwood, Bala Balabaskaran, and Amy Cook) were RevOps leaders before the name "RevOps" in its modern usage was coined. In this book, we'll take you through what it means to embrace RevOps not just as the strategic "pit crew" of your organization, but as a mindset—a transformative approach to achieving predictable growth and operational excellence.

As a serial tech entrepreneur in Utah's "Silicon Slopes," Ryan has successfully exited three companies, including Simplus, which he grew from $0 and sold for $250 million to Infosys with his brother Isaac Westwood, Lance Evanson, and Amy Cook on the team. Now, as CEO of Fullcast, he's leading the charge in transforming how businesses achieve operational excellence. He has invested in over fifty start-ups as a venture capitalist and angel investor. His accolades include Ernst & Young Entrepreneur of the Year and Utah Business CEO of the Year.

Along with Isaac, Lance, Bala, and Amy, Ryan founded Fullcast to solve the complex challenges of Go-to-Market planning and execution—starting with territory planning. Drawing on their experience scaling Simplus, they reunited to take on the next big challenge: eliminating the manual, error-prone processes behind Go-to-Market execution and building a platform that automates and streamlines how revenue teams plan and operate.

"[Ryan's] vision to build a business that helps sales teams cover market opportunities, equitably set challenging but attainable targets, and calibrate future growth and capacity is meeting a major pain point for sales executives," said Tommy Barlow, Vice President of Global Sales at LearnUpon.

A pioneer in the world of RevOps, Bala Balabaskaran is an original cofounder and the chief technology officer of Fullcast. With an incredible wealth of experience as a technology entrepreneur and architect, Bala has a strong track record in designing and implementing large-scale technical systems. He has held executive roles where he built top-tier software engineering and operations teams, excelling in both start-up environments and Fortune 500 companies. Before Fullcast, Bala was the VP of GTM Ops and Tech at Salesforce. While working at Salesforce, Bala led groundbreaking efforts to automate planning and operations, helping the company triple its annual recurring revenue (ARR), expand its sales team threefold, and achieve its most accurate forecasting. After managing an annual planning process that required 1,500 spreadsheets, a team of one hundred, and six months of effort, he decided to leave Salesforce and cofound Fullcast.

Amy has built her career on values that revenue operations leaders hold dear: unity, hard work, alignment, and transparency. Her experience in RevOps spans technology, health care, and other verticals, and she has been fortunate to help several companies grow as the CMO from Series A through acquisition, including Simplus in 2020, PathologyWatch in 2023, and Onboard in 2024. Before Fullcast, Amy spent fifteen years as the founder and CEO of Stage Marketing, a leading full-funnel marketing firm. She also earned a PhD in communication from the University of Utah, worked as an adjunct professor for over twenty-five years intermittently at Arizona State University, University of Utah, and Brigham Young University, and has written extensively on marketing and business.

We're excited to share our experiences, our insights, and our frameworks with you. But enough about us for now. Let's talk about what you can get out of reading *The RevOps Advantage*.

Who This Book Is For

This book is for leaders and teams who are ready to get their revenue engines humming—to align departments, plan and execute efficiently, know how to use data to their advantage, and transform their Go-to-Market. Whether you're a seasoned executive, an emerging RevOps leader, or someone navigating operational challenges for the first time, you'll find actionable insights and frameworks based on research and our experience on what actually works.

Here's who will benefit most:

- **RevOps Leaders:** If you're responsible for planning, operations, or execution, this book is your guide to elevating your role, building alignment across teams, and automating processes to deliver measurable results.
- **CEOs and Founders:** You want to scale smarter and align your organization for growth. This book will help you understand why RevOps is critical to achieving predictable revenue and operational excellence.
- **Sales, Marketing, and Customer Success Leaders:** You're on the front lines of growth and need strategies to break down silos, improve cross-functional collaboration, and make data-driven decisions.
- **Finance and Operations Professionals:** You're tasked with ensuring resources are deployed effectively. This book will show you how to connect strategy and execution seamlessly to improve efficiency and outcomes.
- **Investors and Business Strategists:** Whether you're advising start-ups or scaling enterprises, you'll gain a clear understanding of how RevOps drives valuation, growth, and competitive advantage.

- **Interested Individuals:** If you're curious about RevOps as a career path, this book will give you a comprehensive understanding of the role and its growing impact on modern businesses.

What You'll Get from This Book

Through this book, we'll share frameworks like the RevOps Maturity Model, insights from AI-driven automation, and practical tips to elevate your organization's operational efficiency.

You'll learn how to:

1. Elevate the role of RevOps in your organization and why CEOs must prioritize it.
2. Align planning and execution for seamless Go-to-Market strategies.
3. Build agility into your processes, enabling your team to pivot quickly and stay ahead of the competition.
4. Leverage automation to reduce inefficiencies and focus on what matters most—driving revenue growth.

So buckle up; this journey isn't just about optimizing processes. It's about transforming how your business competes, grows, and wins—and giving it an unfair advantage like the Wood Brothers gave Lotus-Ford in 1965.

Let the race begin.

Part 1

Foundations

1

Why We Need RevOps

The year was 2012. Bala had just started his position as the Vice President of Go-to-Market Technology and Operations at Salesforce. This was the golden age of Salesforce. It was tripling its ARR and expanding its sales team threefold. At the center of this success was the Go-to-Market RevOps team, tasked with aligning planning and operations to keep the company's revenue engine running smoothly.

The tools available to RevOps at the time weren't built for the complexity of the role. Bala found himself at the center of the annual planning cycle. His team endured a painstaking six months of effort involving approximately four hundred managers and leaders across the revenue organization, over 1,500 spreadsheets and a planning collective of four hundred people across the company involved in planning. The executive team was happy.

Bala was tired, and his team memorialized the experience as the "year that shall not be named." The sales team was somewhat satisfied. They took their territories and went to work, but there was no feedback connection between the plan and execution, so a lot of the benefit of this massive amount of work was eroded by the daily practical challenges of running RevOps. Bala finally threw his hands in the air and said, "There must be a better way."

Meanwhile, in another part of California, Amy was leading a Go-to-Market agency that focused on connecting different parts of the revenue engine. For fifteen years, she worked with the executive teams of hundreds of companies to build sales, RevOps, and marketing departments that would work together holistically. It was exhilarating but exhausting work. After helping multiple companies grow from Series A through acquisition, Amy saw common patterns in the companies who succeeded and those who failed. She wished there were a product available to help companies grow efficiently, align on common metrics, and work harmoniously between departments. But she was seeing a lot of revenue (and emotional) pain in companies and losing faith that sales and marketing would ever really be friends.

A few hundred miles away, in the heart of Salt Lake City, Ryan was leading a B2B IT managed services team. Shortly thereafter, he founded and led a Salesforce advisory, implementation, and managed services company focused on Salesforce RevOps products like Configure Price Quote.[4] Like Amy, he saw client after client implement software—and began to see patterns of why some companies were successful and some were not.

As Go-to-Market operators and strategists, we know how hard it can be to achieve efficient growth, especially in the headwinds of difficult market conditions. As consultants for several decades (about seventy-five years between the three of us!), it's hard to see clients that you care about come up short and not achieve their goals.

But there *is a way* for business growth to be easier, systematic, and predictable. Businesses can accurately forecast growth. Data-driven insights can serve as the source of truth for decision-making. Processes can trump politics. Business diagnostics and prognostics can be available at every stage of the customer journey. But it is only possible with a unified Go-to-Market. And a unified Go-to-Market is only possible with a strategic revenue operations function prioritized by the CEO.

This paradigm—what we call the "RevOps FACTOR"—has emerged as a critical function for businesses today. It is the operating system for businesses in a post-pandemic world that must straddle bureaucracy with digital transformation and now faces yet another paradigm shift with artificial intelligence. It's the secret sauce for companies who want to grow predictably and efficiently. More foundationally, it's a function that has become necessary for companies to survive. This book is designed to show how that strategic RevOps function can and should be built.

Revenue Operations is the secret. We'll show you why and how to make it work for you. First, we'll start with a few examples of RevOps in history. RevOps has existed as long as people have been using money—but it has been called by different names, and the modern iteration is quite recent and specific. Next, we'll discuss why RevOps, as we conceptualize it today, is critical for business to thrive. We'll discuss bureaucracy, digital transformation, artificial intelligence, and the need to have RevOps navigate an organization through these.

RevOps Through Time

Revenue operations has been around for thousands of years. At its core, revenue operations is the process of aligning teams, processes, and tools across an organization's revenue-generating departments. As long as there has been revenue, there has been RevOps.

A Look Back

The **Ancient Roman Taxation System** was a case study in RevOps. Revenue operations were highly *aligned*, with tax collectors, governors, and military ensuring that taxes could be collected without rebellion. There was a *centralized data* and reporting system, with detailed censuses and regular reporting. There was *process optimization*, with both poll and land taxes adjusted based on economic status and productivity, respectively. *Tools and technology* such as standardized currency were advanced for their time. The Romans even *forecasted* their revenue. They ranked provinces by type of economic output (e.g., grain from Egypt, silver from Hispania, etc.) to accurately forecast resources to build roads, social programs, and military resources. Caesar Augustus reported that the annual revenue for Rome was 500 million sesterces in 49 BCE, according to the book *The Reckoning: Financial Accountability and the Rise and Fall of Nations*.[5] By today's standards, that is roughly $7.25 billion, according to a subsequent published analysis.[6]

Fast-forward a couple millennia and you have the Ford Motor Company. Under the leadership of Henry Ford, the production of the Model T began in the early 1900s. Manufacturing, Sales, and Customer Success were *highly aligned* to ensure a steady supply of vehicles, which would then be sold and maintained. Ford *centralized reporting* of tracked costs, sales volume, production rates, and customer preferences. Ford thoroughly *disrupted and optimized processes* with the moving assembly line, reducing the time to produce a Model T from twelve hours to just over ninety minutes.[7] Ford utilized only the best machinery and standardized parts, giving them the best *technology and tools* in the industry. And careful revenue *forecasting* enabled Ford to both drop the price of a Model T (from $850 to $260) and introduce a $5 wage for an eight-hour workday to ensure loyalty.[8] By 1918, Ford had reached a 10 percent market share and by 1927, the company produced more than 15 million Model T cars.[9]

Over time, rapid industrialization and modernization produced larger and more complex organizations, many of them becoming increasingly unwieldy. This led to the rise of bureaucracy. Proponents of this dominant organizational philosophy such as Max Weber saw it as the most rational, efficient, and fair organizational system.[10] Hallmarks of this system included division of labor, clear boundaries between departments, strict hierarchy, rigid roles and boundaries, and economies of scale.

While many organizations became more efficient, over time the "iron cage" of bureaucracy reared its ugly head, leading to feelings of alienation (lost freedom), dehumanization (cogs in a machine), and many silos. Bureaucracy became the silent killer, as companies that fully embraced the rigidity of bureaucracy struggled to compete with more agile organizations.[11]

Nokia is a great example of a company failing due to complacency and bureaucracy.[12] Its decline, largely through an inability to recognize, adapt, or react to a platform-and-software-based market shift that led to the rise of smartphones, allowing Apple, Google, and other companies to overtake its market share. In only six years, Nokia went from owning 49 percent of the market share in 2007 to only 3 percent in 2013. Decision-making was slow and inefficient with bureaucratic layers of hierarchy and multiple approvals. This slow decision-making delayed the recognition that software was becoming critical to the success of mobile devices. Like most bureaucracies, departments operated in silos with limited communication and upheld the status quo. Nokia, once known for its innovation, was paralyzed and lacked agility and creativity needed to adapt and win in the market. Its competitors were leveraging single-platform operating systems, iOS and Android, while Nokia struggled with fifty-seven versions of Symbian for its vast array of hardware-based mobile phones.

Other organizations, such as Kodak, Blockbuster, and Polaroid, were subject to the silent killer of bureaucracy and experienced the same decline. The detrimental effects of these silos were especially pronounced in revenue-generating teams, where alignment and cross-functional collaboration are essential.

Revenue Enters the Digital Age

In 1951, when bureaucracy was in its golden age, the Universal Automatic Computer 1, or UNIVAC I, was born. Developed mostly by J. Presper Eckert and John Maunchly, it was the first computer designed for business applications in the United States. The Remington Rand Company, who owned the UNIVAC I, partnered on a marketing campaign with CBS to predict the 1952 United States presidential election. UNIVAC I predicted that Dwight D. Eisenhower would win in a landslide over Adlai Stevenson and win the Electoral College 438 to 93. The Gallup Poll, on the other hand, predicted Eisenhower would win in a close contest. On election night, UNIVAC shined. It had a margin of error of 3.5 percent of Eisenhower's popular vote tally (34,075,029 votes) and was within four votes of the electoral vote total. This historic occasion gave the public greater awareness of computing technology and began the computerized predictions of election night broadcasts.

This pioneering effort, along with many others, began what we now refer to as "digital transformation," defined simply as "the integration of digital technology into business to transform processes and deliver value to customers." While a full history of digital transformation is beyond the scope of this book, a few examples through time stand out.

In the 1970s, General Motors and IBM created an early graphical computer-aided design (CAD) system called the DAC-1, allowing engineers to create, modify, and send designs directly to milling machines. This innovation led to the proliferation of CAD systems in automotive, architecture, and other industries. AT&T developed the UNIX operating system in 1973, which was groundbreaking for its portability, multiuser functionality, modularity, hierarchical file system, and client-server model that laid the foundation for the early infrastructure of digital communication. In 1976, Queen Elizabeth II hit "send" on her first email. The same year, cofounders Steve Wozniak and Steve Jobs had just launched Apple Computer.

In the 1980s, the personal computer was born, making computers accessible for many households. IBM's PC was introduced in 1981, and Apple's Macintosh—with a graphical interface—was launched in 1984. The standardization of the ethernet facilitating local area networks (LANs) in business settings and the introduction of the domain name system (DNS), also helped to advance networking.

In the 1990s, the modern internet was born. While early instances of the internet had been used by the Department of Defense since the 1960s and by research scientists since the 1980s, the World Wide Web as we know it was developed by English scientist Tim Berners-Lee. Mosaic came online in 1993. Netscape Navigator was introduced in 1994. And Microsoft's Internet Explorer came online in 1995.

In the 2000s, we went mobile and social. LinkedIn launched in 2003, Facebook in 2004, and Twitter in 2006. These platforms redefined social interaction. Apple launched the iPhone in 2007, which brought communication, internet browsing, and multimedia onto one device. In 2007, approximately 115 million smartphones were sold globally. In 2024, about 1.22 billion smartphones were sold.

The 2010s got very interesting for digital transformation in business. AWS, Microsoft Azure, and Google Cloud introduced a global system of distributed servers, along with the software and databases that run on those servers, ethereally called "the Cloud."

Data became a critical enterprise asset to drive decision-making, personalize the customer experience, and enhance efficiency. Cloud computing allowed businesses to shift technology infrastructure from a one-time capital expenditure (CapEx) to scalable operational expenditures (OpEx), which improves cash flow management, gives greater flexibility to companies, allows for remote work, and has tax benefits. CRM companies such as Salesforce (started in 1999) and HubSpot (started in 2006) gained popularity as companies became more adept at managing customer relationships in the Cloud. The 2020s—this decade, as we write this book in 2025—has been dominated by the integration of artificial intelligence and automation. AI technology has significantly progressed, with companies like OpenAI and Google introducing large language models (LLMs) such as ChatGPT and Gemini. While digital transformation was about deterministic automation, where armies of engineers automated manual processes, the AI revolution looks different based on the speed at which the change is happening. The automation with AI is self-learning, allowing for autonomous agents to evolve and optimize the automation without it being deterministic.

GTM software companies like Fullcast offer AI-powered solutions to drastically reduce the time to value for strategic tasks such as territory and policy management.

The Clash Between Digital Transformation and Bureaucracy

Today, in a society that many of us call the postmodern digital age, technological advances have transformed how most organizations operate. Vestiges of bureaucracy remain in large, long-standing organizations, but the effects of digital transformation have changed how we define organizations, how we construct our own organizational identities, and how we build systems to reinforce our beliefs about what organizations could and should be. (If you want to deep dive into organizational communication theory, read Amy's PhD dissertation.)

The digital age prioritizes real-time collaboration, automation, transparency, and agile methodologies. Digital communication tools like Slack and Teams have democratized communication, making hierarchical communication structures less appealing and organizational structures more flat and networked. AI and automation have automated away some of the administrative work, allowing more of the organization to focus on strategic activities. CRMs and BI tools have allowed rigid "we've always done it this way" rules to be replaced with centralized data-driven insights. Digital tools have replaced lengthy paper-based processes with immediate access. It's easier than ever to have a distributed virtual work environment (although, even in 2025, this remote-vs.-office debate continues to rage).

Technology's most compelling disruption—for this discussion, anyway—is that its *agile methodologies*, which prioritize flexibility, collaboration, and rapid iteration, challenge the foundations of bureaucracy itself. Lean methodologies, which strive to reduce waste and improve customer satisfaction, are prioritized. But, even with the new-and-improved transformational philosophy, stodgy old bureaucratic principles like overengineered digital processes, rigid compliance rules, and data silos continue to reinforce some of the worst parts of bureaucracy.

Why We Need RevOps Now

The technological advances of the digital age have given us the permission and tools to break down bureaucracy and refocus on alignment and process optimization. It has never been more important for organizations to blend structure with innovation, stability with agility, and thoroughness with speed. This is where Revenue Operations in its most recent incarnation has taken shape.

One of the biggest challenges in scaling revenue operations is ensuring alignment across different functional areas—marketing, sales, and customer success. Too often, these teams operate in silos, each focused on their own part of the funnel without a clear view of the entire customer life cycle.

As Olga Traskova, Vice President of Revenue Operations at Birdeye, explains in a *Go To Market Podcast* with Amy Cook,[13] "Unfortunately, when marketing ops is working on the top funnel and customer success ops is working on retention, they might step on each other's toes, and they might not even realize what's going on on the other side of the process. So what I'm working on now within the team is to ensure that everyone is aware of the entire customer journey, that they understand all of the stages and the processes within the entire customer journey, from lead to cash, and then from extra cash, from the upsells."

A mature RevOps function breaks down these silos by fostering visibility and collaboration across the entire revenue engine. This means aligning marketing, sales, and customer success operations around a unified data framework, shared metrics, and seamless handoffs between teams. When every function understands how their processes impact the next stage of the journey, companies can reduce friction, improve customer experience, and drive more predictable revenue growth.

True RevOps success comes from an end-to-end mindset—one that sees revenue as a continuous cycle rather than disconnected departmental goals. In this section, we'll discuss what RevOps looks like today and introduce a framework for RevOps success.

RevOps Today

Amid complex business operations buoyed by the growth of SaaS in 2015 to 2016, companies recognized the demands for personalized customer experiences, faster Go-to-Market, more efficient territory and capacity planning, and the need to simplify often complex strategies. Leveraging AI and advancements in real-time data analytics required a more collaborative, centralized management model with intentional leadership. The focus of this shift was to improve revenue outcomes via streamlined process and team alignment. In 2016, Evan Liang, CEO at LeanDat, called it RevOps.[14]

At the time, Evan was working alongside sales and marketing teams who were struggling to align their efforts and make sense of their shared goals. Like the DevOps revolution happening in IT and software, he saw the need for a new approach—one focused on collaboration, visibility, and data-driven decision-making. And he wasn't alone.

Large technology companies were organically seeing the same problems and utilizing the same solutions. Google, for example, invests significantly in *forecasting* tools, such as TensorFlow, to predict Google Cloud and Ad revenue across industries, time, and even seasonality. It sets shared OKRs (Objectives and Key Results) across the entire Go-to-Market function. This *alignment* even extends to cross-functional product development. Google *centralizes* its data through tools like BigQuery, and teams use its own product—Looker—to create customizable dashboards.

AI-driven tools such as Campaign Optimization and Smart Bidding, and customer data platforms allow Google and their customers to unify and manage data through *technology*. Continuous *optimization* is a foundational Google tenet, as it utilizes A/B testing, process automation, and pricing optimization for continuous improvement. This RevOps philosophy in action, of course, is all guided by an overarching objective to incrementally increase revenue.

"I have experienced that when RevOps is positioned as a strategic department and empowered with autonomy to work 'in' the business and 'on' the business, it is these revenue operators that have the lenses, strategic and technical skills to communicate across many cross-functional departments to identify and keep the business aligned before a problem arises, and support course correction when necessary," Lonny Sternberg, a revenue operations[15] leader, said.

By 2019, companies with dedicated RevOps groups had surged from 20 to 31 percent[16] in just a year. Forrester validated the trend two years later in 2021,[17] revealing that 57 percent of companies planned to invest in a RevOps function within the next year. Most often, these RevOps teams reported to a chief revenue officer, signaling just how critical RevOps had become to executive strategy and business growth. Companies that implemented a unified GTM strategy across their sales and marketing teams achieved 36 percent more revenue growth and up to 28 percent more profitability,[18] solidifying that RevOps is here to stay.

"I love the juncture of Revenue Operations and business transformations," wrote Christi Lopez, EVP of Sales Operations and Strategy at TRADEBE, in a LinkedIn post.[19] "It is a space that energizes me—seeing strategies come to life and a vision going from 'what if' to tangible results. Most of all, I'm energized by teams working together and doing the gritty, detailed, messy work. Slogging it out, building something each person is proud to be a part of, and enjoying the results together."

Fast Growth

In 2022, LinkedIn ranked the "Director of RevOps"[20] role as the fourth fastest-growing job in America. Companies were looking to fill a job position they had yet to fully understand. Is it sales? Marketing? According to Mike Ciulla at RevOps Co-op,[21] every member of the Go-to-Market team should "have a little RevOps in them."

"At a minimum we want GTM teams to have access to resources that can help them learn, solve problems, and reduce the burden of 'supporting the business' on all things operations," Mike said. "We also need the business teams: the operators in Sales, Marketing, and Customer Success, to be leading RevOps. These domain experts are building plans, adjusting to changes in the market, pivoting, building models, committing to quotas. They're generating revenue."

RevOps has officially leveled up—from back-office support to mission-critical strategy. What triggered this seismic shift? According to RevOps experts at Captivate Talent,[22] the economic climate, tech innovations, and executive leadership all play pivotal roles.

Economic Wake-Up Call: COVID-19, the Great Resignation, and volatile capital markets put an end to the "grow at all costs" mentality. Suddenly, efficiency wasn't just the topic of casual conversation—it marked the difference between thriving and folding. RevOps stepped in to build a more innovative and sustainable path forward.

Tech Revolution: AI, automation, and cutting-edge RevOps tools aren't just making life easier—they're reshaping the entire revenue engine. Those who harness them are setting the Go-to-Market pace and leading the charge.

A Seat at the Power Table: RevOps leaders now report straight to the CEO, influencing the most significant decisions in the business. Revenue operations keeps the GTM machine running, but it's more about creating data-driven strategies that drive where to go next.

Key Shifts Defining the Future of Business

Why is the RevOps paradigm working so well? Because it is vital to four key digital shifts that are redefining the future of business: AI and automation, the growing complexity of scaling in a digital-first world, the increasing importance of data-driven decisions, and the need to thrive during economic uncertainty.

AI and Automation. We're living in a world where artificial intelligence has evolved from being a futuristic gimmick in sci-fi movies to something driving real results. According to Salesforce data, 83 percent of sales teams using AI reported revenue growth this year compared to just 66 percent without it.[23] For RevOps leaders, AI is the superpower we've been waiting for. With the right AI tools, it can automate repetitive, time-consuming tasks that bog down teams, like manual updates, lead routing, and territory adjustments. More importantly, AI unlocks insights faster, enabling RevOps leaders to make smarter decisions with confidence.

But let's be clear: AI is not the pilot, nor can it ever be (sorry, *Terminator* fans). AI might correct errors, analyze data, and predict trends, but it still needs human strategy to guide it. RevOps leaders need to be the ones to operate their AI tool kits, steering their teams based on the best insights and data. This partnership between technology and leadership makes RevOps more effective and strategic than ever before. When AI is applied well, RevOps enables GTM teams to pivot quickly, seize opportunities, and focus on what really drives revenue.

Scaling in a digital-first world. Today, buyers are more informed, more demanding, and harder to reach. We're operating in a multichannel, digital-first world, where customers expect seamless experiences from the first click to the final handshake. Every touchpoint matters, and Go-to-Market teams can't afford to work in silos. RevOps can bring alignment to marketing, sales, and customer success so everyone's flying in formation, not off in separate directions.

Data-driven decision-making. Without RevOps, teams risk missing opportunities or doubling their efforts unnecessarily. But with RevOps, Go-to-Market teams have clarity: Territories are balanced, leads are routed accurately, and handoffs are seamless. It's the kind of efficiency that turns chaos into momentum.

Economic uncertainty. Longer sales cycles, shrinking budgets, and cautious buyers have made it harder than ever to hit targets. Companies can't afford wasted time or resources. RevOps becomes the competitive advantage that separates thriving businesses from struggling ones. By focusing on data-driven decisions and efficiency, RevOps ensures that teams stay agile and laser-focused on revenue growth even when the road ahead feels shaky.

Businesses that thrive in uncertain times are the ones that can pivot fast, make decisions with precision, and eliminate inefficiencies before they drag the team down. If you're doing it correctly, RevOps is what makes this possible. It's the strategic nerve center that connects the dots, keeps the ship steady, and identifies the smartest path through the asteroid field. The future belongs to the companies who get it right.

2

Why We Need Strategic RevOps Leaders

In 2005, Ryan was in the zone, sitting in front of his computer late into the evening, focused on customizing dashboards for their company on SugarCRM. He and Shelly Warren, a talented developer, were knee-deep in building tools that didn't yet exist in the broader market: custom commission reports, forecasting systems, and even a dialer. They were creating the foundation for systems that would later define billion-dollar platforms like Clari and Xactly.

It was a thrill to be solving problems tied directly to revenue generation and operational efficiency. Each tweak to the system felt like another piece of a complex puzzle falling into place. It wasn't the most common way for executives to enjoy spending their time. And yet, here he was, more energized than exhausted, driven by the idea that better systems could mean better results.

These jam sessions with Shelly eventually formed part of a realization that would stay with Ryan throughout his career: Businesses run on revenue, but they thrive on innovation and operational excellence. For every exciting launch or major deal, there's an ecosystem of systems and strategies quietly driving that success. Ryan wasn't just building software tools that night; he was experiencing the power of aligning operations to create sustainable growth.

Now more than ever, the systems, processes, and strategies behind revenue operations matter at the highest level of leadership. Whether a CEO partners with a skilled RevOps leader or really gets into the weeds like Ryan enjoyed doing, the path to growth is built on operational alignment, informed decisions driven by data, and streamlined efficiency.

"Everything in RevOps is context dependent, and so those of us in RevOps are artists in the sense that we have to know the rules, but we also have to know when to break them," said Oscar Armas-Luy, Vice President of Revenue Operations at Garner Health, in a *Go To Market Podcast* with Amy Cook.[24] "There's sort of a dogma of best practices, or standard practices, in RevOps that don't make sense in every single context. Great RevOps people know all the best practices. Extraordinary RevOps people know all of the best practices and the ones to ignore in their particular context. And I think that's what we really have to master."

Above all, there are two things that matter to all CEOs: predictable revenue growth and bottom-line EBITDA (earnings before interest, taxes, depreciation, and amortization). No matter what company a CEO is running, no matter what industry, revenue and EBITDA are the numbers that matter. If you are a RevOps leader, you are in a position to impact both metrics in a meaningful way. This aligns you to the CEO more than you may realize. In this chapter we'll discuss your impact, four ways you can bring strategic value to the CEO, how to communicate your value, and how your value may change depending on the size of the company.

Your Impact as a Revenue Leader

You're not just focused on revenue growth. You're focused on *efficient* revenue growth. The more we speak with revenue operations leaders, the more we realize the outsize impact they're having on companies. However they seem to struggle communicating that impact internally.

The result often sets up the RevOps leader for criticism should a process break down, and little praise when things run smoothly. Leaders can change this cycle of blame with strategic and proactive communication that focuses on the value they bring.

"I think about the strategy and Ops world in three buckets," explained Noah Marks, SVP and Head of Commercial Strategy and Operations,[25] during a recent interview with Amy. "One is strategy-related business partners. These folks are aligned with business leaders in the company. Then, some folks are more systems-process-technology-oriented, which is more holistic. Thirdly, there's an analytics bucket of people focused on what's happening with the trends and datasets, and they are digging in to understand what's happening. Those three areas make the strategy part successful, with the business partners advising on what we should be doing about the business's health and how we can hit or exceed our targets."

Sometimes RevOps leaders short sell themselves because they are internally focused, even though the impact they have on customers and the customer journey is huge. If RevOps leaders do their job right, the people, process, and technology they put in place will directly impact the customers' experience through their journey with the company. Moreover, if you're able to communicate to your CEO and CFO how you've either impacted revenue growth or EBITDA, you will become invaluable to the company.

Let's say, for example, you noticed that the CMO and CRO have purchased software from two different companies but both companies provide similar products. Because you were not siloed to a particular department, you saw the duplication of efforts and spoke to each of them about the opportunity to consolidate to one vendor. You now have the opportunity to impact both the bottom and top line of the company.

In another example, you implement a sales enablement platform. The platform helps to ramp new sales reps in sixty days instead of ninety days. This reduces the cost of ramping up an account executive and gets them selling faster. Again, you've impacted the top and bottom lines of the company.

You find a new AI tool that positively impacts your prospecting efforts. The CRO, sales leaders, and CMO will definitely be talking about the increase in pipeline. They may not even mention the new tools you've deployed. This is why it's important that you articulate your value on an ongoing basis.

Your Unique Strategic Value

Here are a few areas where we believe you bring unique strategic value to the CEO, CFO, and the board:

RevOps leaders serve as the bridge between various departments. You ensure that the CEO and board have the comprehensive insights needed to steer the company toward sustained growth and success.

"I remember sitting in a meeting with Maria Martinez and the CEO, at the time, of a very large telco. The comment he made is telling of a missed opportunity by RevOps. He said, 'I only see your reps when they are assigned to the account, during renewal, or to tell me someone else is taking over the account.' This experience is not very different from how we experience relationships in the SaaS world today," Bala said. "This to me is a failure of the RevOps team. They must continually be looking to ease the customer experience."

Bala emphasized that the customer experience must be the primary focus while you optimize internal processes. "Too often RevOps leaders are focused on optimizing processes and implementing technology to make their lives easier or make the lives of internal revenue teams' lives easier—often at the expense of the customer experience." he said.

Unlike other department leaders who often operate within their silos, RevOps leaders can see the complete picture and make data-driven connections that might otherwise remain isolated. This holistic view allows them to identify trends, inefficiencies, and opportunities across departments. By understanding how these functions impact each other, a RevOps leader can recommend strategies that drive overall success rather than optimizing just one area at the expense of another.

This unique perspective is incredibly valuable to the CEO and board. With insights that span multiple departments, they can highlight areas where collaboration can be improved, resources can be better allocated, and processes can be streamlined, ultimately supporting data-driven decisions that enhance overall business performance.

RevOps leaders are a trusted source for truth (as measured by metrics) outside of individual departments. In this trusted advisor role, your value extends beyond just reporting numbers. You become a strategic partner who anticipates challenges, identifies opportunities, and provides solutions backed by data.

The race toward more efficient Go-to-Market shows 87 percent of cloud companies investing in sales enablement. However, interpreting metrics to ensure Go-to-Market remains on track still requires expertise. The RevOps leader's insights can drive initiatives that enhance efficiency, optimize resource allocation, and improve overall performance.

By consistently delivering accurate and timely data, you build trust and confidence with the CEO and board, solidifying your position as an indispensable asset to the leadership team. This level of trust and reliance on your expertise ensures that your contributions are recognized and valued at the highest levels of the organization.

For example, let's say you notice that the CRO has quietly changed the definition of an SQL (sales-qualified lead). You realize the pipeline isn't as healthy as the executive team and board may think it is. It's your job to call this out.

RevOps leaders democratize data and enable organization-wide business processes. A successful RevOps leader's ability to integrate systems and drive efficiency makes them the glue that holds everything together—key traits that make them stand out. RevOps leaders are like the architects of revenue generation, working across sales, marketing, and customer success to optimize processes and ensure smooth data flow.

Although their title may not always reflect their function, studies show that 23 percent of RevOps professionals have been working in revenue operations for over a decade. The best revenue operations leaders I know have spent time in all disciplines of revenue operations before leading the department. For example, they may have spent time focused on just compensation, territory management, deal desk, or sales enablement before leading the department. They thrive in the data-driven, cross-functional world, ensuring all revenue teams are in sync and delivering results.

"Elevate yourself to looking at the bigger picture and impacting both strategy and execution," said Mudit Garg, SVP and GTM Operator.[26] "Consider yourself as a 'super agent' who orchestrates, is goal oriented, understands the intent and strategy, and pulls in the subagents with specialized skills runtime for best performance"

RevOps leaders are intermediaries between GTM & other departments. One of the tough aspects of being a CEO is balancing the needs of your CRO and CFO. You can act as a commonsense third party in these situations. Here are a few examples:

The CFO may want to cut software that is critical to the growth of the business, but the CRO doesn't know how to articulate this to the CFO, and the CEO doesn't know which side to take. You can help provide the business logic that bridges the gap between the two. As noted by Jonathan Chadwick, former CFO and COO of VMware,[27] "Outside of CEO relationships, the CRO–CFO bond is most important in the organization, especially in a growth business." Effective communication and collaboration can bridge the gap, ensuring that financial prudence aligns with growth objectives.

If you notice an early trend with a new product offering that has a higher win rate, you can flag the C-level executives and help them see where the company needs to double down. You're in a unique position to see this earlier than anyone else.

The board is often skeptical of the CRO's numbers because they've been burned historically by a revenue forecast or inflated pipeline number. If you are working with all the departments and report to the CEO, COO, or CFO, you could provide a no-nonsense set of metrics to the board. You may point out that reps have been converting unqualified opportunities and inflating the pipeline, impacting how much pipeline needs to be generated for the quarter. Calling these things out can be a game changer for the company leadership. These mistakes happen more often than you think.

How to Communicate Your Value

As a RevOps leader, you may not fully realize the size and scope of the impact you have on your organization. However, communicating that impact is crucial, especially to the CEO and CFO, who are always focused on the company's bottom line. Articulating your success not only reinforces your value but also positions you as a strategic partner in driving growth and efficiency. Here are some key strategies to ensure your contributions are recognized.

Share monthly or quarterly highlights. Regularly present clear, concise updates that showcase your achievements and their impact on revenue growth and EBITDA. These reports don't need to cover every detail but should focus on key metrics that tie directly to organizational priorities. Highlight the takeaways that are already influencing growth, as well as insights that could impact future strategies.

For example, you might report on:

- Revenue Growth Metrics: Show progress in metrics like Annual Recurring Revenue (ARR), Net Revenue Retention (NRR), or pipeline growth.
- Efficiency Improvements: Highlight operational enhancements, such as reduced time-to-close or optimized resource allocation.
- Cost Savings: Demonstrate how process automation or streamlined workflows have reduced overhead or improved productivity.

Focus on strategic metrics. Focusing on high-impact metrics can elevate your visibility and demonstrate your ability to drive strategic results. For instance, 58 percent of companies use overall revenue to measure RevOps' impact on organization engagement; 53 percent measure operations efficiency; and 46 percent track improvements in sales cycles.[28] Some have also suggested revenue per employee as the hallmark metric to show RevOps success.

If you focus on improving close rates, you might implement initiatives such as enhanced sales training programs, upgraded CRM tools, or AI-powered lead scoring. Over time, tracking the impact of these programs provides measurable evidence of how your efforts contribute to increased revenue. This metric also signals to leadership that you are aligning your initiatives with core business goals.

By tracking the improvement over time, you'll have measurable evidence of how your initiatives directly contribute to the company's revenue growth. This focused approach highlights your strategic thinking and showcases your ability to drive tangible results.

Reducing sales cycle times is another powerful way to demonstrate value. By streamlining workflows, adopting AI-based technologies, or refining sales methodologies, you can show how these changes accelerate deal closures and boost overall productivity. For example, a detailed analysis might reveal that AI-driven forecasting tools have reduced the average sales cycle by 15 percent. This insight not only underscores your contributions but also reinforces the organization's commitment to innovation.

This analysis can show management how your research accelerates the sales process and enhances overall efficiency, thus reinforcing your value to the organization.

Link initiatives to revenue and EBITDA. Whenever possible, connect your initiatives to the organization's top-line revenue growth or bottom-line profitability. For instance, if a new process reduces customer churn, calculate the financial impact of retaining those customers over time. If an efficiency gain reduces manual labor, estimate the cost savings and reinvestment potential.

After streamlining a complex lead-routing process, you might report:

- An X percent increase in lead response times.
- A corresponding Y percent improvement in conversion rates.
- A total financial impact of $Z in incremental revenue.

Providing these kinds of connections ensures your leadership team understands how your work directly affects the company's success.

Proactively seek feedback. Communication is a two-way street. Regularly seek input from the CEO, CFO, and other stakeholders about what metrics or outcomes matter most to them.

At Fullcast, we recommend measuring the impact of your efforts based on at least four factors:

1. NPS
2. eNPS
3. Effectiveness of your ABM efforts
4. Productivity gains of revenue sources

You can adjust your focus accordingly to ensure your work remains aligned with their strategic priorities. Proactively asking, "What would you like to see more of in our reporting?" can open doors to deeper collaboration.

By consistently highlighting your contributions and tying them to the company's broader goals, you position yourself not just as a manager of operations but also as a critical driver of strategic growth. Clear communication, backed by data and aligned with leadership priorities, ensures your value is not just understood—it's celebrated.

How RevOps Changes from Series A to IPO

RevOps can really drive competitiveness of the organization in its ability to respond to changing market conditions and to be able to take advantage of opportunities that present themselves.

"I knew of a large corporation that required changes to territory to be approved by a central committee involving high-level executives," Bala recalls. "In contrast, Salesforce's approach was to give as much flexibility to the frontline sales manager to manage their business. This allows for the business to respond quickly *but* also means that the RevOps posture must be dynamic enough to accommodate this. That's your accountability as a RevOps leader."

As companies scale, the role of a RevOps leader evolves from a tactical resource to a critical strategic driver—guiding growth at every stage, from early funding rounds to IPO and beyond. Whether you're building from scratch, fine-tuning systems, or optimizing for sustainable growth, a strong RevOps leader ensures that your Go-to-Market engine is always humming.

Early Stages

At the Series A and B stages, the focus is on capturing market share, closing deals, and building momentum. But for many start-ups, this stage can feel chaotic. Teams are small, resources are stretched thin, and tools are often cobbled together with just enough duct tape (and 1,000 spreadsheets) to function. This is where a RevOps leader becomes invaluable. At this stage, RevOps leaders are testing new technologies, providing data and analytics to the board, and creating efficient growth to the board.

RevOps at this stage is about understanding your capabilities and maturing them methodically. It's tempting to chase every opportunity, but if a process or system isn't ready for prime time, the result is chaos. Instead, RevOps leaders identify what's needed now, what comes next quarter, and what's on the horizon—setting the stage for long-term success.

An example of a company that found success at this stage is Airbyte, an open-source data integration platform that rapidly captured market share by focusing on targeted growth strategies.[29]. Within seventeen months of its launch, it rapidly achieved a valuation of $1.5 billion following a $150 million Series B funding round. RevOps played a crucial role in Airbyte's rapid success. The RevOps team streamlined GTM strategies and aligned sales, marketing, and customer success teams, ensuring all departments were working toward shared goals. RevOps built forecasting models to scale effectively as well as expansion models to upsell Airbyte users into paying customers. The RevOps team integrated scalable systems such as CRMs, marketing automation, and analytics platforms. RevOps implemented and documented processes, eliminating chaos and ensuring decisions were data driven. Airbyte's success highlights how a strong RevOps foundation ensures alignment, efficiency, and adaptability during key growth stages.

Growth Stage (Series C+): Scaling with Precision

By the time a company reaches Series C and beyond, the stakes get higher. Growth is no longer just about closing deals—it's about scaling predictably and efficiently. This is where RevOps leaders truly shine, transforming systems and processes into a finely tuned growth engine.

Predictable revenue is the holy grail for any business, and RevOps is the key to unlocking it. By streamlining processes, automating manual workflows, and analyzing data, RevOps creates an operational foundation that makes revenue more predictable, quarter after quarter. With the right data and firsthand insights, RevOps leaders can accurately forecast revenue, manage pipeline health, and identify opportunities for growth, even during market downturns.

Pre-IPO and Beyond: Optimizing for Resilience and Longevity

As a company prepares for an initial public offering (IPO), every part of the business comes under scrutiny. Investors and boards expect accuracy, predictability, and a clear path to sustainable growth. This is where RevOps leadership becomes a cornerstone of success.

In the pre-IPO phase, RevOps leaders focus on driving alignment, visibility, and precision across the GTM organization. They refine forecasting models, improve pipeline visibility, and ensure that sales, marketing, and customer success operate as one unified team. This level of discipline not only satisfies investor expectations but also creates a foundation for post-IPO growth.

Navigating the post-IPO world brings a new layer of complexity. Compliance and regulatory reporting become essential components of day-to-day operations, and RevOps leaders can play a pivotal role in ensuring these requirements are met. From tracking revenue recognition to providing audit-ready data, they ensure reporting processes are airtight, helping the company meet shareholder expectations and maintain trust. In addition to regulatory compliance, transparent reporting gives investors and the board clear insights into performance, forecasts, and growth opportunities. This transparency builds confidence and positions the business for sustained success in the public markets.

ZoomInfo's transition to a public company showcased the critical role of RevOps in navigating the complexities of the IPO process.[30] The Go-to-Market intelligence platform leveraged RevOps to streamline workflows, improve pipeline visibility, and deliver audit-ready data to meet investor expectations. This approach not only ensured compliance with regulatory standards but also fostered alignment across sales, marketing, and customer success teams. By maintaining transparent reporting and focusing on predictable revenue growth, ZoomInfo positioned itself for sustained success in the competitive public market.

Becoming a Great RevOps Leader

Great RevOps leaders rarely are in the spotlight like a singular heroic salesperson may be, but their influence is key to helping the company scale and grow. In this section, we'll discuss characteristics that make a good RevOps leader and how to become the leader your CEO trusts and prioritizes.

Characteristics of a Good RevOps Leader

After interviewing hundreds of RevOps leaders and being part of the RevOps movement since the beginning, we believe that a few key capabilities separate RevOps leaders from the rest of the pack on the operational side:

1. **Drive Cross-Functional Alignment:** They unify departments to operate as a single, revenue-driving force.
2. **Provide Data-Driven Insights:** Every recommendation is anchored in clear, reliable data.
3. **Champion Growth and Innovation:** They identify opportunities for efficiency, improvement, and revenue growth. It's easy to get distracted with the latest tech innovations. The danger with chasing shiny objects is that it causes wasteful tools fatigue for your organization.

    However, with clear business objectives in place and proven strategies at hand, a RevOps leader can focus on the ideal technology stack with as much care on its overall impact to the organization while avoiding the risks of inertia and fatigue from having too many tools that don't talk to each other and destroy agility.

RevOps leaders are the backbone of a thriving, agile, and competitive organization. Their behind-the-scenes efforts lay the foundation for long-term success.

A great RevOps leader starts by identifying goals that cross multiple departments. The end-to-end customer journey should be your guiding principle, serving as your north star. By focusing on this broader perspective, you can align your efforts in RevOps with the needs of marketing, sales, and customer success teams, ensuring that all initiatives contribute to a seamless customer experience.

When you boil it down, success in RevOps is all about effective collaboration and building trust across teams. RevOps professionals often act as the glue between teams, uniting stakeholders with different priorities. This requires empathy, strong communication, and the ability to mediate when tensions arise. In such situations, curiosity becomes a valuable tool, helping you focus on understanding others' perspectives instead of getting caught up in conflicts.

As a RevOps leader, it's also incredibly important to align your goals directly with your CEO's priorities. You need to deliver the clarity executives need to make bold decisions. The key lies in transparency. By clearly documenting RevOps' core functions— forecasting, planning, compensation design, lead management, and more—you can highlight your team's current capabilities, identify gaps, and demonstrate progress. This approach enables CEOs and boards to understand:

- What's ready to execute now?
- What's in motion?
- What's coming next?

If your organization has not yet invested in AI-driven digital transformation, the opportunity to do so has never been more exciting. Recent advancements in AI are revolutionizing the RevOps function. We'll talk more about this in chapter 2.

Characteristics of a Strategic RevOps Leader

Ryan and Amy were fortunate to be part of the incredible journey of Simplus, a Salesforce advisory, implementation, and managed services company that began in 2014 and was acquired by Infosys in 2020. At the beginning, we were generalist systems integrators. At the end, we were seasoned RevOps professionals specializing in implementing revenue-focused software. When we reflect on what fueled Simplus' growth and eventual acquisition, we believe we became trusted RevOps consultants by prioritizing focus, culture, and discipline—hallmarks of what it means to go from being a good operational leader to a great strategic leader.

Focus. Early on at Simplus, we were stretched thin. Like many start-ups, we tried to do too much—integrating multiple platforms, supporting various services, and chasing every opportunity. But Ryan and Amy understood that operational focus was key to scaling effectively, and we diligently toed the line to focus first on Salesforce, and then even more diligently on CPQ software.

We zeroed in on quote-to-cash solutions within the Salesforce ecosystem. This decision transformed the business. We stopped trying to be everything to everyone and instead became the best at one thing. Equally important to our focus was positioning ourselves strategically within the Salesforce ecosystem, which can only be done with a deep understanding of the lay of the land. We knew where to put our flag in the sand. What we didn't know is that this would position us incredibly well to help define and build within the burgeoning RevOps ecosystem.

For RevOps leaders, this lesson is clear: Focus, positioning, and alignment drive success. When you get the team, tools, and processes behind a unified strategy, you unlock growth.

Culture. Simplus was built on values that mattered: stewardship, critical thinking, and an underdog spirit. They believe that businesses thrive when every individual feels valued and heard.

That culture permeated everything they did—from executive meetings to the way they treated customers.

We remember a defining moment during the pandemic. Faced with a significant drop in revenue, we had a choice: layoffs or collective sacrifice. Instead of cutting jobs, the team unanimously agreed to take a temporary pay cut. That decision wasn't made because leadership mandated it; it was a natural extension of the culture we'd built together. Later, as revenue regained momentum, we were able to back pay everyone on the team.

For RevOps leaders, this highlights an essential truth: Culture drives alignment. A high-performing RevOps team succeeds when sales, marketing, and customer success are aligned not just through tools and processes, but through shared values and trust. This isn't something that happens overnight, either. It takes a lot of hard work and mutual respect between leaders and employees.

Discipline. One of the most critical lessons we learned at Simplus was the importance of financial rigor. We started as a boot-strapped company, and that experience shaped how we approached growth. Every dollar was intentional, every investment strategic. Later, when we brought on outside funding, we deployed it with the same discipline we had in our early days. In 2020, after aggressively growing for six years, all our hard work paid off. We sold the company to Infosys for $250 million.

RevOps leaders face a similar balancing act—how to fuel growth while maintaining efficiency. The Simplus journey taught us that success comes from focus, culture, and discipline. The Simplus story is, at its heart, a RevOps story. It's about focus, efficiency, and bringing Sales, Marketing, and Customer Experience teams together to achieve something remarkable.

"As a Revenue Operations leader, I see firsthand how powerful it is when Sales and Marketing move in lockstep," wrote Shefali Raghavan, Vice President of GTM Strategy and Operations at G2, in a LinkedIn post. "A unified Go-to-Market strategy isn't just a nice-to-have; it's the key to winning."

Checklist: What CEOs Should Look for in a Strategic RevOps Leader

Hiring a strategic RevOps leader is one of the most impactful decisions a CEO can make to drive sustained growth and operational excellence. However, not every candidate possesses the unique blend of skills, experience, and vision required to excel in this role.

CEOs should seek leaders who embody strategic thinking, execution, and cross-functional influence. In a Sharebird post,[31] Nick Rico, Senior Vice President of Growth & GTM Strategy at Lucid Software, said these are the three main qualities that RevOps leaders all have:

1. *Positive energy:* The ability to move with relentless passion and a positive attitude. This sets the tone for others, ignites momentum, and fosters a culture of winning together.
2. *Ability to execute:* Everyone wants "strategy" in their title, but execution is just as critical. Surround yourself with doers—people who are ready to take on any challenge, whether it's their idea or not.
3. *Comfort at all levels:* From interns to executives, the best leaders show composure in every situation. Those who operate with low ego and high adaptability can step in and fill any gap within a team.

CEOs also need leaders they can trust—professionals who can align diverse teams, navigate complex systems, and translate data into actionable strategies. This is not a role for someone who only understands the technical side of operations or the interpersonal dynamics of leadership. A truly strategic RevOps leader bridges both, operating as a visionary who understands how to optimize systems while keeping a firm eye on the company's revenue and EBITDA goals.

Below are key questions CEOs ask themselves when evaluating candidates for this vital role. If you're aspiring to be a strategic RevOps leader, consider how your skills, experience, and mindset align with these expectations. Are you the person CEOs are looking for?

Leadership Skills

- Does the candidate bring a proven track record of aligning sales, marketing, and customer success?
- Can they turn complex data into actionable strategies?
- Are they collaborative, adaptable, and aligned with your company's values?
- Can they communicate and influence effectively at the executive level?
- Are they willing to speak up in executive meetings about ways to pivot to meet revenue goals?
- Do they have the skills and experience with your tech-stack, including your CRM, marketing automation software, and AI-enabled RevOps software (if you have one)?

Operational Vision

- Do they prioritize reducing technical debt and optimizing systems?
- Can they guide your team through a clear RevOps maturity model?
- Do they have a vision for leveraging technology and automation effectively?

Strategic Impact

- How do they align RevOps with CEO priorities?
- Can they demonstrate measurable success in revenue growth?
- Can they demonstrate measurable success in providing data-backed insights?
- Can they demonstrate measurable success in operational efficiency and cross-functional alignment between Sales, Marketing, Customer Success, and Finance?

Conclusion

In this chapter, we've explored the transformative impact RevOps leaders have on their organizations, from shaping efficient revenue growth to aligning cross-functional teams with CEO priorities. First, we looked at the ways RevOps leaders create measurable value, whether by streamlining sales cycles, reducing costs, or implementing technologies that enable better decision-making. Their ability to provide clear, data-driven insights makes them indispensable partners to CEOs, CFOs, and boards.

As companies scale, the role of RevOps evolves, adapting to the unique challenges of each growth stage. From building foundational processes in early-stage start-ups to driving precision and compliance in IPO-ready enterprises, RevOps leaders guide their organizations through the complexities of growth while ensuring alignment and accountability.

We explored the characteristics of strong RevOps leaders. Great RevOps leaders go beyond operational efficiency; they anticipate challenges, foster collaboration, and ensure that every initiative contributes to the company's broader goals. To close, we included a practical checklist to identify the right candidates for this vital role—leaders who can bridge technical expertise and strategic thinking to propel organizations forward.

The role of the RevOps leader is both dynamic and essential. By understanding their impact, honing their strategic value, and communicating effectively, these leaders position themselves not just as operators, but as indispensable members of an organization's leadership team.

In the next chapter, we'll break down how to structure your revenue engine, starting with the most important element: your people. From there, we'll explore the processes that create alignment and the technology that powers innovation. Let's dive in.

3

State of Revenue Operations in 2025

For the better part of two decades, Ryan, Bala, and Amy have been living and breathing RevOps. As pioneers and leaders of the RevOps movement, we're surrounded every day by businesses that have achieved transformational change by adopting RevOps principles and practices. Indeed, we are proud to have helped lead many of these businesses to RevOps success.

At the same time, we recognize the RevOps industry as a whole is still in a state of transition—RevOps remains a nascent field. While some forward-thinking revenue leaders are already reaping the benefits of RevOps, far more are still familiarizing themselves with RevOps, developing strategies for how to infuse RevOps into their organizations, and gaining internal buy-in and funding to implement RevOps.

As we discussed in chapter 1, RevOps represents a fundamental mindset shift in how businesses generate revenue. As a result, legacy approaches for generating revenue look different from the RevOps approach—and are sometimes incompatible with a modern RevOps mindset.

Today, businesses cannot rely solely on outbound, in-person sales to deliver strong, predictable revenue streams. Whether a business is operating in a B2B or B2C environment, customers are often doing their own research online first—before they ever speak to a sales rep. Similarly, customers' buying decisions are more complex.[32] Customers increasingly expect that in-person interactions will give way to digital sales processes. They also increasingly expect that sales reps will rely on customer data, not personality and rapport, to personalize every interaction.

In response, businesses are finding a proven, scalable solution for organizing and coordinating all of the disparate, disconnected functions of the organization that support revenue-related processes. It is these pain points that are driving businesses to embrace RevOps.

RevOps is becoming a more mature and widespread practice every year. As RevOps practitioners, we viscerally feel this mindset shift in our everyday work. As industry thought leaders, we are committed to methodically assessing and quantifying it. That's why we developed a comprehensive survey to quantitatively evaluate how RevOps is unfolding in the real world, and quantify priorities and future directions for RevOps-minded businesses.

Highlights from our State of Revenue Operations 2025 survey—which included participation by nearly 100 business leaders—are organized around seven key findings. Each main finding includes a synopsis of applicable survey results, plus analysis and commentary on what the survey results mean for the state (and future) of RevOps.

If you are a RevOps leader who's been at it since the beginning, we hope you'll walk away from this chapter with a newfound appreciation for how dramatically RevOps has evolved. And if you're new to RevOps, we hope this chapter convinces you that RevOps is more than just another passing business fad; it truly is the most expeditious path forward for an organization to achieve its revenue goals.

Developing the State of Revenue Operations Survey

RevOps is not merely a policy change or a piece of software or a planning tool. It is an approach and a mindset that brings together multiple interrelated parts of an organization to work in a coordinated fashion toward a common goal. Thus, when we developed our State of Revenue Operations 2025 survey, we knew we needed a survey capable of shedding light on the industry's progress toward the RevOps way of doing business.

Our sixty-one-question survey does more than just capture overall trends and attitudes about RevOps. It also asks questions intended to draw out the nuanced priorities, concerns, and considerations that are at the forefront of leaders' minds as they work toward a RevOps transformation.

Profile of Our Survey Takers

To ensure the survey captured the perspectives of executive-level leaders in the RevOps field, we selected and invited people to take the survey who were established as seasoned revenue operations leaders. We also posted the survey to each of our personal LinkedIn profiles. This personalized, targeted approach yielded the high-quality, representative sample size we were seeking.

In total, we received ninety-six responses. Nearly 80 percent were C-suite leaders or VPs, and 95 percent were director-level and above. Meanwhile, more than three-fourths—79 percent—were leaders in sales and operations.

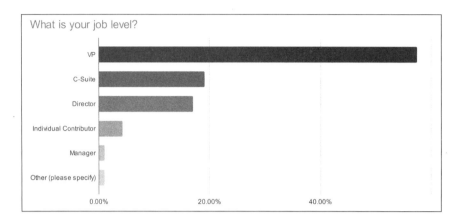

Our survey takers told us that they hail largely from mid-market and enterprise businesses. The average size of their companies is about eight thousand employees, with company size ranging from just five to 100,000 employees. Their RevOps team has, on average, fifty-four people.

The average survey taker is a US-based male with a college degree and an average age of forty-four. They make an average of $316,000 annually, and have almost fourteen years of experience, primarily in tech and software.

Seven Key Findings About the State of Revenue Operations

The State of Revenue Operations 2025 survey provides a range of granular, nuanced insights about the state of the RevOps field. We identified seven overarching takeaways from the survey that rose above others because of the important light they shed on the state of RevOps. Let's dive into the seven key RevOps findings from the survey:

RevOps Is a Strategic Role Growing in Importance

Modern RevOps is fast becoming a core growth strategy for many organizations, serving as the connective tissue across sales, marketing, and customer success. Among the RevOps leaders who participated in our survey, 93 percent say their job encompasses sales operations, 66 percent say their job encompasses customer success ops, and 64 percent say it encompasses marketing ops.

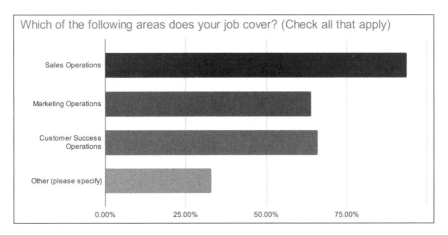

While sales, marketing, and customer success are the three most common areas that fall under the RevOps umbrella, RevOps leaders oversee a far broader range of business functions—everything from success operations and partner operations to billing to data science and data management.

The following is a list of all of the functions that RevOps leaders reported that they oversee. Needless to say, RevOps leaders are extensively involved end-to-end in the revenue engine.

List of Business Functions That RevOps Leaders Report Overseeing, in Alphabetical Order

Analytics	Deal Desk	Payments
Back Office and System Operations	Demand Gen Ops	Pricing and Monetization
BDRs	Enablement	Product Launches
BI CoE	Enablement and Sales Strategy / GTM	Program Management
BI Reporting	Enablement and Training	Revenue Pricing and Packaging
Billing	Enterprise Technology	Security
Business Operations	Entire business	Sales and Business Growth
Channel	F&I	Sales Data and Technology
Channel Ops	Finance Ops	Sales Enablement
Commercial Ops	GTM Systems	Sales Systems
Compliance	GTM Tool Stack	Sales Tools and Technology
Customer Data Management	Incentive Comp	Services and Partner Ops
Customer Support	Lender Relations	Strategy, Planning and Analytics
Data Science and Analytics	Market Development Ops	Strategic Partnerships
Data Analytics / Engineers	Operations	Strategic Programs
Data Science and Engineering	Partner Ops	

The survey also quantified and ranked the most common strategic and operational activities that RevOps leaders oversee. Once again, the list is extensive, reflecting the many hats that RevOps leaders wear.

The two most common types of responsibilities of RevOps leaders are Go-to-Market strategy and planning and sales process optimization. Nearly 89 percent of RevOps leaders reported being involved in both of these activities.

The following table presents a ranked list of the nineteen top job responsibilities of a RevOps leader. Notably, at least half of RevOps leaders identified the vast majority of these job responsibilities—sixteen of the nineteen responsibilities—as one of their personal responsibilities.

Job responsibility	Percent
GTM strategy and planning	88.31%
Sales process optimization	88.31%
Forecasting and revenue modeling	87.01%
CRM management and optimization (Salesforce, HubSpot, etc.)	84.42%
Pipeline management	83.12%
Data governance and hygiene	81.82%
Territory management	79.22%
Marketing and sales alignment	76.62%
Productivity	76.62%
Quota management	74.03%
Lead management and routing	72.73%
Systems implementation	71.43%
Capacity planning	70.13%
Deal desk and approvals	63.64%
Commission management	58.44%
Customer success and retention strategies	55.84%
Sales enablement and training	53.25%
Contract and pricing governance	48.05%
Risk assessment and mitigation	25.97%
Compliance and security (GDPR, SOC 2, etc.)	11.69%

Our survey also found that RevOps is gaining broad buy-in and senior leadership attention, with proportionately greater investments in expanding RevOps capabilities and head count. A strong majority—79 percent—say they have a formal RevOps department. Moreover, nearly all business leaders consider RevOps important for revenue outcomes, with 70 percent rating it very important and 98 percent rating it at least somewhat important.

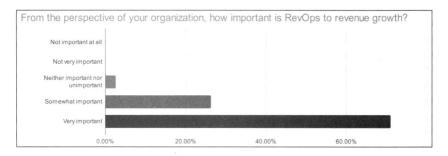

Finally, nearly 81 percent of RevOps leaders characterize the RevOps industry as growing, including 39 percent who say RevOps is growing rapidly. Nearly 60 percent of RevOps leaders say they expect their revenue team will add new tools to their tech stack in the next twelve months—on top of an average of thirteen tools that RevOps leaders already say comprise their tech stacks.

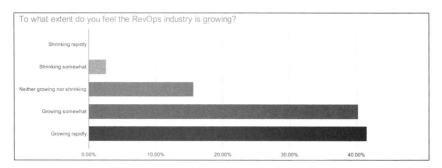

Takeaway: RevOps leaders should continue to elevate RevOps as a strategic partner in driving revenue, given its recognized impact on growth and its expanding influence across industries.

Major KPIs Focus on Business Outcomes

RevOps is increasingly driving bottom-line revenue outcomes—not just internal process improvements. RevOps leaders are responding by turning to KPIs that can track revenue outcomes. Our survey found that the top three KPIs that RevOps leaders are tracking all revolve around top-line growth metrics.

The following is a list of the major KPIs that businesses report using to track RevOps success, ranked from most popular to least. Included alongside each KPI is the percentage of RevOps leaders who say they are using the KPI in their organization.

- **Forecast accuracy (76.32%)**: How effectively RevOps improves predictability and planning
- **Operational efficiency (72.37%)**: How much RevOps streamlines operations and reduces friction
- **Annual recurring revenue (ARR) (68.42%)**: How RevOps contributes to bottom-line revenue growth
- **Sales cycle improvements (65.79%)**: How much RevOps streamlines and automates sales processes
- **Pipeline generation (63.16%)**: How RevOps contributes to strengthening the sales pipeline
- **Win rate (61.84%)**: How RevOps contributes to a higher portion of deals that successfully close
- **Upsell/cross-sell rate (55.26%)**: How RevOps boosts sales reps' ability to upsell and cross-sell
- **Revenue per employee (42.11%)**: How RevOps increases the average revenue generated by each sales rep

- **Cost savings (40.79%):** How RevOps contributes to reducing expenses
- **Deal sizes (32.89%):** How RevOps boosts the size of deals

Significantly, the list captures the vast majority of commonly used metrics for measuring RevOps success; only about 11 percent of RevOps leaders reported that they use a KPI other than the ten common KPIs listed above.

Takeaway: Businesses should be regularly reviewing KPI metrics dashboards with stakeholders to help keep RevOps efforts aligned with what the business cares about most, which is predictable growth and efficiency. In fact, these KPIs should serve as a north star guiding every RevOps initiative, whether that's investing in analytics and clean data to boost forecast accuracy, or refining lead qualification to increase win rates and pipeline.

Sales Process Improvement and Pipeline Generation Are Top RevOps Priorities

RevOps leaders are focused on improving core sales processes and pipeline development to drive revenue. When asked to rank the relative importance of nine RevOps priority areas, RevOps leaders overwhelmingly ranked sales process improvements at the top, followed closely by pipeline generation. These two areas had the highest weighted average scores (6.9 out of 9) and the most No. 1 rankings by respondents, indicating that RevOps leaders are strongly focused on optimizing the sales engine and feeding it with sufficient pipeline.

The following list provides the average ranking of nine RevOps priority areas—the result of an exercise in which RevOps leaders were asked to prioritize the relative importance of each area. In this table, the higher the score, the higher the priority.

RevOps priority areas	Average score
Pipeline generation	6.86
Sales process improvements	6.82
Rep productivity	6.17
Forecasting	5.82
Data hygiene	5.68
Reporting and dashboards	4.16
Team alignment	4.03
Tech integrations	2.79
Revenue attribution	2.69

Business leaders were least likely to indicate they're using RevOps for revenue attribution and tech stack integrations—likely due to a focus on more immediate revenue drivers.

Takeaway: To extract maximum value from RevOps investments, RevOps teams should focus on securing quick wins with pipeline development and sales process improvements first. Subsequently, they can tackle longer-term initiatives like attribution modeling and complex integrations.

The RevOps Tech Landscape Is Expansive and Underutilized

Technology is central to RevOps, and most organizations have a large (and growing) RevOps tech stack. RevOps leaders report using about thirteen tools on average in their revenue tech stack—a figure that reflects the expanding ecosystem of tools being managed under the RevOps umbrella, including CRM, marketing automation, sales engagement, and business intelligence. Moreover, 85 percent of RevOps report using real-time dashboards and analytics tools to plan throughout the year.

The most common order management system that RevOps leaders use is Salesforce (69%). The most commonly used billing system is NetSuite (61%), and the most commonly used payroll system is ADP (47%). For document management, the most commonly used system is Docusign (83%).

A majority of RevOps leaders who took our survey—58 percent—report that they're not using a territory management system; of the ones who are, 15 percent use Salesforce, followed by 11 percent who use Fullcast. A sizable minority of RevOps leaders—28 percent—also do not use a commissions platform; of the ones who do, the most popular are Xactly (23%) and CaptivateIQ (18%).

Looking ahead, most RevOps leaders are continuing to invest in new technology: Fifty-nine percent of RevOps teams plan to add even more tools in the next twelve months, while another 26 percent say it's a possibility.

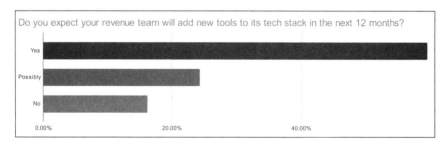

However, with this expansive tech stack has come a significant challenge: underutilization. Business leaders estimate that about 30 percent of the tools in their tech stack are underutilized or sitting unused. In fact, only 10 percent of business leaders feel they are using their tech stack to its full potential—that is, fully adopting and leveraging new features. Most leaders acknowledge only partial use, with 44 percent saying some tools aren't fully deployed, and an additional 11 percent reporting having "a lot" of unused tools.

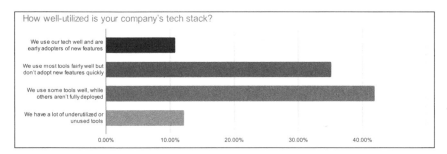

RevOps leaders cite numerous reasons for technology underutilization. The most commonly cited root causes are lack of training and enablement resources and too many tools to learn and use.

Causes of technology underutilization	Percent that cited
Lack of training and enablement resources	54.17%
Too many tools to learn and use	44.44%
Lack of clear ROI from tools	43.06%
Poor integration between platforms and tools	41.67%
Lack of alignment between teams	36.11%
Tools don't align with existing workflows	26.39%
Other	12.5%
Insufficient vendor support	9.72%

Takeaway: RevOps leaders often find themselves with more technology than their teams can absorb, or with systems that don't seamlessly integrate. In response, RevOps leaders should invest in team training and better integration of existing platforms to boost utilization of their tech stack. Streamlining the tech stack (or consolidating overlapping tools) also can be effective at boosting efficiency.

Better Managing Sales Processes Is an Effective Way to Provide Revenue Lift

To optimize revenue, RevOps leaders report overwhelmingly that they invest in documenting their sales processes; only 6 percent report that they lack documentation for sales processes. The most common method that RevOps leaders use for sales process documentation is Google and Microsoft docs, spreadsheets, and slides (54%).

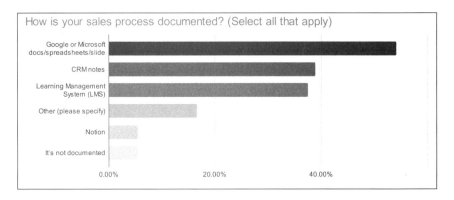

Meanwhile, to monitor sales reps' ability to follow established sales processes, a strong majority—67 percent—report using dashboards with activity metrics, while nearly as many—66 percent—report also using sales managers to monitor process adherence.

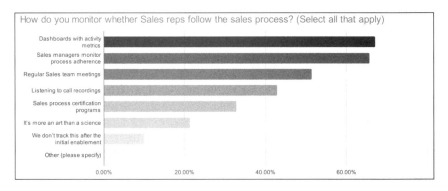

At the same time, RevOps leaders acknowledge that their sales processes aren't perfect. To the contrary, even with an invaluable boost from adopting RevOps, execution gaps in the sales process still cost many companies significant revenue. RevOps leaders estimate that an average of 17 percent of their organization's total revenue is lost due to breakdowns and inefficiencies in the sales process. These execution gaps commonly manifest as leads slipping through the cracks, deals stalled due to process errors, and inconsistent sales practices.

Another persistent RevOps challenge is achieving strong alignment across all Go-to-Market teams. Misalignment can manifest as conflicting KPIs, handoff issues between departments, and differing views on strategy—all of which can hurt execution. When asked to rate the alignment of sales, marketing, and customer success functions in executing a unified revenue strategy, RevOps leaders gave their organizations an overall average rating of just 6.7 out of 10. Meanwhile, RevOps leaders gave a similar rating to the strength of alignment among sales leadership (an average of 7.5 out of 10). These lukewarm ratings indicate that while teams may share high-level goals, coordination and unity of effort have room for improvement.

Takeaway: Closing even part of the enormous revenue leakage happening in organizations is a viable strategy for potentially recapturing millions of dollars in lost revenue. RevOps leaders should prioritize stopping revenue leaking by improving sales processes, including tightening process adherence, improving training, and supporting reps with better tools and playbooks.

RevOps Planning Isn't Happening as Often as It Should

A core tenet of RevOps is a commitment to continuous refinement and improvement. When revenue-related processes and sales territories are not continuously revisited, they tend to become less effective over time.

Unfortunately, many RevOps leaders acknowledge RevOps planning isn't happening in their organizations as often as it should. When it comes to adjusting and refining sales territories, a majority—58 percent—say they only make territory adjustments once a year. Just 8 percent revisit territories twice a year, and only 13 percent do so quarterly. What this means is that most RevOps leaders are allowing problems with territory assignments to potentially fester for many months without resolution. Even as RevOps leaders acknowledge this reality, 72 percent of them simultaneously acknowledge that one of the biggest challenges associated with territory management is ensuring equitable distribution of opportunities.

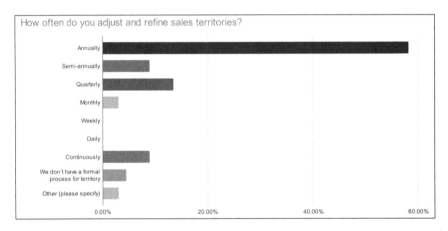

Other major challenges that RevOps leaders face with territory management include managing account and rep transitions (70%), understanding total addressable market within territories (45%), and adapting to market shifts and territory expansions (25%).

To set sales quotas, RevOps leaders almost unanimously agree that they use only five main factors. The following is a list of these five factors, plus what portion of RevOps leaders report using each factor when setting quotas.

Factors When Setting Quotas	RevOps Leaders Using
Historical sales performance	91.04%
Top-down revenue targets	83.58%
Bottom-up rep productivity modeling	73.13%
Market potential and TAM analysis	59.7%
Competitive benchmarking	22.39%

Once sales quotas are set, RevOps leaders overwhelmingly prioritize tracking performance to plan throughout the year. More than 85 percent report monitoring performance using real-time dashboards and analytics tools, while less than 3 percent reported having no formal or structured approach for monitoring performance.

Takeaway: The RevOps leaders who treat RevOps planning as a continuous exercise and aspire toward continuous improvement should keep doing what they're doing. For the many companies that still do RevOps planning in a more ad hoc manner, they should redouble their efforts to close these continuity gaps.

RevOps Leaders Are Moving Decisively on AI

Effective RevOps relies on copious datasets to gain insights into revenue-related processes and outcomes. Often, these datasets are too voluminous, complex, and wide-ranging for RevOps teams to even make sense of—much less keep up with. That's where AI shows tremendous potential. AI helps RevOps leaders gain—and maintain—a masterful understanding of what an organization's data reveals about RevOps health and how the organization might use its wealth of data to drive improved RevOps outcomes.

An impressive 82 percent of RevOps leaders told us in our survey that they expect AI will have at least a somewhat positive impact on their organizations over the coming twelve months. Moreover,

RevOps leaders reported that they already are moving decisively on AI. Not only have they already integrated three AI tools on average into their tech stack, but they also have been using AI technology to enhance a wide range of RevOps tools and processes. The most common RevOps applications for AI technology are call transcription and analysis, chatbots, and lead scoring.

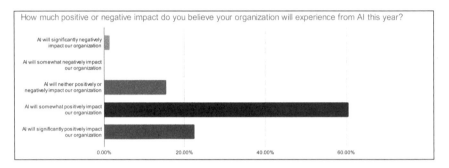

The following is a list of the eleven most common RevOps applications for AI technology, alongside the portion of RevOps leaders who reported using AI for each application.

AI Applications	Portion That Use
Call transcription and analysis	70.31%
Chatbots	46.88%
Lead scoring	39.06%
Automated lead routing	37.5%
Support AI Agent	31.25%
Sales forecasting	29.69%
Deal insights and recommendations	29.69%
Personalized content creation	28.13%
Prospecting AI Agent	21.88%
Territory balancing	15.63%
CRM policy management	4.69%

Even as RevOps leaders have already made numerous wide-ranging investments in AI, they're showing no signs of stopping. The following is a list of the top eleven applications for AI that RevOps leaders are planning to invest in over the next twelve months, including the portion of RevOps leaders who have identified the application as an area of planned future investment.

AI Applications	Portion That Plan to Invest
Deal insights and recommendations	40.35%
Prospecting AI Agent	38.6%
Sales forecasting	35.09%
Personalized content creation	26.32%
Call transcription and analysis	24.56%
Automated lead routing	22.81%
Lead scoring	22.81%
Territory balancing	17.54%
Chatbots	15.79%
Support AI Agent	15.79%
CRM policy management	12.28%

Unquestionably, RevOps leaders are moving decisively to incorporate AI into their RevOps tools and processes. But RevOps leaders simultaneously acknowledge that they are not moving as fast as they'd like. The biggest barriers to even more widespread use of AI in a RevOps environment are bandwidth constraints (59%), budget constraints (51%), and dependence on legacy systems (32%).

Takeaway: RevOps leaders who are ignoring or underinvesting in AI are doing so at their own peril. AI isn't a passing fad or bells and whistles with no substance. AI will enable organizations to supercharge many of their RevOps investments—and get outsize results that are more than the sum of their parts.

The RevOps Career Pathway Shines Bright

Modern-day RevOps is still so new to the revenue operations industry that very few of today's RevOps leaders made a conscious, strategic decision to become a leader in the RevOps field. To the contrary, most RevOps leaders fell into the industry as it's been still evolving. For them, the transition was logical, organic, and seamless—playing off their strengths and talents. And they are unequivocal that RevOps shines bright as a career pathway.

Our survey respondents shared story after story about how they'd begun their RevOps career journey somewhere else: sales, sales ops, marketing ops, project management, even software development and legal. Then, they transitioned to RevOps as a result of a business need, a suggestion from a colleague, or even simply reading about RevOps.

The following are just two of these inspiring stories that showcase two very different ways that RevOps leaders stumbled into the world of RevOps:

- "I originally started in legal, but transitioned into RevOps at the request of the VP of Operations after closing the largest deal in company history. Initially, I was advised to kill the deal as it was perceived as unfavorable. However, after a deeper analysis, I uncovered its true value—turning it into a game-changing opportunity for the company."
- "I created the revenue operations team here out of need. The disparate operational teams that supported various areas of the business needed to be centralized to be effective. Aligning the team under a broader rev ops umbrella addressed a business problem of silos and imbalance. The biggest leap in my career to bring me to

RevOps though started through a business operations role at the company."

In our survey, we also asked RevOps leaders to zero in on the most important skill sets for RevOps success, and what their best advice is for the next generation of RevOps leaders.

The following is a ranked list of the top six skills and experiences that RevOps leaders say are critical to RevOps success. Two skill types—data analytics and reporting, plus cross-functional collaboration—rose to the top of the list, with an impressive 89 percent of RevOps leaders identifying these skills as critical.

RevOps Skills and Experiences	Percent That Selected
Data analytics and reporting	86.76%
Cross-functional collaboration	86.76%
Leadership and stakeholder management	83.82%
Process optimization and automation	67.65%
CRM and tech stack management	61.76%
Financial and forecasting expertise	44.12%

We followed up by asking RevOps leaders to identify what are the most effective strategies that current and future RevOps leaders should prioritize using to build out robust professional networks to support their career growth. Four key networking strategies rose to the top of the list, selected by 45 percent to 69 percent of RevOps leaders.

RevOps Networking Strategies	Percent That Selected
LinkedIn networking and thought leadership	68.75%
RevOps-specific communities (e.g., Pavilion, RevOps Co-op)	67.19%
Industry events and conferences	59.38%
Internal mentorship or leadership development programs	45.31%

Notably, RevOps leaders identified LinkedIn as the single most important way to network. LinkedIn beat out multiple types of in-person networking opportunities, including industry events, mentoring, and leadership development—reflecting the strength and robustness of LinkedIn's RevOps network. LinkedIn, of course, should not just be about making connections with other RevOps professionals. As RevOps leaders noted, an investment in LinkedIn also should involve regularly developing and posting RevOps thought leadership content.

Finally, we asked RevOps leaders to offer their best advice for those aspiring to lead a RevOps organization someday. RevOps leaders emphasized that RevOps is not for those who like stability and predictability. RevOps leaders need to be fearless, proactive, and constantly looking to disrupt the status quo. They also need to always be in charge, leading the C-suite in articulating what directions the organization needs to go and setting the pace for change—as opposed to the other way around. "Provide your boss insights into how the business is doing—proactively. Don't wait to be told what reports to generate," one RevOps leader recommended.

RevOps leaders also shared insights into the make-or-break soft skills that every RevOps leader needs to be able to masterfully execute: Exceptional agility, intuitive understanding of human behavior, effective relationship-building skills, and management of diverse stakeholders. "Don't be constrained with a one-size-fits-all playbook," another RevOps leader shared. "You have to be agile and capable of adapting to new ways of operating, capable of dealing with hard personalities, and willing to put in effort where the payoff is most certain while guarding against burnout at the same time. You can't do everything, so pick your battles."

Takeaway: Clinching a position as a RevOps leader is a wide-open field for everyone who's willing to work tirelessly and strategically as an innovator, visionary, and disruptor. Especially given the rapid expansion that the RevOps field is undergoing, aspiring RevOps leaders have endless opportunities to contribute significant, quantifiable impacts—and ultimately to get noticed. Along the way, aspiring leaders should prioritize not just building technical skills like data analytics and platform management, but also their soft skills.

Conclusion

RevOps has emerged as a critical business strategy for driving alignment across sales, marketing, and customer success—and for keeping all teams focused on a shared revenue strategy. While some businesses already are fully reaping the benefits of RevOps, it's still a work in progress for most organizations.

Forward-thinking leaders are working toward achieving greater RevOps maturity by focusing on improving sales workflows, expanding their tech and AI tool sets, and knowing how to effectively measure, track, and report on progress. Simultaneously, leaders are focusing on aligning teams, closing execution gaps, and honing their soft skills to fully realize the potential of RevOps. By focusing on these key areas, leaders will become well-positioned to realize the RevOps future they envision—an ambitious vision that will bring them greater influence, broader scope, and forward-looking investment, paired with a clear-eyed view of challenges.

Part 2

The Fullcast FACTOR Framework

4

FACTOR Framework for RevOps Success

Whether you've just landed your first role in RevOps or you've been given the monumental task of bringing order to a chaotic organization, you're stepping into a function that is as critical as it is complex. If you're feeling overwhelmed, you're not alone. Many RevOps professionals start their journey with an inbox full of urgent requests, a lack of clear documentation, and the expectation that they will somehow create immediate operational harmony. So where do you begin?

The answer is the FACTOR Framework. This structured approach to RevOps success provides a blueprint for how to organize your efforts, prioritize your time, and build the foundations for long-term impact.

- **F**orecasting and planning
- **A**lignment of departments
- **C**entralization of data

- **T**echnology focus
- **O**ptimization and execution
- **R**evenue impact

Mastering RevOps isn't about fixing everything at once—it's about knowing where to focus. Let's break down the FACTOR Framework and why it's your key to success.

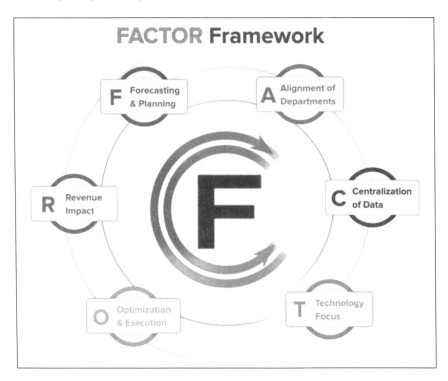

Forecasting and Planning: The Bedrock of RevOps Success

A predictable revenue stream is every CEO's dream. In an unpredictable world, RevOps provides stability by leveraging historical data, market trends, and real-time analytics to build accurate revenue forecasts. This proactive approach allows companies to allocate resources effectively, mitigate risks, and make informed business decisions.

RevOps teams work closely with sales, marketing, and finance to create revenue models that are both aspirational and achievable. They analyze past performance to identify trends, track external market conditions, and prepare for different revenue scenarios. Planning is not a one-time exercise but an ongoing process, requiring frequent adjustments as new insights emerge. Without precise forecasting, revenue leaders are left reacting to changes instead of proactively strategizing. RevOps ensures predictability, enabling leadership to make data-driven decisions with confidence.

We'll explore more about forecasting and planning for your revenue engine in chapter 5.

Alignment of Departments: Breaking Down Silos

The greatest challenge in revenue operations isn't technology or process—it's alignment. Siloed teams create inefficiencies, misaligned goals, and poor customer experiences. RevOps fosters alignment by establishing shared KPIs, unified data sources, and cross-functional collaboration.

For organizations to operate efficiently, sales, marketing, and customer success must work toward common revenue goals. When these departments operate independently, miscommunication and inefficiencies slow down progress. A shared vision, consistent communication, and standardized processes ensure seamless handoffs between teams. A customer-centric approach also plays a crucial role, ensuring that the prospect's journey is frictionless from initial engagement to long-term retention. True alignment leads to higher conversion rates, better customer satisfaction, and improved operational agility.

We will talk more about how to align departments, break down silos, and focus on the people behind your revenue engine in chapter 6.

Centralization of Data: The Single Source of Truth (SSOT)

In an ideal world, every revenue team would have a single, reliable source of data. In reality, most companies operate with fragmented CRMs, disparate data silos, and conflicting metrics. RevOps leaders must champion the centralization of data to ensure accuracy, accessibility, and actionable insights.

Data fragmentation is one of the biggest challenges for modern revenue teams. Different departments often use separate tools, leading to conflicting records and decision-making based on incomplete information. When data is not centralized, revenue teams struggle with redundancies, inconsistencies, and a lack of transparency. To counteract this, organizations must integrate data across systems to create a unified platform.

With a structured data governance strategy in place, teams can ensure information remains accurate, consistent, and available in real time. By improving data transparency and eliminating inefficiencies, RevOps enables teams to make faster and more informed decisions.

In chapter 7, we'll dive into all things data and cover all of the ways it can be used to dive your revenue goals forward.

Technology Focus: The Right Tools for the Right Outcomes

Technology can be an enabler or a hindrance, depending on how it is deployed. Many organizations adopt new tools without considering long-term integration, leading to inefficiencies and unnecessary complexity. A strategic approach to technology is crucial for RevOps success.

Automation has become a driving force in modern revenue operations, allowing teams to streamline workflows and eliminate manual tasks. However, technology must be carefully selected and integrated to ensure that systems work together cohesively. A RevOps leader must understand the nuances of different platforms, ensuring that they enhance efficiency rather than create additional complexity. Scalability is another key factor; selecting tools that grow with the business prevents frequent disruptions and unnecessary migrations. Ultimately, technology should serve people, not the other way around, and should always be evaluated for its real impact on productivity and revenue growth.

Technology will be the focus on chapter 8, where we will explore all the different types of tech and specific examples of what you can add to your RevOps tech stack.

Optimization and Execution: The Agile RevOps Mindset

RevOps is not a static function—it is a continuous cycle of testing, learning, and improving. Companies that embrace agility can adapt faster to market changes, optimize their Go-to-Market strategies, and execute with greater precision.

Optimization requires a mindset of constant improvement. A successful RevOps leader regularly assesses workflows, eliminates inefficiencies, and refines processes to improve overall performance. Decision-making must be data-driven, using analytics to identify opportunities for improvement. Collaboration across departments ensures that all revenue teams remain aligned in their objectives.

While it may sometimes frustrate IT teams, a good RevOps leader will always be on the lookout for better tools and processes, ensuring that the organization is never complacent. The willingness to experiment and iterate is what allows RevOps to stay ahead of changing market dynamics and drive ongoing success.

The backbone of optimization and execution is the processes of your revenue engine. We'll explore all of the best processes and practices you should be using in chapter 9.

Revenue Impact: The Ultimate Measure of Success

At the end of the day, RevOps success is measured by its impact on revenue. It's not just about new business; it's about driving sustainable revenue growth across multiple streams. Companies must focus on acquiring new customers, retaining existing ones, and maximizing upsell opportunities. Operational efficiency also plays a crucial role, as reducing costs while maintaining revenue growth contributes directly to profitability.

Revenue impact is the culmination of all RevOps efforts. When forecasting is accurate, teams are aligned, data is reliable, technology is optimized, and processes are continuously improved, the result is a high-functioning revenue engine that drives sustained growth. RevOps leaders must continuously monitor these factors, ensuring that revenue goals remain on track and adjusting strategies when needed.

This holistic approach to revenue management allows organizations to scale effectively while maintaining profitability. Think of the two images below as a three-dimensional cube. The FACTOR Framework identifies the main components of RevOps. The second illustration shows the departments that revenue operations supports from a traditional model. Both of these are guided by the people, processes, systems/tech, and data components that make up a true RevOps function within an organization.

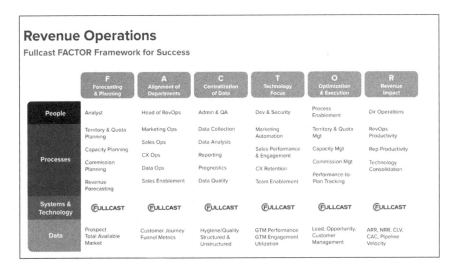

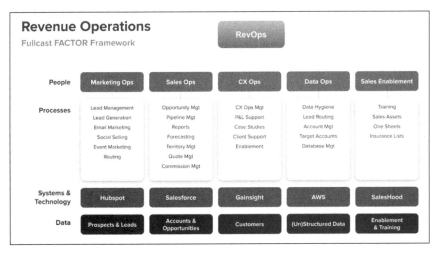

Conclusion

By mastering forecasting, alignment, data centralization, technology, optimization, and revenue impact, RevOps leaders can build a high-performing revenue engine that scales with the business. In the chapters ahead, we'll explore each pillar in detail, providing actionable strategies to implement and refine the FACTOR Framework within your organization. Use this framework as your foundation for success—and unlock the full potential of RevOps in your business.

5

Revenue Forecasting
and Planning

Revenue forecasting has always been a numbers game, but how RevOps decision-makers act on results has changed dramatically since the 1990s. Businesses continuously refine their approach to predicting revenue, from back-of-the-napkin projections to spreadsheet-driven models and now AI-powered analytics.

These days, AI promises more precise, AI-driven forecasting. However, the road to adoption has been anything but smooth. Many companies feel stuck in a time-consuming cycle of compensating for incomplete data, grappling with biased inputs, and trudging through outdated methodologies.

A groundbreaking Gartner study found that only 45 percent of sales leaders have "high confidence in their company's forecasting accuracy."[33] According to Gartner's States of Sales Operations Survey, skepticism to this degree results in "actions that are based on intuition instead of evidence, which often results in reduced commercial outcomes."

These are problems that AI alone can't fix.

For RevOps Leaders, Go-to-Market Specialists, and Sales Territory Managers, the challenge isn't just adopting AI; it's rethinking how we collect, analyze, and trust the data that fuels it.

New technology innovations are met with new obstacles as businesses race to integrate AI into their revenue strategies. But poor data quality, overreliance on hazy historical trends, and disconnected tech stacks all limit AI's capacity to generate scalable forecasts.

The truth is, forecasting is only as good as the data it captures and analyzes. Without addressing foundational customer data issues and learning from past forecasting missteps in earlier forms of technology, AI becomes just another tool producing flawed predictions at scale.

In this chapter, we accept the reality that the future of revenue forecasting isn't just about AI adoption. We recognize that it's about creating a more innovative, more connected data ecosystem that allows AI to deliver its full potential. But how?

To better understand ways to move forward with revenue forecasting, we need to step back and learn from the evolution of this predictive process that started humbly with early forms of SaaS-based CRM in the 1990s to a virtual whirlwind of algorithmic real-time AI-supported data analytics and machine learning that is transforming modern revenue operations and the Go-to-Market strategies that support them.

The History of Revenue Forecasting

In the early days of sales forecasting, the 1990s witnessed a move toward process automation and the foundational years of CRM software. Tools like ACT! and GoldMine emerged, allowing sales teams to track their pipelines and manage deals more systematically.

1990s: Process Automation and CRM Foundations

During the 1990s, technology focused on sales efficiency as businesses sought better ways to analyze their processes and improve forecasting accuracy. However, CRM adoption was often inconsistent, implementation was expensive, and many organizations struggled with fragmented systems that fed into entrenched data silos.

In 1999, Salesforce introduced SaaS-based CRM, with big promises to deliver greater accessibility and scalability than traditional on-premises solutions. Around the same time, "you've got mail" became the business buzzword of the decade as email secured its role as a critical sales channel, delivering more direct and scalable communication with prospects.

These advancements laid the groundwork for modern sales forecasting, but organizations still faced hurdles with data integration and system adoption across departments.

2000s: Digital Transformation Begins

The 2000s launched the early beginning of digital transformation in sales forecasting as businesses embraced online channels for lead generation. Websites and digital content attracted prospects, and email marketing and automated follow-ups helped sales teams nurture leads at scale. Improved web-based analytics helped sales and marketing teams gain valuable insights about customer buying behavior, which allowed for more data-driven forecasting. But were these innovations helping sales teams sell more effectively?

Forrester research found that salespeople worked an average of 52.3 hours per week, but only 23.3 percent of a sales rep's time was devoted to direct customer engagement or selling activities.[34] Moreover, spam concerns and decreasing engagement rates forced a pivot in email marketing as customer inboxes overflowed with a constant trail of promotions and offers.

Sales teams needed more time for selling, and they needed solutions to ensure they were reaching out to the right customers. Companies leveraged improved forecasting accuracy with a better selection of marketing automation tools, which streamlined lead management and tracked customer interactions more effectively.

By the end of the decade, predictive analytics was utilizing historical data and emerging AI models to anticipate trends and refine forecasting methodologies.

2010s: Data-Driven Sales and AI Emergence

During the 2010s, sales and marketing teams saw sales forecasting evolve into a highly data-driven discipline bolstered by platform data integration. Go-to-Market teams centralized customer information from CRM systems, marketing automation tools, and sales engagement platforms to gain greater visibility into customer buying behavior.

By utilizing a single source of truth, sales teams could track buyer journeys and engagement more effectively with improved forecasting. However, managing volumes of customer data was a challenge, and it required robust infrastructure and processes to maintain data quality and usability. Early statistics show companies were collecting approximately two zettabytes (equal to 2,000 exabytes, or 2 billion terabytes) of customer data in 2010.[35]

The emergence of AI-enabled tools transformed forecasting and lead scoring, allowing businesses to predict deal outcomes with greater precision. Platforms like Clari and Gong led revenue intelligence, using AI to analyze conversations, identify trends, and provide actionable insights. While these innovations improved forecasting accuracy, they also increased reliance on expensive software ecosystems.

Meanwhile, the rise of social selling on LinkedIn and other platforms further changed how sales teams engaged with prospects, blending digital networking with data-driven sales strategies. By the end of the decade, AI and automation had become central to modern sales forecasting, laying the groundwork for even more sophisticated predictive models in the years ahead.

2020s: The Age of AI and Revenue Operations

AI-driven sales forecasting and revenue operations helped define the 2020s, when more advanced real-time pipeline visibility and predictive accuracy emerged. Now, with machine learning and AI-enhancing forecasting models, GTM teams can anticipate deal outcomes with greater confidence, enabling more strategic decision-making.

The shift toward a RevOps model has further aligned Go-to-Market (GTM) teams, ensuring that sales, marketing, and customer success work from a unified data-driven approach to forecasting and growth.

Research from McKinsey & Company found that 92 percent of organizations have plans to increase their AI investments over the next three years.[36] There's no question that companies are sold on AI's impact on RevOps, but only 1 percent of leaders call their companies "mature" on the deployment spectrum. This means that AI is fully integrated into workflows and drives substantial business outcomes, according to McKinsey researchers Hannah Mayer, Lareina Yee, Michael Chui, and Roger Roberts. "The big question," they ask, "is how business leaders can deploy capital and steer their organizations closer to AI maturity?"

Managing increasingly complex integrated tech stacks also presents new challenges, as businesses must consistently capture customer data across multiple platforms. Tools like Gong and Gainsight accelerate the adoption of conversational intelligence, providing deeper insights into customer interactions. AI chatbots and virtual assistants are streamlining sales cycles by handling routine engagements. Additionally, advanced scenario planning tools are helping organizations navigate economic shifts and evolving buyer behaviors with greater agility. As AI continues to refine sales forecasting, the focus remains on balancing automation with human-driven strategy to maximize revenue growth.

Agility, Forecasting, and Growth Inside Nokia

Nokia is a great example of a company failing due to complacency and bureaucracy. Rob Levey, a seasoned RevOps advisor and executive who worked at Nokia as the VP of Global Channels and Operations between 1999 and 2005, witnessed this firsthand. Nokia's decline, largely through an inability to recognize and adapt or react to a platform-and-software-based market shift, which led to the rise of smartphones, allowing Apple, Google, and other companies to overtake its market share.

In only six years, Levey saw Nokia go from owning 49 percent of the market share in 2007 to only 3 percent in 2013. Decision-making was slow and inefficient, with bureaucratic layers of hierarchy and multiple approvals, according to Levey. This slow decision-making delayed the recognition that software was becoming critical to the success of mobile devices. Like most bureaucracies, departments operated in silos with limited communication and upheld the status quo. Nokia, once known for its innovation, was paralyzed and lacked agility and creativity needed to adapt and win in the market. Its competitors were leveraging single-platform operating systems (iOS and Android), while Nokia struggled with fifty-seven versions of Symbian for its vast array of hardware-based mobile phones.

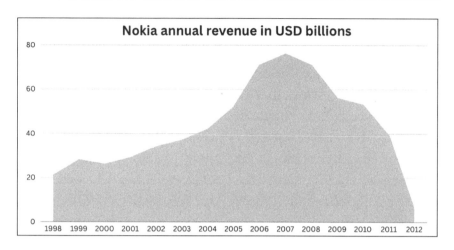

The Unknown Start-Up within Nokia. In 1999, a company within Nokia was created in an attempt to create the elusive third leg, along with the hugely successful mobile phone and infrastructure groups. It was called Nokia Internet Communications (NIC), and was the consolidation of several acquisitions, most notably an Enterprise Firewall company that ran Check Point on an appliance.

In 1999 NIC generated close to $40 million in revenue with a sales team of thirty-five people, primarily based in the United States, the United Kingdom, Germany, and France.

Levey was hired out of the United Kingdom by Greg Shortell, who was about to be appointed VP of Worldwide Sales. He asked him if he would like to become his Head of Sales Operations—with a catch. He needed to relocate from London to Dallas, Texas. Levey was newly married, and he proceeded to move with his four-month-old firstborn in November 1999.

"From a SalesOps perspective, I did not really know what I was doing, but I knew we needed a solid sales compensation plan since we were hiring reps like crazy," Levey said. "We also had a crazy good product that enterprises around the world were deploying. It was a hardware appliance that was being installed in data centers around the world and protecting companies with what was called a Security Firewall. At one stage, 99 of the Fortune 100 companies were using the Nokia/Check Point appliance."

With hyper growth came a need to track the business. In 2000, they became one of the first companies to deploy a CRM. This was a database that a company called Salesforce was promoting to help track your opportunities and your sales reps' "Rolodex" of contacts. In those days, sales orders would come in via fax. You were completely blind; reps would call potential customers in their territory, schedule meetings over the phone, and ultimately close deals. Your first visibility to the deal (apart from talking over the "grapevine") was the fax machine with a purchase order coming in.

Deploying Salesforce and "encouraging" sales reps around the world to enter their contacts into a company database and then track their deals was completely foreign to them. To say there was resistance was an understatement. Levey personally traveled around the world for months, explaining the "why," and then training the team on how to use the tool.

"That really was the beginning of sales forecasting," Levey says.

Fast-forward three years. In 2002, Levey's team generated $350 million in annual revenue with a total sales team of 240. Head count grew from thirty-five to over three hundred with annual revenue growing from $40 million to over $500 million over a period of five years.

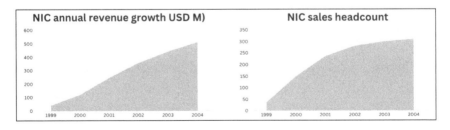

Some Sales Ops Lessons Learned. Levey says he truly did hire a global sales force, and at one point, he was issuing up to five compensation plans a week with multiple currencies and multiple managers, each wanting their own "special" exceptions. Working with human resources was key to ensuring that compensation details were correct and that they could be issued within two days of a sales rep's start date. They had no systems to help them, so this was all communicated via email and Excel spreadsheets.

"It might have been easy to simply do what I was asked to by my boss," Levey said. "But my boss was often too tied up in deals or hiring or executive meetings to provide too much direction. So, I dug into numbers, spoke to loads of sales folks, and generally put up my hand to provide any assistance, anywhere. If there was a project that needed attention, I was invariably involved or eager to help."

Marketing and CX Alignment. Even twenty-five years ago, alignment between Marketing and Sales was crucial. Events were the primary lead drivers in those days, so the handoff from Marketing to Sales, the messaging, and of course the "swag" were all key components of the sales process. There were no BDRs then, so this was a full cycle run by AEs—from lead to purchase order.

"In those days, we spoke about four-legged sales calls," he said.

The systems engineer was the "linchpin" of the deal. They did not say much but understood the customer's network almost better than the customer, and tech prowess definitely helped close the deal. Just as important was the customer support team, or post sales. This was hardware being installed into some of the largest and most secure data centers in the world. The customer relied on and got support excellence.

Strong Leadership and Collaboration. Every story talks about the leadership team, but this team was made up of some genuine pioneers and truly good people, Levey recounted. Kent Elliott, the CEO from Canada, became a three-time successful exit founder. Greg Shortell, Levey's boss, was one of the best CROs he said he had ever worked with. And Dan McDonald, the CMO, was one of the most creative marketers in Silicon Valley at the time. But the real leadership, Levey says, came from the promotion of young leaders, including Sales Manager Gord Boyce, who went on to be CEO of Forescout Technologies, and Head of Customer Support Nanhi Singh, who became Chief Customer Officer of Imperva.

Levey's own personal collaboration between the CFO and Chief Product Officer, in particular, was what he remembered the most. They were selling a product that was mostly manufactured in Mexico. So, all those orders coming off the fax machine needed to be sent to the manufacturing team. His quarterly forecast was less about revenue and more about the orders that the manufacturing team needed to plan for. When they launched the mid-range appliance, the Nokia IP330 Security Appliance Firewall VPN, orders increased from two hundred appliances to over 1,500 per month within six months of the launch.

"Developing a rapport with sales reps and sales leaders was key," Levey said. "This involved staying informed about new hires and departures, assigning territories, supporting promotions, explaining compensation plans to new reps, navigating introductions to the German Works Council, and handling many other key responsibilities."

Nokia's story serves as both a cautionary tale and a testament to the power of agility, leadership, and forecasting in Sales Operations. While the company as a whole succumbed to bureaucratic inertia, the NIC division demonstrated the transformational impact of having clear, data-driven visibility into the business. By deploying one of the earliest CRM systems, NIC shifted from reactive order-taking to proactive pipeline management. This gave SalesOps and leadership the ability to forecast demand, anticipate resource needs, and guide strategic decisions. Early investment in forecasting discipline can fuel rapid growth, even within a larger organization struggling to keep pace with change.

Understanding the Basics of
Successful Sales Forecasting

Is your CRM drowning in bad data? Incomplete and inaccurate CRM records undermine your Go-to-Market strategies and create a distorted view of customer relationships. Recent statistics published in the *AI Journal* report 85 percent of companies blame poor data quality as the primary barrier to AI success in 2025.[37]

Add in forecasting bias and an unhealthy overreliance on subjective sales inputs, and you're stuck with skewed predictions that mislead your decision-making process. The truth? Sales teams often work off gut feelings and outdated information rather than solid, actionable insights.

Poor data quality makes it challenging to create reliable forecast scenarios, especially when RevOps leaders must figure in market adjustments and new variables. If your forecasting process is buried under these challenges, it's time to ask: How long can you afford to ignore the cracks in your data-driven strategy?

Through his experience working with teams to build a centralized revenue operations function, Louis Poulin, CRO and a leader in RevOps implementation, has seen his share of common challenges that delay AI adoption success.[38]

"Teams were realizing, like lots of companies, there were silos of operations resources and different agendas and priorities that spanned the marketing organization," Louis explained during a recent *Go To Market Podcast* with Dr. Amy Cook.[39] "There were lots of inefficiencies and disconnects that were preventing efficiency, preventing automation, and lacking a cohesive view of customers."

Louis often sees a lack of agreement on where teams have problems and where they have opportunities. "Teams often asked what we could be doing across the organization to help enable and fuel revenue growth in the future?"

For effective revenue forecasting, RevOps leaders must avoid the six most common challenges facing GTM teams hoping to implement AI-sourced solutions for successful revenue growth.

The Six GTM-Stalling Challenges of AI Adoption

1. Incomplete and Inaccurate CRM Records

When key customer details are missing, outdated, or inconsistent, AI can't accurately identify patterns. As far back as 2011, studies showed lead generation campaigns lacking clean data ended up wasting almost 30 percent of each sales rep's time. According to Gartner research, dirty data can cost companies around $15 million every year.

Recommendation: Employ AI and ML models that auto-complete missing fields and cross-check records with external databases for real-time validation.

Data Enrichment Tools: Consider solutions like **ZoomInfo**, **TigerEye**, **6Sense**, and **Apollo.io**, among others. Also, augment your captured profile data with industry-specific and/or regional and country-specific customer data providers.

AI-Powered Data Validation: Platforms like **Salesforce Einstein** and **Clari** use AI to detect and flag discrepancies in CRM records.

2. **Forecasting Bias and Subjective Sales Inputs**

   Human behavior plays a significant role in forecasting bias. "Optimism bias often leads sales teams to overstate revenue projections, assuming the best-case scenario for deal closures," experts at BoostUp explained.[40] "Conversely, pessimism bias can result in conservative forecasts, where teams underestimate opportunities to avoid pressure from unrealistic targets. Recent data bias is another factor, where teams overemphasize recent trends, ignoring broader historical patterns critical for reliable forecasting."

   Even systemic issues like inconsistent data collection processes and siloed operations between departments can misalign forecasts. AI models learn from these inaccuracies and then reinforce flawed assumptions instead of providing trustworthy data-driven insights.

Recommendation: Implement tools that incorporate unbiased deal insights, eliminating personal bias through activity-based scoring and real-time pipeline analysis.
Predictive Analytics Platforms: Clari, **Aviso**, and **Gong** reduce bias by analyzing historical patterns, deal signals, and activity data. **Salesforce Einstein Forecasting** and **BoostUp** contribute to removing forecast bias.
Deploy Behavioral and Sentiment Analytics: People.ai evaluates sales behaviors to identify inconsistencies in forecasting and suggests objective adjustments.
Gainsight and **Gong** are also great choices to track customer sentiment and evaluate attrition risk.

3. **Overreliance on Historical Sales Data**
   AI models that are trained mainly on past trends struggle to consider new variables, such as economic shifts and competitive disruptions. This leads to outdated predictions.

Recommendation: Use solutions that weigh leading indicators (e.g., marketing engagement, buyer readiness) alongside lagging historical data.

Predictive Analytics Tools: Clari, **Aviso**, and **Gong** integrate AI to factor leading signals like market trends and competitive dynamics.

Dynamic Forecasting Models: Platforms like **Anaplan**, **Fullcast**, and **Aviso** enable scenario modeling that combines historical data with predictive signals like seasonality and buyer intent.

4. **Data Quality Issues**

    Data quality issues—such as duplicates, inconsistencies, and missing information—undermine AI's ability to generate accurate revenue forecasts. A recent survey found that more than half of respondents to Monte Carlo's survey reported 25 percent of their revenue was impacted by data quality issues.[41]

    When AI is fed bad data, it amplifies errors rather than correcting them, leading to misleading insights and poor decision-making.

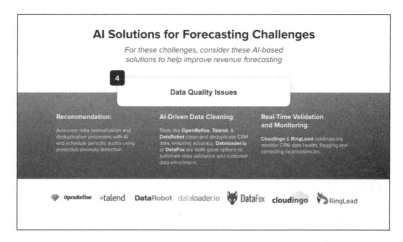

Recommendation: Automate data normalization and deduplication processes with AI and schedule periodic audits using predictive anomaly detection.

AI-Driven Data Cleaning: Tools like **OpenRefine**, **Talend**, and **DataRobot** clean and deduplicate CRM data, ensuring accuracy. **Dataloader.io** and **DataFox** are both great options to automate data validation and customer data enrichment.

Real-time Validation and Monitoring: Cloudingo and **RingLead** continuously monitor CRM data health, flagging and correcting inconsistencies.

5. **Complex, Disconnected Tech Stacks**

   When critical sales, marketing, and customer data is fragmented across multiple systems, AI struggles to generate reliable forecasts, leading to inconsistencies and missed insights.

   "One of the things that connects all of this is the flow of data from point A to point Z, meaning from the time you start prospecting a customer to the point where you convert into an opportunity, you can't lose sight of the integrity of the data flowing through," Prasad Varahabhatla, a RevOps innovator, said during a *Go To Market Podcast* with Dr. Amy Cook.[42] "That is the one big thing around revenue operations—you need to start focusing on where you can think about this as one continuum, as compared to three, four, or five different processes."

Recommendation: Consolidate systems with AI-powered connectors creating a centralized repository of sales and operational data.

Integration Platforms: MuleSoft, Zapier, and **Boomi** and similar solutions use AI to integrate disparate systems, enabling unified data flows.

AI-Driven Orchestration: Workato and **SnapLogic** synchronize tech stacks, streamlining workflows between CRM, marketing, and financial platforms.

6. **Forecast Scenarios Accounting for Market Adjustments** Without integrating factors like economic shifts, competitive changes, and unforeseen disruptions, AI-driven forecasts risk being static and misaligned with current market realities.

Recommendation: Leverage external market intelligence in combination with internal data for agile forecasting that adapts to volatility.

Scenario Modeling Tools: Anaplan, Adaptive Insights, and all the major cloud providers—**AWS, Azure, GCP**—allow for market scenario simulations based on macroeconomic trends.

Sentiment and Trend Analysis: Crunchbase and **ZoomInfo** analyze external market data, including news and social sentiment, to adjust forecasts. **Sprinklr** and **Brandwatch** offer solutions to monitor social media mentions and trends.

- **The bad news is that these are daunting problems for any RevOps team.**
- **The good news is that AI solutions are available to help address these challenges.**

"AI, obviously, is very transformational for where we are today," Louis said during his *Go To Market Podcast* episode.[43] "As I think about applying that into the revenue operations space, I think about things like automated process enablement. So rather than having people manage processes that need to be automated, either having software step in and workflow step in to automate that, either with human intervention or even identifying areas for opportunity, then building and putting forward processes and building links between disconnected processes for one continuous flow. That is a huge piece that just didn't exist even three years ago. I'm seeing more of that functionality being built into some of these core platforms that run revenue operations."

Unless your operational foundation is well thought out among RevOps teams, AI won't magically fix your sales and revenue forecasting.

Louis recently listed four key prerequisites to ensure that AI-driven insights are accurate, reliable, and actionable. They are:

- Integrated Customer Data Sources
- Trusted GTM Forecasting Processes and Models
- Integrated GTM Technology Stack
- Cross-Functional Revenue Growth Alignment

Are You Prepared for AI Forecasting Solutions?

How can you be sure you are prepared? Let's break down each fundamental prerequisite to ensure your revenue operations are ready to adopt AI solutions to advance revenue forecasting.

1. **Integrated Customer Data Sources**
    *   **CRM system (Salesforce, HubSpot)**
    *   **Trusted customer data and third-party data sources**
    *   **Past sales performance and revenue attainment baselines**
    *   **Market trends and economic indicators**

    You can't trust AI to forecast revenue if your data is messy. Go-to-Market teams need trusted customer information and third-party data sources to create reliable forecasting. These external sources are especially key for understanding buying behavior and market conditions and generating reliable forecasts.

    "Depending on where your organization is in the SaaS life cycle, you might find that some elements are most important than others," said Jose Aleman, Director of Global Sales Operations.[44] "So this is a good time to think about what relative weight you will want to assign to each of these categories."

    AI models also need insight on historical sales performance and revenue attainment baselines. This data helps identify key trends, seasonality, and potential risks. In turn, forecasts can be adjusted to account for broader shifts in the industry or economy.

    "The RevOps team's job is to be the plumbers of the revenue process and flows," Louis said. "You look for leaks, you plug them, and you do that through technology, process, and data."

2. **Trusted GTM Forecasting Process and Models**
   - **Pipeline-driven forecasting model tied to revenue goals**
   - **Analysis on both top-down and bottom-up approaches**
   - **Historical trend analysis**
   - **Robust revenue scenario "what if" modeling**

Sixty-two percent of platform businesses recognize the critical role of real-time data in their growth strategies, according to a PYMNTS survey.[45] Their study found that "companies leveraging real-time insights are more agile, allowing them to respond quickly to market changes and customer needs."

For GTM teams to ensure sales targets align with corporate goals, they need real-time data backed by AI-sourced solutions. Without this framework, AI insights risk disconnecting from actual revenue results, giving you inaccurate forecasts that don't get you anywhere.

Data, including top-down analysis, bottom-up insights, and historical trends, fuel AI. A top-down strategy offers the macro-level view, taking into account the business's overall goals and the market's state. At the same time, bottom-up forecasting guarantees that AI incorporates the frontline, real-time sales data that truly generates income. This potent combination of both strategies raises the accuracy of AI forecasting. Additionally, powerful "what-if" scenario modeling allows teams to test predictions against market changes.

By putting these components in place, RevOps teams prepare the way for AI to provide more accurate, data-supported revenue forecasts that support more intelligent, strategic decision-making.

3. **Integrated GTM Technology Stack**
   - **Leveraging tools to unify data and improve accuracy**
   - **Avoid tech sprawl and align GTM teams around a set of two or three core platforms managing revenue**
   - **Deploy AI and ML to identify new revenue opportunities**

Leveraging tools that consolidate customer, sales, and revenue data ensures that AI-driven insights use accurate and consistent information. AI models risk pulling from fragmented or siloed data without this integration. The result? Unreliable forecasts and misaligned Go-to-Market strategies and tech sprawl.

A recent study reported that 77 percent of US technology decision-makers have "moderate to extensive levels" of tech sprawl.[46] "This sprawl can result in unsustainable costs, slower IT delivery, reduced operational resilience, and increased security risks," Biswajeet Mahapatra, a principal analyst at Forrester, said.

Teams can avoid tech sprawl by operating around a streamlined set of core platforms, such as CRM, marketing automation, and revenue intelligence. A simplified stack reduces data inconsistencies, enhances cross-functional collaboration, and allows AI-supported forecasting to reflect a single source of truth.

"Today, we are in this capital efficiency mode where the mantra is to do more with less. And I believe RevOps really helps businesses get the most from their tech stack," Saket Kapoor, a RevOps expert and GTM leader, said during a *Go To Market Podcast* with Dr. Amy Cook.[47] "I read somewhere that an average B2B enterprise software company has somewhere from twenty to twenty-five core systems in their GTM stack alone. Imagine the waste! RevOps takes a hard look at what's working and what's not, and finds the most efficient way to drive revenue using the tools you already have." With this in place, GTM teams can use AI tools and machine learning (ML) to identify new revenue opportunities.

4. **Cross-Functional Revenue Growth Alignment**
    - **Alignment across Sales, Marketing, Customer Success, Partner, Pro Serve, Finance, Rev Ops, etc.**
    - **Clear accountability and revenue forecasting ownership across the GTM**
    - **Data ownership spanning all customer-facing teams**

    Did you know only 36 percent of companies organize their customer data into a unified database? In addition to this, Customer Data Platform research found only 78 percent of surveyed companies use centralized data as part of their customer data strategy.[48]

    AI models rely on data from the entire organization. When this data is inaccurate, outdated, or incomplete, it skews forecasting models and robs the RevOps team of opportunities to understand and identify key touchpoints within the entire client life cycle.

    AI adoption also requires that GTM teams have clear ownership and accountability for revenue forecasts. All teams interacting with customers must share data ownership to guarantee that AI-driven insights are founded on reliable, superior data from each phase of the revenue funnel.

    Without a clear framework, forecasting results feel disjointed and interfere with AI's capacity to recognize patterns and hazards.

Revenue Forecasting: AI Systems and Solutions to Consider

Revenue Forecasting AI Systems & Solutions

Solution	Great For...	Ideal Customer	Capabilities & Benefits
GONG	Extracting insights from customer conversations & track deal sentiment	Sales teams relying on verbal interactions for revenue.	Conversation analytics, deal tracking. Provides AI-driven visibility into customer engagement trends and risks.
Clari	Offering complete pipeline visibility & integrates with major CRMs and BI tools	Enterprises seeking holistic pipeline and forecasting solutions.	AI-driven forecasting, risk identification. Reduces surprises and increases forecast accuracy.
salesforce Revenue Cloud	Comprehensive, customizable; integrate seamlessly with Salesforce ecosystem	Organizations already using Salesforce.	CPQ, revenue recognition, forecasting. Provides real-time insights based on deal stages. Heavy focus by Salesforce on AI agents to enrich customer insights.
Outreach	Combining engagement data with pipeline health metrics	Sales teams using Outreach's engagement tools.	Pipeline health tracking, engagement-driven insights. Simplifies forecasting for engagement-driven teams.
Salesloft	Combining sales engagement w/ pipeline analytics for E2E visibility. Actionable RT insights on deal progression.	Sales teams looking to align engagement data w/ revenue forecasting.	AI-driven engagement tracking and forecasting. Deal health analysis & pipeline visibility. Aligns sales activity metrics with revenue outcomes for more reliable forecasting.

Revenue Forecasting AI Systems & Solutions

Solution	Great For...	Ideal Customer	Capabilities & Benefits
ebsta	Enhances pipeline visibility through email and calendar engagement data; integrates seamlessly with Salesforce.	Small to mid-sized businesses integrated into Salesforce's ecosystem, and large enterprises looking for advanced analytics and pipeline accuracy.	CRM enrichment, engagement analytics, deal scoring. Improves pipeline accuracy and helps sales focus on deals likely to close.
FULLCAST	Streamlines revenue operations planning; enables dynamic scenario modeling	Enterprises with complex sales & revenue operations	Quota planning, revenue modeling, operational alignment. Increases forecast reliability through strategic adjustments.
Seam AI	AI-driven forecasting with real-time updates and high accuracy.	Mid-to-large enterprises focused on AI-driven precision.	Predictive analytics, real-time adjustments. Reduces forecast errors and proactively identifies pipeline risks.
aviso	Scenario-based forecasting; lightweight integration with multiple CRMs.	Teams needing advanced forecasting and deal intelligence.	AI predictions, risk scoring, scenario planning. Improves accuracy with scenario-based insights and reduces forecasting bias.
Gainsight	Customer health scoring, renewal & upsell forecasting, churn prediction, and revenue tracking reporting.	B2B SaaS companies with a mature Customer Success discipline and a need for centralized customer data management	Great new AI offering and expanded capabilities within the platform (LMS, in-product messaging, etc.), improved forecast accuracy, cross-team collaboration, focus on retention & growth.

Key Takeaways and Call to Action

RevOps leaders are constantly testing, adapting, and refining their approaches to stay ahead in the GTM game. There's no perfect formula for GTM teams. However, experimentation and continuous learning will give organizations the flexibility to thrive.

Teams should remember that every business is unique, and the right solution requires careful alignment with goals and data strategies. As you evaluate your revenue forecasting plan, consider this an opportunity to test, refine, and evolve your approach—ultimately paving the way for more proactive, data-driven decision-making.

Nobody has this all figured out! We're in a time of experimentation with rapid advances in AI capabilities.

As RevOps leaders, we're all navigating uncharted territory regarding AI-driven revenue forecasting. With rapid advancements in Go-to-Market and AI capabilities, businesses constantly test, refine, and adapt their strategies to see what works.

There's no one-size-fits-all solution—only continuous learning, iteration, and innovation. The companies that succeed won't be waiting for a perfect playbook but those embracing experimentation, refining their data foundations, and staying agile as AI evolves.

AI-powered forecasting tools help overcome traditional forecasting limitations.

Teams that use traditional forecasting methods rely on static models, gut-instinct, or historical yet outdated data, which leads to inaccurate conclusions and missed opportunities. In contrast, AI-powered forecasting tools analyze large volumes of real-time data, identify hidden patterns amid this data, and adjust predictions based on dynamic market conditions.

By leveraging AI, teams can pivot from reactive planning to proactive strategy to stay ahead in a dynamic and unpredictable market.

Know that there is not a single right approach or one system or tool that is best for every company.

Every company has unique data structures, customized sales processes, and targeted market dynamics, so there's no universal, one-size-fits-all approach to AI-powered forecasting. The best system for one organization might not be the right fit for another, and success depends on aligning technology with specific business needs, data quality, and operational workflows.

Companies must experiment with new strategies, refine processes, and adapt modern AI-sourced forecasting strategies to balance AI automation and human insight. The key isn't chasing a perfect solution—it's building a flexible, data-driven approach that evolves with the business.

Revenue forecasting isn't waiting for teams to catch up—it's already happening, and it's shaped by those daring enough to challenge the status quo.

The companies that will dominate tomorrow's RevOps aren't clinging to outdated models or unthinkingly following "best practices." It's the companies that embrace AI, experiment with new strategies, and relentlessly adapt to the ever-changing landscape that will lead the GTM charge. If you're not actively rethinking how you forecast revenue, you're already falling behind.

AI-Powered Revenue Forecasting Worksheet

Call to Action: Critically evaluate your plan for revenue forecasting. Identify where you have challenges that can be helped through the adoption of AI tools. Select a few AI tools to test to address key blockers.

Step 1: Evaluate Your Current Revenue Forecasting Process

1. **Describe your current revenue forecasting methodology:**
   (e.g., historical data analysis, manual projections, CRM-based predictions)

   _____

   _____

2. **What are the main challenges in your forecasting process?**
   (e.g., data accuracy, real-time insights, scalability, human bias)

   _____

   _____

3. **How frequently do you adjust your forecasts?**

   _____

   _____

4. **Who are the key stakeholders involved in your forecasting process?**

   _____

   _____

Step 2: Identify AI Opportunities

1. **Which areas of your forecasting process could benefit from AI?**

   _____

   _____

2. **What key blockers could AI help address?**

   _____

3. Have you used AI tools for forecasting before?

_____

Step 3: Select AI Tools to Test

1. Research and list at least three AI tools that could improve your forecasting process:

AI Tool	Key Features	Potential Impact on Forecasting
1.		
2.		
3.		

2. Which AI tool will you test first, and why?

_____

3. What success metrics will you use to evaluate the AI tool's effectiveness?
(e.g., improved accuracy, reduced manual effort, faster reporting)

_____

_____

Step 4: Implementation and Review

1. Set a timeline for testing AI tools:
   - Start Date: _____
   - Evaluation Date: _____
2. After testing, what improvements did you observe?

_____

3. **Will you continue using the AI tool or explore other options? Why?**

_____

_____

Final Thoughts: AI has the potential to revolutionize revenue forecasting by providing deeper insights, reducing errors, and improving efficiency. By following this worksheet, you can take a strategic approach to integrating AI into your forecasting process.

Next Steps:

- Share findings with your team.
- Refine forecasting processes based on insights gained.
- Continue evaluating AI tools for greater efficiency.

GTM Planning

RevOps planning cannot be a once-a-year activity. For an organization to sustain effective RevOps, the organization must commit to engaging in RevOps planning year-round. For better or worse, there's not a single right way to do this planning. Rather, organizations need to develop their own tailored approaches to RevOps planning—approaches that blend discipline, clarity, and inclusivity.

"Annual planning is one of the most critical activities that RevOps plays," said RevOps executive Katerina Ostrovsky in a *Go To Market Podcast* with Amy Cook.[49] "We work very closely with other parts of the business—finance, specifically, but also product. We have this unique perspective that the organization relies on for data to make decisions."

Ryan Westwood approaches continuous RevOps planning by scheduling quarterly strategic off-sites for Fullcast revenue leaders;

the quarterly session in October of each year is dedicated to annual RevOps strategy. Ryan's carefully structured, tightly orchestrated RevOps planning sessions integrate methods like Salesforce's V2MOM (Vision, Values, Methods, Obstacles, and Measures) framework and budget allocation[50]; the goal is to provide an opportunity for executives to evaluate what Fullcast should start, stop, or continue doing to improve alignment with long-term revenue goals.

Ryan also employs playbooks to provide clear direction and foster accountability on RevOps goals. These playbooks, updated and signed at each off-site, clarify roles, reinforce company culture, and serve as a compass for decision-making throughout the year. Alongside this, his emphasis on ruthless prioritization ensures that the company focuses only on what will deliver the most value to customers, avoiding distractions from competing interests or the loudest voices in the room.

A well-structured RevOps plan balances revenue growth with operational efficiency, sales team enablement, and executive alignment. In an interview with Kluster, Brandon Bussey, Director of Revenue and Account Operations at Lucid, said he has four overarching goals when it comes to RevOps planning.[51]

"One of the goals is to increase the total amount of bookings," Bussey said. "This is important because we have an aggressive growth target, so we need to make sure our goals are aligned with that. The second goal is increasing average bookings per rep across the board. I've seen companies that increase the overall number of bookings, but it's a 'the rich get richer and the poor get poorer' situation—that is not success.

"The third goal is transparency and visibility upward into our executive team," Bussey continued. "Our exec team doesn't have a traditional sales background, so a lot of it is educating them and showing them the key metrics. The last goal is creating a vibrant culture in the orgs that we support."

No matter how an organization chooses to do RevOps planning, every part of the organization that is involved in revenue planning needs to be involved, aligned, and engaged.[52] That's why sustaining successful RevOps planning requires extensive up-front thought and planning. The purpose of this chapter is to introduce the multiple discrete elements that comprise successful RevOps planning: territory planning, quota management, capacity planning and forecasting, establishing a commission structure, data analytics, and business enablement. It doesn't matter if this planning takes place at an executive off-site brainstorming session or by analyzing spreadsheets in the office. What's important is that organizations build clear structures and frameworks to effectively guide, coordinate, and sustain all of their RevOps planning activities. By the end of this section, we hope you'll begin conceptualizing your own blueprint for how to transform RevOps planning from a functional necessity in your organization into your organization's competitive advantage.

Territory Planning

Territory management is one of the most critical components of effective RevOps planning. It serves as the blueprint for aligning Go-to-Market resources with the company's strategic goals, ensuring that every rep, team, and function has the best chance of success. Well-balanced territories lead to improved quota attainment, rep retention, and overall productivity. Yet, territory balancing is often overlooked or approached with oversimplified methods, which can result in inefficiencies, low morale, and revenue leakage.

Research from *Harvard Business Review* reveals that optimizing territory design can increase sales by 2 to 7 percent,[53] even without additional resources or changes to the overarching sales strategy. This significant impact highlights the importance of territory management not just as a sales exercise, but as a strategic function that influences the entire GTM engine.

At its core, territory balancing is a resource allocation exercise. It ensures that opportunities are distributed equitably, maximizing revenue potential while maintaining fairness and transparency. For sales representatives, territory design directly affects their earning potential and workload, making it a highly sensitive issue. A well-designed territory plan enables reps to focus their efforts on deals that yield the highest returns, reducing wasted time and frustration.

Transparency in the balancing process fosters trust, demonstrating to sales teams that the playing field is level. Conversely, unclear or biased territory assignments can lead to disputes, overcompensation to resolve conflicts, and ultimately, missed quotas or increased turnover.

Territory management becomes even more vital during challenging economic times. When budgets are tight and hiring freezes are common, optimizing existing resources becomes a necessity. Balanced territories allow organizations to achieve more with the same, or even fewer, resources. This makes it a key lever for operational efficiency and growth.

Steps for Balancing Territories. The first step in effective territory management is aligning the process with corporate goals and defining the ideal customer profile (ICP). Companies must consider whether their strategy prioritizes expanding market share, retaining existing customers, or targeting specific segments. A useful tool for this analysis is the BCG Growth Share Matrix,[54] which categorizes accounts into four types:

- **Stars:** High market share and high growth—ideal opportunities to prioritize.
- **Cash Cows:** High market share but low growth—stable and profitable accounts.
- **Question Marks:** Low market share but high growth—potentially high-reward accounts requiring strategic investment.

- **Dogs:** Low market share and low growth—accounts that may not justify significant effort.

This matrix provides a framework for understanding account potential and distributing opportunities fairly among team members. For example, a Cash Cow account in North America may be a Question Mark in a less established market like Asia-Pacific, demonstrating the need to localize the criteria.

Balancing territories also requires a mix of criteria tailored to each organization's goals and structure. Commonly used criteria include:

1. **Geography:** Often used to align resources with time zones, cultures, or regional strategies. However, as remote selling becomes more prevalent, companies are increasingly moving away from geography-based designs.
2. **Historical Performance:** Balancing high-performing accounts with newer opportunities to maintain a mix of stability and growth potential.
3. **Revenue Potential:** Allocating territories based on the total addressable market (TAM) and account value (ACV).
4. **Account Size:** High-ACV accounts may require in-person selling and longer sales cycles, while low-ACV accounts may favor more automated approaches.
5. **Industry:** Useful for specialized teams targeting specific verticals like financial services or government.
6. **Propensity to Buy:** Grouping accounts based on predictive metrics to assign high-value opportunities equitably.
7. **Account Score:** Aggregating multiple criteria into a single, weighted metric for simplicity and accuracy.

These criteria are often combined in a hybrid model, adjusted to reflect corporate strategy and regional dynamics.

Territory balancing is not a static exercise. Economic changes, new data, and evolving business goals necessitate ongoing adjustments. Establishing feedback loops ensures that changes are informed by field insights and fosters trust across the organization. Managers can review proposed adjustments to integrate field knowledge and maintain existing relationships, while transparent communication about the changes builds buy-in.

Example Scenarios for Territory Balancing. Effective territory balancing is not a one-size-fits-all process, as each organization's needs, goals, and resources vary significantly. One example is the *High-Velocity Hunter Model*,[55] which is ideal for companies with high-volume SMB sales. In this scenario, territories are often designed based on industry or account density. For instance, financial firms, which tend to be quick and high-value deals, might be distributed evenly across territories to ensure equal opportunity. Similarly, urban ICP accounts located in dense markets like Manhattan or San Francisco could be assigned strategically to maximize efficiency and throughput for sales representatives.

Another approach is the *Transition from Geo to Strategic Model*, which suits enterprise sales teams adapting to the rise of remote selling. Instead of relying on geographic boundaries, territories may be defined by factors such as annual recurring revenue (ARR) potential, time zones, or existing customer relationships. This method minimizes disruption to customers while aligning territories with strategic priorities, such as focusing resources on accounts with the highest potential for growth.

The *Focused Farmer Model* is particularly effective for companies with limited head count aiming to maximize impact without overextending resources. In this model, territories are balanced to include an equal number of high-ARR accounts while prioritizing retention and account expansion. Reps are also tasked with managing flagged accounts at risk of churn, ensuring that customer retention remains a top priority. Each of these scenarios highlights the importance of tailoring territory balancing strategies to the specific needs and goals of the organization, enabling RevOps teams to align resources effectively and drive sustainable growth.

Quota Management

Ryan was on a call with a customer when they revealed something stark: Forty to 50 percent of sales representatives were failing to meet their quotas.[56] This wasn't just a minor hiccup—it's a systemic issue affecting countless organizations. In fact, according to Forrester, the average quota attainment for B2B sales organizations is only 47 percent.[57] The problem in these organizations isn't a lack of talent or effort from the sales teams. Instead, the issue stems from the way territories, quotas, and compensation plans are too often designed.

Sales reps aren't being set up to succeed. Ineffective quota-setting and poorly designed territories are hamstringing reps before they even have a chance to start. Companies often fail to align these elements with the realities of the market, creating barriers that even the most talented sales teams struggle to overcome.

To tackle the 40–50 percent quota attainment failure rate for Ryan's client, Ryan's team focused on implementing methods to help this company quickly assign realistic, data-driven quotas. By breaking down the process into manageable components—such as the products being sold, the industries targeted, and the geographies covered—they made it easier for the organization to create plans that set sales reps up for success.

Effective quota management is a delicate balance. If you set quotas too high, and you risk demotivating your sales team and missing targets. As Go-to-Market executive Marc Maloy warned in a LinkedIn post,[58] "If AE attainment was 60% or less this year AND you're planning on a 10% or more quota increase next year, you will miss the plan next year."

In fact, increasing quotas too aggressively often backfires. "Generally, higher quotas have a negative correlation to absolute dollars sold," Maloy wrote. Instead of stretching quotas beyond reach, leaders should focus on incentive structures that drive performance. "Do yourself and your team a favor. Keep quotas flat and accelerate commission early. You will sell more in the end, and your team will feel like it's winning."

By keeping quotas realistic and structuring incentives wisely, RevOps leaders can drive higher sales performance while maintaining a motivated, high-energy sales force. Quota management provides the foundation for aligning individual targets with broader organizational goals. When quotas are realistic, data-driven, and clearly communicated, they not only enhance productivity but also help retain top talent by fostering trust and transparency.

Steps for Setting Quotas. The first step involves setting high-level revenue targets at the organizational level. This typically done by senior management or the finance team, taking into account a variety of factors:

- *Market Conditions:* The current state of the market, including demand for the product or service, competitive landscape, and economic climate, can significantly impact revenue potential.
- *Growth Projections:* Historical data and future forecasts can provide insights into expected growth rates and help set realistic targets.
- *Strategic Priorities:* The company's overall strategic goals, such as market expansion, product launch, or customer acquisition, should be considered when setting revenue targets.

Then, incorporate field-level insights from managers and sales representatives who have firsthand knowledge of customer behavior and regional dynamics. This dual approach ensures that quotas are both achievable and aligned with corporate objectives.

Another critical component is centralizing data and using it as the foundation for quota-setting decisions. Quota planning should rely on clean, accurate data from a secure, centralized source to minimize confusion and ensure consistency. Factors such as historical performance, market trends, account potential, and resource allocation should all be considered. By using a data-driven approach, teams can eliminate bias and create more equitable and attainable quotas.

Let's look at a hypothetical scenario to explore this further. Imagine a SaaS company that sells an AI-powered analytics platform. Historically, their sales reps have closed an average of $800K in ARR per year, but the company is aiming for 25 percent growth this year. Market research suggests that demand is increasing, but new customer acquisition is expected to slow due to economic uncertainty.

Given these factors, the RevOps team decides to set quotas by balancing historical performance with future projections. They analyze past deal cycles, win rates, and territory potential, determining that a reasonable stretch goal would be a 20 percent increase per rep rather than the full 25 percent, allowing room for market fluctuations. This means the new quota is set at $960K ARR per rep instead of an arbitrary $1M, ensuring it remains challenging but achievable.

Additionally, to support reps in hitting these targets, RevOps adjusts account coverage and prioritization—assigning larger, high-potential accounts to senior reps and providing additional marketing support for underperforming segments. By tying quotas to real-world conditions rather than a top-down revenue goal, the company fosters a more sustainable, performance-driven culture.

Scenario modeling. Scenario modeling is an important tool for refining quotas before finalizing them. By running "what-if" scenarios, organizations can assess the potential impact of changes in market conditions, territory assignments, or head count. This step allows teams to identify potential challenges and adjust quotas proactively, ensuring that targets remain achievable under various circumstances.

For example, consider a situation where a company is expanding into a new market. Scenario modeling can help estimate how long it will take for new sales reps to ramp up, what portion of the market they can realistically capture in the first year, and how this will impact overall revenue goals. Alternatively, if the economic outlook suggests a slowdown in demand, scenario modeling can provide insights into how quotas might need to be adjusted to reflect lower purchasing volumes without demotivating the sales team.

In addition to its role in planning, scenario modeling should be used throughout the sales cycle to monitor progress and adapt to changing conditions. For instance, if a new competitor enters the market midyear, scenario modeling can help assess how this might impact sales velocity and inform necessary quota adjustments. By integrating scenario modeling into the broader quota management process, organizations can remain agile and proactive, responding to changes in real time rather than being caught off guard.

Getting Buy-In for Quotas. Transparency and collaboration are crucial to gaining buy-in from sales teams. Clearly communicate the rationale behind quota assignments and provide visibility into how they are calculated. Engage managers and representatives in discussions about the quotas, incorporating their feedback where appropriate. This collaborative process builds trust and reduces resistance, ensuring that sales reps feel confident in their ability to meet their targets.

To maintain effectiveness, quota management should be a continuous process rather than a one-time event. Regularly review and adjust quotas to account for changes in the business environment, such as economic shifts, new product launches, or team expansions. Monitor progress throughout the sales cycle, using real-time data to identify trends and make necessary course corrections.

Finally, it is important to prioritize fairness and equity in the quota-setting process. Ensure that quotas are aligned with the potential of each territory, account, or region, rather than distributing them evenly without regard to market conditions. This approach not only motivates sales reps but also avoids the frustration and turnover that can result from unrealistic or unbalanced targets.

By following these actionable steps, organizations can transform quota management into a strategic advantage. A well-executed quota plan aligns teams, motivates individuals, and creates a clear path toward achieving both personal and organizational success.

Capacity Planning and Forecasting

Capacity planning and forecasting are a critical component of RevOps strategy, ensuring that an organization has the right resources in place to meet its revenue goals. It bridges the gap between high-level growth ambitions and the operational realities of the sales, marketing, and customer success teams. Done effectively, capacity planning and forecasting provide a road map for resource allocation, hiring, and workload management, helping organizations scale efficiently and avoid the pitfalls of over- or underinvestment. And with less than half of companies having faith in their forecasts, according to Gartner,[59] capacity planning and forecasting need to be major parts of your planning cycle.

Capacity planning and forecasting can seem like an abstract and archaic concept—until the real-life consequences of doing subpar planning work become apparent. Many organizations learn this lesson the hard way. As Bala puts it, capacity planning typically starts off in a smaller organization with figuring out the size of the budget and the size of the head count based on this budget. Instinctively, capacity planners develop basic rules of thumb to help them simplify and streamline this work: "Five sales reps per sales engineer." Using simple ratios and other rules of thumb enable the teams that do capacity planning to essentially go on autopilot. But as the company grows, eventually the rubber hits the road. Companies finally realize they have a capacity planning problem, Bala says, when eight people in eight different revenue-related roles suddenly show up for a customer meeting—and there's just one customer in the meeting.[60]

Capacity planning. Capacity planning begins by translating revenue targets into actionable staffing and resource needs. This requires a clear understanding of productivity metrics such as average deal size, sales cycle length, and quota attainment rates. Analyzing these metrics helps RevOps leaders determine how many sales reps, customer success managers, or other GTM roles are needed to achieve specific revenue goals. For instance, if the company plans to grow revenue by 20 percent in the coming year, capacity planning identifies the additional head count required and establishes timelines for ramping up those resources.

Forecasting. Forecasting complements capacity planning by providing a data-driven outlook on future needs. It considers factors like expected market growth, upcoming product launches, and shifts in the competitive landscape. Scenario modeling is especially valuable in forecasting, enabling teams to test different assumptions and assess their impact on resource requirements. For example, how would a faster-than-expected product adoption affect the number of sales reps needed? Or how might economic slowdowns influence demand? Forecasting allows organizations to prepare for a range of possibilities, ensuring they remain agile and ready to pivot.

Capacity planning and forecasting also involve identifying bottlenecks within the GTM engine and addressing them proactively. This could mean reallocating resources to high-performing regions, hiring for under-resourced roles, or improving enablement to boost productivity. For instance, if a particular territory consistently outperforms others, adding more reps or resources in that area could further accelerate growth. Similarly, if onboarding times are longer than expected, investing in more effective training programs can improve productivity and ramp up speed.

RevOps leaders must work closely with cross-functional teams to ensure alignment between sales, marketing, and customer success. Involving field managers and team leads in capacity planning and forecasting discussions provides critical on-the-ground insights, helping refine projections and resource allocation. Regularly reviewing and updating plans ensures they remain relevant as market conditions or strategic priorities evolve.

A key benefit of effective capacity planning and forecasting is the ability to prevent burnout and attrition while avoiding over-hiring. Stretching resources too thin leads to unmanageable workloads, dissatisfaction, and turnover among top performers, while overinvesting results in wasted resources and inefficiencies. Striking the right balance ensures that teams are supported, productive, and motivated.

Setting Commission Structure

Commission structures are a fundamental part of sales compensation, designed to motivate and reward sales teams for achieving their targets. And research shows commissions work. Nearly 60 percent of salespeople say working for commissions or bonuses motivates them to do a better job at work.[61] However, they must be thoughtfully designed to balance seller motivation, company financial stability, and long-term organizational goals. In dynamic and uncertain market conditions, setting and managing commission structures becomes even more critical. Below are actionable steps for creating effective commission structures that drive results while maintaining fairness and flexibility from Gartner.[62]

Before diving into the details of a commission plan, convene key stakeholders, including leaders from sales, finance, HR, and operations, to define the guiding principles for your compensation strategy. These principles should align with the company's overall goals and values. Consider questions such as:

1. How will the commission structure balance company cash flow and seller earnings?
2. Should top performers receive higher incentives compared to others?
3. What mechanisms will be in place to adapt to market fluctuations or unforeseen events?

This foundational step ensures alignment across the organization and provides a framework for decision-making throughout the process.

Design a Balanced Commission Plan. Unlike traditional sales commission structures that focus solely on hitting quotas, RevOps takes a more holistic approach, balancing incentives across revenue, profitability, and customer retention. A successful commission structure should incentivize desired behaviors while maintaining financial viability. Start by identifying the key metrics that align with your company's goals, such as revenue, profit margins, or customer acquisition. Define payout curves that reward performance proportionally, ensuring that exceptional results are recognized without creating undue pressure on cash flow.

For example, consider adjusting payout thresholds to motivate sellers at every performance level. Removing overly aggressive minimum thresholds ensures that reps who achieve partial success are still rewarded, fostering a positive and motivated sales culture. Similarly, decreasing the slope of payout curves can provide stability in volatile markets by reducing extreme variations in earnings.

Adapt and Monitor Continuously. Commission structures are not static—they must evolve with changing business needs, market dynamics, and organizational priorities. Regularly review the plan's performance, using data to assess its effectiveness and identify areas for improvement. For example, if a particular payout curve is leading to excessive costs or demotivated sellers, make adjustments in real time to address these issues.

Establish clear feedback mechanisms to gather input from the field. This includes engaging sales managers and representatives to understand how the structure impacts day-to-day operations. Incorporating their insights helps refine the plan and ensures it remains aligned with both corporate objectives and seller realities.

In times of significant disruption, like economic downturns or market shifts, it may be necessary to implement phased adjustments to your commission structure. For the short term, provide stability by introducing guarantees or draws to protect sellers' income during uncertain periods. For the long term, use refined forecasts to create plans that reflect more stable conditions, ensuring that sellers remain motivated as the market stabilizes. By balancing immediate needs with long-term strategy, organizations can maintain morale while positioning themselves for future growth.

Three Ways to Build a Killer Sales Comp Plan

Incentive plans drive behavior—but are you driving the right behavior?

Erik Charles, a RevOps advisor and a leading expert in revenue and incentive management, believes that a well-designed sales compensation plan is both an art and a science. It should align with company goals, motivate sales reps, and adapt to changing business dynamics.

1. **Sell Your Comp Plan to Your Sales Team**

Before you can expect your reps to sell to customers, you need to sell them on the compensation plan. If they don't see a clear, compelling opportunity to earn, they won't be motivated to perform.

"The approach should be, 'I've got an amazing opportunity for you to make some coin,'" Erik says. That's the first pitch. The second pitch is selling them on their territory—whether it's geographic, vertical, or segment-based. A rep needs to believe their patch is full of potential.

2. **Keep It Simple and Transparent**

A comp plan should be easy to understand. Erik suggests a simple test: Ask a rep how much they'll make if they close a specific deal. If they can't answer quickly, the plan is too complex. Every dollar spent on incentives should be driving results—not confusion.

3. **Adapt as Business Needs Change**

"The idea of building a plan in Q4 that triggers in Q1 and not touching it for another twelve months is insane," Erik says. Business challenges don't follow the calendar, so your comp plan should be flexible enough to adjust to market shifts, sales cycles, and company strategy.

A killer comp plan isn't about paying the least; it's about paying for performance in a way that fuels growth. And if your top rep makes more in commissions than you do, that might just mean you've built a fantastic plan.

GTM Enablement

Business enablement is at the core of RevOps success, ensuring that teams across sales, marketing, and customer success have the tools, resources, and strategies they need to excel. RevOps is the glue that connects high-level business strategy to execution because RevOps leaders are often responsible for the strategies that keep a business enablement plan running smoothly, from aligning territories and quotas to implementing scalable capacity plans.

GTM enablement isn't just about sales training—it's about aligning every revenue function for seamless execution. While some argue that Sales Enablement belongs strictly under Sales Leadership, others see it as a cross-functional role tied to Revenue Operations. RevOps leaders often oversee Sales Ops, Marketing Ops, Demand Gen, and GTM Strategy, making collaboration between Enablement and RevOps essential.

"If you lump Sales Operations and Revenue Operations together and see them as the same role, then I disagree that Sales Enablement should only belong under Sales Leadership," said Dedra Estrada, Global VP of RevOps at Corsearch. "It's not cut and dried either—it depends on the Sales Leadership and equally on the RevOps leader. Regardless, there has to be synergy. Oftentimes, the RevOps leader also has responsibility for Marketing Operations, Demand Generation, and GTM Strategy—all areas that an Enablement leader should be linked to and find value in. RevOps (and, in most cases, Sales Ops) are mislabeled as postmortem analysts, but I am 1,000 percent okay with being labeled tactical."

Providing the Right Tools and Technology. A critical element of business enablement is ensuring that RevOps teams have the tools they need to do their jobs effectively. Enabling RevOps with the right technology leads to better outcomes for the entire organization. For example, using AI-driven tools to automate repetitive tasks, such as updating territories or quotas, frees RevOps professionals to focus on higher-value strategic initiatives. This shift not only reduces operational inefficiencies but also enhances agility by allowing teams to respond in real time to changes in the business landscape.

In speaking with numerous VPs of RevOps across industries—from SaaS start-ups mid-market to enterprise organizations in many industries—Ryan identified a common, pressing challenge: the fragmentation of operational systems leading to inefficiencies, misalignment, and lost revenue opportunities. RevOps leaders consistently expressed frustration with the lack of a centralized, adaptive platform that could streamline processes, enforce governance, and provide real-time visibility across their GTM motions.

This insight drove Ryan to prioritize building solutions that don't just automate tasks but actively solve RevOps-specific pain points—simplifying complex workflows that were once managed on spreadsheets, ensuring seamless handoffs between teams, and enabling data-driven decision-making. For RevOps professionals seeking to optimize their operations, this focus on software-driven enablement is essential.

Building Confidence Through Enablement. Effective enablement also instills confidence in frontline teams. Sales teams perform best when they know the organization has done its due diligence in setting fair quotas, assigning clear territories, and designing well-structured compensation plans. By providing sales reps with these foundational elements, along with the tools and training they need, business enablement fosters trust and motivation. Sales teams feel supported, knowing the company is committed to their success.

Define Enablement Goals and Priorities. Start by identifying the specific skills, knowledge, and tools your teams need to succeed. Align these needs with your organization's strategic objectives. For instance, if your company is launching a new product, prioritize training on the product's value proposition and its fit within the market. Similarly, if entering a new market is a focus, equip teams with region-specific insights and strategies. Clear goals help ensure enablement efforts are targeted and impactful.

Invest in Training and Development. Training is at the heart of effective enablement. Develop programs that address core competencies, such as product knowledge, sales techniques, and customer engagement strategies. Provide ongoing training to adapt to changes in the market or company offerings. Interactive sessions, role-playing exercises, and microlearning modules can keep training engaging and actionable.

Additionally, create a central knowledge repository where teams can access updated resources, including playbooks, case studies, and competitive analyses. A well-maintained library of resources empowers teams to find answers quickly and independently.

Conclusion

Planning is the foundation of any effective RevOps strategy. As we've explored in this chapter, robust planning across key areas transforms abstract goals into actionable steps that drive measurable results. Territory management ensures that resources are distributed equitably, enabling teams to maximize revenue potential while maintaining fairness and morale. Quota management aligns individual targets with organizational goals, empowering sales reps to perform at their best. Capacity planning and forecasting anticipate resource needs and bottlenecks, ensuring teams can scale efficiently. Thoughtful commission structures motivate teams while balancing financial sustainability. Data hygiene and planning create the backbone for reliable decision-making, and business enablement ensures that every team member is equipped to succeed.

Each of these components reinforces the others, forming a cohesive system that aligns strategy with execution. Leaders who approach planning holistically, embrace collaboration, and leverage tools and data to their fullest potential will not only achieve their revenue goals but also position their organizations for long-term success.

RevOps planning is more than a set of processes; it's a mindset. By adopting a disciplined, strategic approach, you can turn planning into a competitive advantage, ensuring your revenue engine runs smoothly, efficiently, and with the agility needed to thrive in an ever-changing business landscape. The key is to start now—because the best time to plan for success is before the year begins.

6

Alignment Across Departments

The People in Your Revenue Engine

Sometimes, being a leader in a company feels a lot like coaching Little League baseball. As someone who works in RevOps and has also coached countless Little League games, Steve Settle, Senior Director of Revenue Operations at Customer.io, draws a powerful analogy between managing revenue operations and guiding a young baseball team.[63] Like a coach carefully positioning players to maximize their strengths, RevOps leaders must ensure sales, marketing, and customer success teams are aligned and working toward a common goal. Without alignment, revenue motions fall apart—just as a poorly coached baseball team will struggle to make plays.

Settle describes the early stages of a company like T-ball, where everything is simplified for new players. "A coach walks up to the batter, offering a lot of hand-holding by positioning them right next to the tee, and they say, swing," he explained. "The batter starts to do circles, and eventually, they hit the ball. And then once they hit the ball, everyone's pointing and saying run to that base. Sometimes they run to the opposite base." The same is true in early-stage start-ups—there is a lot of trial and error, course correction, and hands-on guidance to get things moving in the right direction. The company is still defining its product-market fit, sales processes are being built on the fly, and marketing is experimenting to find the right messaging.

But as the company matures, RevOps must step up to a more strategic leadership role, much like a baseball coach transitioning young players from T-ball to kid pitch. "The growth stage is when you start to introduce pitching," Settle said. "You wonder if it's going to hit the backstop. You don't know if it's going to reach halfway to the plate, and if it hits the catcher's glove, you're excited but don't know if that's a strike." This uncertainty mirrors the experimentation phase of a growing company, where RevOps must fine-tune demand generation, refine the ICP, and figure out which revenue motions will scale efficiently.

At its core, RevOps is about making sure every player on the team knows their role and is set up for success. When alignment is achieved, the entire organization benefits—not just internally, but in the way customers experience the company. "When you've got it fully aligned, the teams are working together really well," Settle explained. "It is a significant improvement, not just in working within the company, but for the customer experience."

Misalignment, on the other hand, can be devastating. Without a strong feedback loop between marketing and sales, companies lose valuable insights into what messaging and outreach tactics are resonating with prospects. Sales might pursue leads that aren't a good fit, or marketing might continue running campaigns that generate low-quality pipeline. Without customer success operations feeding insights back into marketing and sales, companies struggle with churn and miss out on opportunities for upsells and renewals.

Settle believes that alignment is not a one-time fix—it needs to be adapted to each stage of business growth. "If you think about what the business needs at the early stage, it's about establishing product-market fit and building product awareness," he said. "On the marketing side, they're going to provide insights into our target customers and determine the messaging we will use. Sales complements that because they can also provide feedback on what's actually resonating with the people they're talking to." But if sales and marketing aren't aligned, this feedback loop breaks down, leaving both teams to operate in the dark.

As a company grows, RevOps must take a more proactive role in structuring processes for scale. The key, according to Settle, is to always view processes through the lens of the customer experience. "When you start to make sure that everything you're doing is going through the lens of how the customer will actually view this process and how the customer is going to interact with this process, that solves the experience part of it," he said.

But customer experience alone isn't enough—RevOps must also solve for scalability. Processes that work for a ten-person sales team might crumble under the weight of a two-hundred-person global sales force. "That's why, when working cross-departmentally, I can create something that works for a sales operations process, for example," Settle explained. "But then you start to think about the marketing operations process, and that's where you have to work cross-functionally. There is so much interconnectedness as you think about the entire customer journey."

One of the most common mistakes companies make is building processes in isolation without considering how they affect the rest of the revenue engine. A sales automation workflow that works well for SDRs, for example, could create bottlenecks for marketing automation efforts or cause confusion in customer success handoffs. The solution? RevOps must be deeply embedded in all revenue functions, ensuring that every new process is designed with cross-functional alignment in mind.

Great RevOps leadership is like great coaching. It's about bringing the right players together, developing their skills, and making sure the entire team is working toward a shared goal. At an early-stage company, RevOps is hands-on, guiding individual players and ensuring fundamentals are in place. In the growth stage, RevOps becomes more strategic, helping teams experiment and refine their approach. And in the enterprise stage, RevOps must scale operations, optimize efficiency, and ensure every part of the revenue engine is connected.

Settle's approach to RevOps is simple: Align the team, build for scale, and never lose sight of the customer experience. When these elements come together, RevOps doesn't just drive revenue—it creates a well-oiled, high-performing machine that keeps winning, quarter after quarter.

In this chapter, we'll break down how to structure your revenue engine, starting with the most important element: your people. We'll also look at the structures of some well-known companies and some standard RevOps organizational charts for your own RevOps team, whether it's a young start-up or a large enterprise.

What Does a Good Team Look Like?

Asking one person to take on all RevOps responsibilities—from strategy to operations to tactics—is like asking a quarterback to play every position on the field. Even Peyton Manning or Tom Brady can't win a game by themselves. Joe Montana famously said, "In football, it is not a QB's game . . . even though the media likes to make it into that. It takes the whole team."[64] Similarly, RevOps succeeds when every player knows their role and works together to move the revenue engine forward. You need the playmaker setting up strategy, the defenders keeping operations tight, and the running backs executing high-performance plays.

Core Elements

To build a truly effective revenue engine, you need a team that covers both strategy and execution. At the same time, you need a team that aligns across sales, marketing, and customer success. Defining the roles, responsibilities, and leadership structure of this team is essential to launching a winning RevOps team.

Building a winning revenue engine is as much about the human element as it is about strategy. In a conversation with Cody Guymon, a seasoned RevOps leader with a track record at organizations like Vivint and Qualtrics, he emphasized how empathy is the cornerstone of effective leadership in RevOps. He describes this essential RevOps leadership skill as the ability to listen, understand, and truly connect with the people you support, whether that's sales, marketing, or customer success.[65] By developing a deep understanding of the challenges and motivations of each team, RevOps leaders can bridge the gaps between disparate teams and create a unified force that drives success.

"RevOps is a job that changes every year," Guymon said. "My biggest piece of advice is to listen to sales reps. Listen to the sales leaders because they're on the front lines. They understand what's happening in the moment, so they're going to know if there's momentum in a certain vertical or not, and what sales methodology is really landing and what messaging is landing in the market. Just stay curious."

Core Functions

In RevOps, every role should have a clear purpose tied to driving revenue outcomes. While titles and specific responsibilities might vary by organization, there are four core functions that should exist within any RevOps team:

1. *Strategic Planners:* These are the architects of the revenue strategy. They focus on forecasting, long-term planning, and aligning revenue goals with business objectives. Their work ensures that RevOps is not just a tactical function but a driver of growth.

2. *Operational Doers:* This group ensures that processes run smoothly across the entire customer life cycle. From lead routing to territory management, they focus on operational efficiency and remove roadblocks for customer-facing teams.

3. *Data Specialists:* The lifeblood of any RevOps organization is data and analytics. These specialists gather, analyze, and interpret metrics to provide actionable insights. They build the dashboards and reports that allow leadership to make informed decisions.

4. *Technology Managers:* The tech stack champions who ensure the team has the tools it needs to succeed. They evaluate, implement, and maintain the platforms that support RevOps operations, from CRMs to AI-driven analytics tools.

Core Positioning

The success of RevOps depends heavily on how it's positioned within the organization. In companies where RevOps reports directly to the CEO or CRO, its influence and alignment with strategic priorities are stronger. But this isn't a one-size-fits-all model—what matters most is having a leader who can balance strategic thinking with operational execution.

Whether the title is Head of RevOps, VP of Go-to-Market Strategy, or something else, we are strong proponents of hiring a RevOps leader as part of the leadership team to help fine-tune Go-to-Market operations. This leader needs to foster collaboration across traditionally siloed departments, ensure accountability for shared revenue goals, and advocate for RevOps as a critical function in the organization. A strong RevOps leader sets the tone for how the team operates, emphasizing agility, data-driven decision-making, and customer-centricity.

"Think of the RevOps leader as the company wheel's hub, with all revenue operations branches meeting at the center," Guymon said. "The result is a streamlined, collaborative process that breaks down department silos. This provides the RevOps leader with a comprehensive view of each angle of the RevOps team. You need to know where the puck is going. Armed with valuable data insights and analytics from each department, the RevOps leader can drive informed, data-supported decision-making across the entire organization."

Core Relationships

To understand where RevOps fits within an organization's hierarchy, let's use an analogy from RevOps expert Whitney Merrill and inspired by *Star Trek*.[66] Just as the Starship *Enterprise* relies on a structured command system to navigate unknown territories and achieve mission success, companies today must have a strategic RevOps team behind the scenes to keep the company moving toward revenue targets.

Like the *Enterprise*, modern companies operate at warp speed. Yet, 68 percent of companies lack a structured plan for every Go-to-Market launch. However, those that establish even a basic framework experience a 10 percent increase in Go-to-Market success rates.[67] This highlights the importance of a well-structured RevOps function and its leadership reporting structure.

On the *Enterprise* or in business, the ship's captain—whether it's Captain Kirk or a modern-day CEO, CRO, or CFO—sets the course, steering the organization toward success. The chief engineer, like Scotty in *Star Trek*, plays a critical role too, much like a RevOps leader. This executive keeps the GTM engine running smoothly, optimizing operations and ensuring everything stays efficient. And then there's AI, the ship's computer, handling automation, responding to commands, and enhancing decision-making.

At the top, the CRO or CEO provides strategic direction, making sure the company stays on track and grows. Meanwhile, the RevOps leader, much like the chief engineer, keeps the GTM engine fine-tuned—making sure sales, marketing, and customer success teams have everything they need to operate at full speed. Just as a starship can't go anywhere without a working propulsion system, a company can't scale without a well-structured and optimized revenue engine.

For RevOps to be truly effective, it needs to report to a senior executive who understands its strategic value. In many companies, RevOps sits under the CRO to stay tightly connected with revenue teams. Others place it under the CFO or COO, especially when financial planning and operational efficiency are top priorities. More and more, businesses are recognizing the need to elevate RevOps leadership directly into the executive team.

"Founder-led GTM isn't just for day one," wrote Sangram Vajre, cofounder and CEO of GTM Partners, in a LinkedIn post. "Yes, in the early days, you're cold calling, demoing, building pipelines with your own hands. But even at scale—GTM is still a team sport that starts at the top."

Survey results from members of Fullcast's Advisory Council, which includes over one hundred RevOps professionals across the nation, show that RevOps most commonly reports to the CRO (49.98%), though a growing number of organizations place it under the CEO/President (17.35%) and COO (15.31%) to align with broader business strategy. Reporting to the CFO (12.24%) highlights RevOps' role in financial planning, while reporting to the CCO (4.08%) and CMO (2.04%) remains less common. These trends reflect the evolving strategic importance of RevOps within executive leadership.

No matter the reporting structure, the key takeaway is clear. RevOps must be a strategic driver of revenue success. When sales, marketing, and customer success are aligned and operating as a cohesive unit, the company is positioned to move faster, adapt to change, and achieve long-term growth.

Core Mission

Modern Go-to-Market leadership demands what Captain Kirk relies on aboard the *Enterprise*—a command center with strategic maneuverability, real-time insights, and the ability to operate at warp speed. Achieving this level of agility requires a new structural approach, one that fully integrates automation, data-driven decision-making, and cross-functional coordination. A well-maintained revenue engine must not only be operated from within RevOps, but also be accessible and controlled from the executive level to enable rapid, strategic pivots when necessary.

This structural shift is not a prepackaged solution but one that must be deliberately built and tailored to each organization's unique mission and GTM needs. The role of the RevOps leader is comparable to stepping onto the bridge of the *Enterprise* in the midst of a critical mission. When the captain calls for an immediate jump to warp speed or full power to the shields, the chief engineer must assess the situation and provide an honest, tactical response. Whether the answer is "just a few more minutes" or "not possible," that communication determines the outcome of the battle.

Trust and collaboration between RevOps and GTM leadership are paramount. Much like Kirk and Scotty's dynamic, the relationship between the CRO and RevOps leader is defined by moments of high-stakes decision-making. When systems fail or challenges arise, the CRO must rely on RevOps to navigate the complexity and deliver solutions in real time.

A prime example of this is the end-of-quarter deal push. In the final hours before revenue closes, when high-stakes negotiations hinge on deal terms, approvals, and signatures before midnight, a single roadblock can determine whether the company hits its target. In these moments, RevOps is the command center, fielding urgent calls on whether a deal can be structured, identifying creative solutions, or clarifying why a last-minute pivot is not possible. The ability to act decisively in these situations requires not just technical and process mastery but an established position of authority within the GTM leadership team.

Without direct executive alignment and a well-defined leadership role, RevOps risks being relegated to a reactive, support-based function rather than the strategic command center it must become. When properly positioned, RevOps serves as the engine room and the bridge—driving execution while providing the visibility and control necessary to navigate the unpredictable challenges of modern revenue operations.

Creating a Unified RevOps Culture

RevOps thrives when there's a culture of collaboration and shared ownership. The team needs to build trust across sales, marketing, and customer success by proving that their work leads to better outcomes for everyone. Whether it's accelerating deal cycles, improving forecast accuracy, or increasing customer retention, the RevOps team must consistently demonstrate its value.

Tyler Morrow, AVP of Enterprise Sales, had some great insight about the dynamics between RevOps and sales teams in a conversation on the *Go To Market Podcast* with Amy.[68] "When RevOps makes decisions that affect people's territories or books, that's effectively messing with their W-2 at the end of the day," Morrow said. It was a reminder that for a unified RevOps culture to work, transparency, and communication aren't just nice-to-haves; they're essential.

Too often, collaboration between RevOps and sales or customer success teams is overlooked. RevOps might operate in the background, focusing on strategy and processes, while sales teams are laser-focused on hitting their numbers. Decisions made by RevOps, like territory changes or account assignments, can feel disruptive to sales reps if they aren't involved in the process. This disconnect can breed frustration and erode trust.

Morrow had some great advice about how you can avoid this. First, involve sales reps, especially frontline AEs, in RevOps decision-making when possible. For example, if RevOps is scoring accounts or making adjustments to territories, gathering input from the people closest to the customer helps avoid costly mistakes. It's a practical way to show that RevOps isn't working against the team but with them to ensure success.

Second, redefine what a "win" means for the organization. Success isn't just about individual reps closing deals. It's about building a cohesive system where RevOps, sales, marketing, and customer success work together toward shared goals. By expanding the definition of a win to include operational efficiency, accurate forecasting, and strategic alignment, you reinforce the value of teamwork across the entire revenue engine.

Finally, sales leaders play a crucial role in building this culture. "Sales leaders aren't successful because of themselves—they're successful because of the team they've built around them," Morrow said. For RevOps to thrive, leaders need to foster relationships between their teams and RevOps. It's about showing reps that the decisions coming from RevOps are there to help them hit their numbers, not create roadblocks.

A unified RevOps culture isn't built overnight. It's the result of transparent communication, collaborative decision-making, and leaders who understand that no one succeeds alone. By focusing on these principles, you can transform RevOps from a behind-the-scenes function into a trusted partner that helps everyone win.

How Should a Good Team Be Structured?

While RevOps can take different forms depending on company size and industry, the core structure remains fairly consistent across most organizations. Louis Poulin, a seasoned RevOps leader who built the RevOps department at AWS, PayPal, Buildertrend, and other major enterprises, has seen firsthand how RevOps structures mature over time and change in different industries. In a conversation with us about RevOps organizational models, he emphasized that while every company's structure will differ, the core components—sales operations, marketing operations, customer success operations, and data—must be integrated effectively at every stage of growth.[69]

As Poulin states, the foundation of any RevOps function is always the consolidation of sales operations, marketing operations, and customer success operations under a single umbrella. "Those are always there," he explained. "Those are non-negotiables." These teams work together to drive alignment across Go-to-Market strategy, data, and process execution.

At its heart, RevOps is not just about systems and automation—it's about people. The way teams are structured, how they collaborate, and who owns what responsibilities determines whether RevOps is successful or simply another layer of bureaucracy. In an optimal model, RevOps is embedded deeply into the revenue engine, ensuring that sales, marketing, and customer success are working from a unified playbook rather than operating in silos.

A traditional RevOps team typically consists of the following core groups:

1. *Sales Operations (Sales Ops):* Focuses on territory planning, forecasting, deal desk management, sales enablement, and CRM optimization to ensure the sales team operates efficiently.
2. *Marketing Operations (Marketing Ops):* Manages lead generation, campaign tracking, and marketing automation platforms to ensure seamless customer acquisition efforts.
3. *Customer Success Operations (CS Ops):* Supports post-sale engagement, renewals, churn prevention, and upsell/cross-sell initiatives, ensuring that revenue growth extends beyond the initial sale.

These three functions must be tightly integrated. When RevOps is structured correctly, marketing passes well-qualified leads to sales, who then close deals and provide critical data for customer success teams to engage customers in a meaningful way. However, if these teams operate separately—each with their own tools, processes, and KPIs—the result is misalignment, inefficiencies, and lost revenue opportunities.

That's where AI-powered analytics and real-time data come in—transforming attribution from a guessing game into a strategic advantage, according to Doug Topken, an expert in Global CRM and Customer Data. "It's connecting the dots within RevOps. It enables us to collaborate better, and AI helps us understand what's happening within the funnel and throughout the opportunity stages. For example, once it's closed, we sometimes lose sight of the order because we move on once the opportunity closes. Attribution models are being built to show us the customer's lifetime value and marketing's actual value."

By mapping every touchpoint—from marketing campaigns to sales interactions and customer success engagements—leaders can identify the most effective channels, allocate budgets more efficiently, and confidently refine forecasting models.

Beyond the core teams, some RevOps organizations include business process engineering functions, responsible for optimizing the full end-to-end revenue journey. These specialists ensure that:

- Processes are well-defined and scalable.
- Key stakeholders are involved in decision-making.
- Any changes to the revenue engine are properly approved and implemented.

Having dedicated process engineers within RevOps can be a major advantage. These teams can report directly to RevOps leadership, or they can be embedded within different revenue functions as subject matter experts in their respective areas.

Where Data, Analytics, and Technology Fit In. Another key consideration in RevOps structure is who owns data, analytics, and revenue technology. Poulin strongly believes that CRM ownership should sit under RevOps, not IT or an independent data team. "I find it nearly impossible to separate CRM out these days," he said. "If you don't own the core platforms like Salesforce, Gainsight, or Fullcast, it just feels like you're one degree separated from where you need to be."

In some organizations, data and reporting teams are housed separately under finance or IT, which can create obstacles for RevOps. "I like having the data reporting and analytics teams under me,"

Poulin explained. "But it's not a showstopper if they sit elsewhere—as long as RevOps still has the ability to define what's being tracked and how data is reported back to leadership." Without this level of oversight, organizations risk fragmented reporting, poor visibility, and ultimately, bad decision-making.

A common problem that occurs when RevOps does not own its data tools is tech sprawl—where different teams purchase overlapping or redundant technology without a unified strategy. If IT owns all revenue-related tools, customer-facing needs often take priority, leaving internal revenue teams with outdated, inefficient platforms. "If it's sitting in IT, all the customer needs bump the internal needs," Poulin said. "So you wind up with antiquated tools that aren't providing value back to your organization."

Why Enablement Belongs in RevOps. One often-overlooked component of RevOps is revenue enablement, which includes training, adoption, and change management for new processes and tools. Poulin emphasized that enablement should sit under RevOps, not be outsourced to other departments. "If you don't have enablement resources under you," he said, "you're constantly begging and borrowing for help to get sales teams trained on new processes."

Enablement is what bridges the gap between strategy and execution. Without it, new sales processes, CRM updates, or marketing automation rollouts are doomed to fail because teams won't fully adopt them. Having a dedicated enablement function within RevOps ensures that as tools and processes evolve, the entire revenue organization is kept up to speed.

Here is a standard hierarchy chart for a RevOps team that Poulin has seen at companies like PayPal, Buildertrend, and more:

Standard Model
Paypal, Buildertrend

RevOps Head

Enablement	Marketing Ops	Sales Ops	CX Ops	Data	Business Process Engineers
Saleshood	Hubspot	Salesforce	Gainsight		Data reporting/ analytics
					Snowflake, PowerBI, Databricks, AWS

While the above model is generally accepted as a traditional RevOps model, what's best for an organization depends on several factors, such as its size and stage of business.

Start-Up Stage

In the early stages of a company, resources are limited, and every decision carries significant weight. Speed and adaptability take precedence over rigid processes, and RevOps is typically a small, scrappy team focused on enabling revenue growth with minimal overhead.

At this stage, RevOps is often just an extension of sales operations, with a strong focus on lead management and opportunity tracking. The goal is to establish a functional system that allows marketing and sales teams to collaborate efficiently without getting bogged down by bureaucracy. He pointed out that while sophisticated tools and automation may not yet be in place, foundational processes are critical. "At its core, no matter what, you need a CRM," Poulin emphasized. "You need to start with a CRM and build disciplines around having a CRM system that makes sense."

The leadership structure in a start-up is typically flat, with the CEO closely overseeing revenue-generating functions. A RevOps leader, often wearing multiple hats, works alongside marketing, sales, and customer success leadership to ensure alignment. Poulin described this as a period where RevOps is more about providing tactical support than driving deep strategic initiatives. "At this stage, you're not thinking about complex forecasting models or optimizing conversion rates at every touchpoint. You're making sure that leads don't fall through the cracks, that sales teams have what they need, and that customers receive a seamless onboarding experience." The RevOps team is often just a few people, responsible for keeping the organization moving forward without introducing unnecessary complexity.

Because start-up teams are lean, RevOps professionals must be generalists, handling everything from CRM administration to reporting and basic process optimization. The tools at this stage are often rudimentary—email, spreadsheets, and a lightweight marketing automation platform like HubSpot or Marketo.

Customer success operations remain a secondary focus in the early stages, primarily because most start-ups are focused on acquiring new customers rather than optimizing retention and expansion. However, as Poulin pointed out, laying the groundwork for customer data tracking is essential. "You might not have a dedicated CS Ops team early on, but you need to start collecting data that will be useful when retention and expansion become bigger priorities. Otherwise, you'll be scrambling to figure out customer behavior patterns later." Even if a start-up does not yet have a full-fledged customer success operations team, it should still have a clear way to capture customer interactions, satisfaction metrics, and early indicators of churn risk.

At this stage, RevOps functions best as a flexible, high-touch team that enables sales and marketing to move quickly. The start-up phase is about minimizing obstacles rather than enforcing structure. The focus should be on simplicity and efficiency when implementing processes in a start-up. Sales, marketing, and customer success should have sufficient structure to operate effectively, but avoid the complexity of enterprise-level processes, which tend to slow things down. While some degree of RevOps structure is necessary, overcomplicating processes too early can lead to inefficiencies and bottlenecks.

As the company grows, this structure must evolve, introducing automation, clear role definitions, and structured handoff mechanisms. But in the start-up stage, the primary objective is to keep the revenue engine running with minimal friction, allowing the organization to scale without being weighed down by premature process constraints.

Here's an example of how a basic hierarchy chart could look like at this stage of your business:

At this stage, the lead handoff process is often informal but highly responsive. Let's explore a hypothetical example of how this could work:

1. *Lead Capture:* Marketing runs a simple campaign, such as a LinkedIn ad or webinar, capturing leads in a spreadsheet or a basic CRM.
2. *Lead Qualification and Sales Handoff:* Without an SDR team, marketing quickly reviews the lead and directly pings the sales rep (often the founder or a small sales team) via Slack or email.
3. *Sales Engagement:* The sales rep reaches out personally, scheduling a call and manually logging notes in a shared document or CRM.

4. *Closing and Customer Success Handoff:* Once the deal
    is signed, the sales rep introduces customer success
    via a simple email or a shared document outlining
    next steps.

At this stage, speed and adaptability matter more than rigid processes. While this high-touch approach works, it is sometimes difficult to scale.

Growth Stage

As the company scales and enters mid-market, the increasing complexity of managing revenue operations requires a more structured approach. The number of customers expands, teams grow, and processes that worked in the start-up stage begin to strain under pressure. The organization must move beyond ad hoc systems and manual processes to establish scalable, repeatable workflows that can support sustained growth.

If we go back to our baseball analogy,[70] this is when the RevOps leader steps onto the pitcher's mound to take on more responsibility. "The growth stage is when you start to introduce pitching," Settle said. "You wonder if it's going to hit the backstop. You don't know if it's going to reach halfway to the plate, and if it hits the catcher's glove, you're excited but don't know if that's a strike. There's more refinement when we think about the growth base. But the idea is, you're starting to try new things. You've defined your ICP, and now you're trying to create that demand generation engine to figure out what's going to work, what campaigns to run, and what you can do to really accelerate your growth."

At this stage, RevOps evolves from a tactical, hands-on function to a more specialized department with clear roles and responsibilities. Poulin described this transition as the point where RevOps must become more structured to support an expanding Go-to-Market motion. "Customer success becomes more critical. Then I also think your data and reporting become more critical. You're going to be looking for a bigger depth of metrics and KPIs that you're going to be reporting. Having the right dashboards, the right visibility that you can then share with the different revenue leaders across the organization becomes more important," he explained. At this stage, companies must shift from simply tracking basic sales and marketing data to developing robust analytics that inform strategic decision-making.

To facilitate this growth, RevOps teams introduce dedicated roles such as Sales Operations Manager, Marketing Operations Manager, and Customer Success Operations Manager, each responsible for refining and optimizing their respective areas. The leadership team expands as well, often incorporating a CRO who oversees revenue functions holistically. A well-structured RevOps function at this level ensures smoother integration between departments.

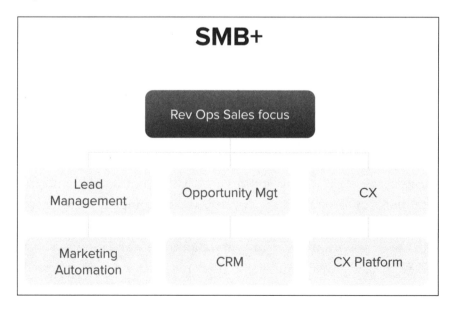

"The introduction of data and looking for additional optimization opportunities through the existing tool suite becomes key here," Poulin said. He also warned against unchecked tech sprawl (adding tools without a clear strategy) stressing that growth-stage companies need to be highly intentional about their technology investments.

"If you don't pay attention to this now—and I would extend that to data hygiene as well—you should really start to focus as you start to get into a rapid growth situation," Poulin said.

Beyond specialized RevOps roles, new supporting positions emerge. CRM Administrators become essential for maintaining data integrity and system efficiency, while Marketing Automation Admins help scale demand generation efforts. Deal Desk Managers streamline contract approvals and pricing processes, ensuring that sales teams can close deals faster. Meanwhile, SDRs take on the crucial role of lead qualification, allowing Account Executives to focus on closing deals. Marketing also begins to introduce campaign execution specialists who manage and optimize lead generation efforts. On the customer success side, structured onboarding and retention programs are established to improve customer satisfaction and reduce churn.

Another key shift in this phase is the company's increasing reliance on automation and AI. "It's really interesting because it's allowing organizations to scale much more quickly than we could even three or four years ago," Poulin noted. "If you set up and enable a lot of really intelligent AI features, like Gainsight, to really monitor health and customer sentiment, you can get a really good early warning system of where you need to focus your sellers' time and attention." By leveraging AI-driven insights, companies can proactively identify customers who may churn or who present cross-sell and upsell opportunities, significantly improving revenue efficiency.

With this growth comes the need for stronger handoff mechanisms between teams. RevOps must ensure that leads transition seamlessly from marketing to sales and from sales to customer success. It's crucial for mid-market businesses to have one continuous end-to-end customer journey. This is more important than it is for small- or medium-sized businesses. Alignment is also key. Everyone needs to be focused on the same priorities and accounts as they move through the pipeline and funnel. Resources must be used for the opportunities that will bring the most value to the company.

By the time a company reaches this level of maturity, RevOps is no longer simply about keeping things running; it is actively shaping the Go-to-Market strategy. The focus is on building repeatable, scalable processes, improving operational efficiency, and optimizing revenue growth. This is the stage where companies refine their approach, experiment with different tactics, and develop the systems that will allow them to sustain and accelerate their trajectory.

Let's look at a basic structure of how a RevOps team may start to evolve during the growth stage within a company:

At this stage, RevOps remains heavily sales-focused, prioritizing optimization, end-to-end visibility, and data integrity. Your organization's RevOps team may shift to have roles like customer experience to be under RevOps at this point. As the company gains traction, dedicated teams emerge, and RevOps introduces more structured processes while keeping flexibility intact.

1. *Lead Capture and Qualification:* Marketing implements lead scoring within a CRM to prioritize high-intent prospects, and SDRs handle initial outreach.
2. *Sales Handoff:* SDRs pass qualified leads to account executives through structured workflows, ensuring clear ownership.
3. *Sales Engagement and Deal Progression:* The CRM tracks interactions, and automated reminders ensure timely follow-ups.

4. *Customer Success Integration:* A structured onboarding
   process kicks in, with sales providing a formal handoff
   via an internal meeting or an automated workflow.

This is the phase where the foundation for scalable processes and technologies is laid, setting the stage for long-term success. Automation is starting to play a bigger role, but human oversight remains key to preventing friction in the process.

Enterprise Stage

As companies reach the enterprise stage, RevOps transforms from a growth enabler into a mission-critical function, responsible for orchestrating complex revenue processes across global teams. This is where operational scale, specialization, and strategic oversight become paramount.

At this level, RevOps is no longer just a support function—it is an integral part of the business strategy, ensuring that every revenue-generating motion is optimized, data-driven, and aligned with corporate objectives.

"You get much more specialized, and your team will be larger," Poulin said. "Your revenue is larger, and you take more of a focused approach to the different organizations you're supporting—sales, CS, and marketing." The ability to support complex sales motions, integrate systems across multiple regions, and maintain high-quality data across vast customer segments becomes the differentiator between a RevOps team that drives efficiency and one that simply maintains the status quo.

At this stage, RevOps leaders oversee distinct teams specializing in sales operations, customer success operations, marketing operations, and revenue technology. Each function is led by senior managers or directors responsible for ensuring their teams support the company's global Go-to-Market strategy. The RevOps leader typically reports to the CRO aligning revenue operations with executive decision-making.

A key challenge at the enterprise level is balancing standardization with regional flexibility. Global teams need consistency in processes and reporting, but local market nuances must be accounted for.

"Something I hate to see when companies globalize is assuming that anything built in the United States will automatically work in Europe or Asia," Poulin said. "That's completely false. You still need to take into consideration local Go-to-Market motions, regional regulations, and cultural differences." Successful enterprise RevOps teams establish global frameworks while allowing regional teams the flexibility to customize their execution—so long as data and processes remain aligned at a corporate level.

At this scale, the complexity of revenue data and reporting reaches a new level. Enterprise RevOps teams must integrate data across multiple systems, ensuring that sales, marketing, and customer success teams are working with a single source of truth. It's now important to completely own your data at this stage instead of working with third-party agencies.

"The optimal model is I would love to have data rolling into me as a leader of revenue operations because then all my efforts around processes, systems, and reporting are fully synced," Poulin said. "Otherwise, you're constantly trying to reconcile competing priorities from finance or data science teams that don't necessarily align with what sales and marketing need."

Security also becomes a greater concern at this stage, particularly regarding customer and revenue data. While Poulin has owned security functions within RevOps, he prefers working in close partnership with an enterprise security team. "Enterprise security can be something different, and I don't think it really does anything as long as they're setting corporate standards for data protection," he said. "If security dictates how we manage and protect data, RevOps can then interpret that within the tools we manage, like Salesforce, Gainsight, and other Go-to-Market systems."

Another critical function that expands at the enterprise level is enablement. With more employees, products, and processes to manage, training and change management become essential for maintaining efficiency. Constantly needing to ask for assistance to train sales teams on new processes or system changes is a consequence of not having enablement resources under RevOps. In a large-scale organization, enablement ensures that revenue teams adopt new technologies, understand evolving sales methodologies, and align with company-wide goals.

One of the biggest risks at the enterprise stage is operational inefficiency caused by disconnected tools and redundant processes. RevOps leaders must manage tech sprawl carefully, consolidating systems where possible and ensuring data remains structured and actionable. "Too many organizations don't pay attention to this soon enough, and then it becomes a really big problem," Poulin warned. "As we introduce AI into the mix, AI is only as good as the data that's available. If you curate a really solid set of data now, it's going to allow you to do things that your competitors aren't able to do."

Ultimately, enterprise RevOps is about driving strategic impact at scale. It is no longer about just making sales, marketing, and customer success work together—it is about optimizing every aspect of the revenue engine to ensure efficiency, predictability, and long-term growth.

"At this stage, RevOps leaders need to be thinking beyond just supporting Go-to-Market teams," Poulin said. "They need to be influencing company strategy, ensuring that revenue operations is not just an operational function, but a competitive advantage."

With a RevOps team under the CRO and CEO, here's an example of how a RevOps team may look at this stage:

Enterprise

RevOps Sales focus

Product Mgt	Lead Management	Opportunity Management	CX	Data	Enablement
	Marketing Automation Hubspot	CRM Salesforce	CX Platform Gainsight	Dashboards	Enablement, training, comms, awareness

Security

Many founders reach a point where growth stalls, despite doing everything "right." This isn't always a failure of execution—it's a failure of perspective. If you're only focused on scaling your company within an existing market, you'll eventually hit a ceiling. True, lasting growth comes from expanding the market itself, not just competing within it.

"I talk to a lot of founders hitting a wall at a certain point in scaling their revenue," wrote RevGenius Cofounder Jared Robin in a LinkedIn post. "Got me thinking, does GTM have a ceiling? If you're playing in somebody else's market, it does. The ceiling you hit is because you're trying to grow your company vs. grow your market."

Case Study: How AWS Structured Their RevOps Team

As AWS grew into a multibillion-dollar enterprise, the need for a structured and scalable RevOps function became critical. Poulin, who led RevOps at AWS during this period of rapid growth, built a specialized organization that mirrored the company's evolving Go-to-Market strategy. Over six and a half years, his team transformed from a small, tactical function into a highly specialized revenue operations organization capable of supporting AWS's global sales engine.

At the time, RevOps as a formal discipline had not yet been fully embraced in many organizations. While AWS had strong alignment between sales and marketing, customer success was largely treated as a separate function. "Revenue operations really hadn't taken hold in a lot of organizations," Poulin recalled. "Sales and marketing were very aligned. We were questioning—'should it be part of RevOps or not?'" Because of this, his team's primary focus was on optimizing sales and marketing operations, ensuring that lead and opportunity management were seamless so that customer success teams could access the necessary data without operational roadblocks.

AWS's sales structure was divided into two primary segments: commercial sales, which accounted for the vast majority of revenue, and public sector sales, which operated under a different set of requirements. The majority of the revenue at the time was tied to commercial sales, with a sizable public sector/SLED (state, local government, and education) sales team focused on government entities. However, the selling motions were largely similar, meaning that RevOps could maintain consistency in its approach across both teams.

Each of the sales teams had distinct needs, and RevOps played a crucial role in ensuring that territory planning, deal desk operations, and pipeline management were handled efficiently. "We were tracking the right KPIs, generating the right reporting, and making sure that sales leadership had the insights they needed to make strategic decisions," Poulin explained.

As AWS expanded globally, RevOps had to balance standardization with regional flexibility. AWS initially centralized operations in North America, but as its international presence grew, Poulin added regional RevOps teams in London, Tokyo, and Sydney to support local markets. "We eventually put resources in London, in Tokyo, and in Sydney to be able to address local APAC, Japanese, and European needs in addition to what we were doing in the United States," he said. His team ensured that while core processes and reporting remained globally consistent, regional teams had the flexibility to adapt based on their specific market conditions.

However, one of the biggest mistakes enterprises make is assuming that what works in the United States will work everywhere else. "Something I hate to see when companies globalize is assuming that anything built in the United States will automatically work in Europe or Asia—that's completely false," Poulin said. While some level of standardization is necessary, AWS's RevOps team ensured that regional sales strategies were tailored to accommodate local nuances while still maintaining the integrity of AWS's global revenue data and reporting structures.

AWS also invested heavily in revenue technology under Poulin's leadership, with Salesforce at the center of its operations. "We were basically a Salesforce shop," he said. As RevOps scaled, AWS brought Salesforce development in-house, hiring close to fifty Salesforce developers and quality assurance (QA) engineers to build custom solutions that integrated seamlessly with the company's revenue operations.

AWS didn't stop at just development. QA, security, user interface/user experience (UI/UX), artificial intelligence/machine learning (AI/ML), customer data management, training, adoption, change management, communications, revenue enablement, segmentation, and territory management were also embedded into the RevOps structure to ensure that AWS's Salesforce environment remained secure, compliant, and efficient. While AWS had a dedicated enterprise security team, RevOps was responsible for ensuring Salesforce, FinancialForce, and other GTM tools were aligned with corporate security policies.

As AWS's sales organization grew, it became clear that RevOps needed to play a direct role in enablement and change management. New sales motions, tools, and processes were being introduced regularly, and without structured training, adoption suffered. "Enablement reported directly to me," Poulin explained. "And we built an internal team to ensure adoption of changes, awareness of new processes, and methodical approaches to implementation."

Having enablement embedded within RevOps allowed AWS to deploy changes quickly and at scale, ensuring that sales teams could keep pace with evolving Go-to-Market strategies. Without an enablement function, Poulin noted, organizations often struggle to roll out new initiatives effectively, leading to low adoption and inefficiencies.

By the time Poulin left AWS, his RevOps team had grown from three people to 150, structured into six primary functions:

1. *Sales Operations Programs:* Delivered strategic and operational support for all customer-facing teams, including Commercial Sales, Public Sector, Solution Architecture, Partners, and Professional Services.
2. *Development:* Built and maintained internal systems with a dedicated team of Salesforce developers, QA engineers, and Agile/Scrum resources.
3. *Administrators:* Managed system configuration, user support, and global operations to ensure smooth day-to-day functionality.
4. *Enablement and Change Management:* Led change management initiatives, training, enablement, UI/UX design, and the Voice of the Customer (VoC) program to drive adoption and continuous improvement.
5. *Data and Analytics:* Owned customer data management, territory planning, segmentation, variable compensation analysis, and predictive insights.
6. *Revenue Technology and Security:* Oversaw the full tech stack, including CRM systems, and ensured compliance, governance, and data security across all tools.

This RevOps model ensured that AWS could support its complex, multi-tiered sales organization while maintaining efficiency, data integrity, and process alignment. AWS's RevOps team became a key driver of operational efficiency and revenue growth, proving that a well-structured RevOps function is not just an internal support system but a strategic force that enables sustained enterprise success.

Case Study: How RevOps Failed in a Large Silicon Slopes Tech Company

While some companies successfully scale their RevOps functions into highly efficient, strategic teams, others struggle with misalignment, lack of ownership, and internal resistance. Poulin experienced this firsthand when he joined a very large tech company in Silicon Valley. This particular company had a RevOps model that ultimately failed due to structural missteps and cultural dysfunction.

At this company, Poulin was part of a newly formed Global Business Operations group, created to drive internal business process optimization. His role focused on lead-to-opportunity management, meaning he was responsible for defining a global process that aligned lead management (owned by marketing) and opportunity management (owned by sales). On paper, this structure seemed logical. However, in practice, the RevOps model was deeply flawed. "Marketing ops and sales ops were completely separate. I didn't report to either of them. I reported to a different leader altogether," he explained. "So while I was supposed to be optimizing processes, Marketing Ops and Sales Ops could just go off and do whatever they wanted."

This setup left RevOps without direct ownership over systems, data, or decision-making—a fundamental mistake that undermined the function's ability to drive change. When internal business process engineering is done without ownership of key systems, direct alignment with sales and marketing leadership, or control over data, it becomes an uphill battle. Without these elements, RevOps teams are left dependent on other departments to approve and implement changes. Even well-designed processes can be dismissed if individual teams decide they don't align with their priorities, leading to a cycle where great ideas are proposed but never adopted. The result at this particular company was a cycle of inefficiency, where good ideas were proposed but never implemented because RevOps lacked the authority to enforce them.

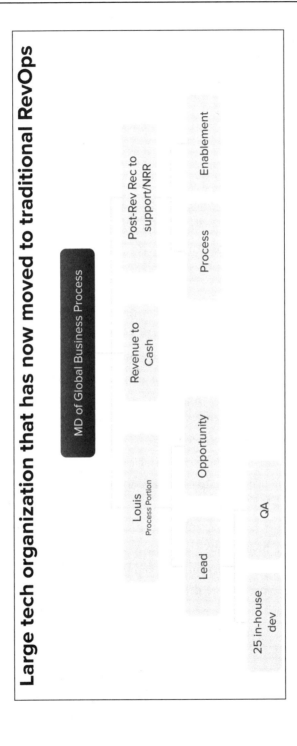

Adding to the dysfunction, many of the leaders of this company came from the same organization and attempted to implement a copied-and-pasted model that had worked there. However, what had been successful at one place did not translate well into the new organization. "They tried to just cut and paste it into this company," Poulin explained, "and it actually didn't work." The result was a fragmented, ineffective RevOps structure that failed to unify sales, marketing, and customer success.

One of the biggest issues was the hostile relationship between sales and marketing. "Before they had a RevOps council, it was literally Sales and Marketing absolutely hating each other, not talking to each other, and trying to undermine each other," Poulin recalled. Instead of collaborating to create an effective revenue engine, these teams were working against each other, making it nearly impossible to implement meaningful process improvements. "There were so many disconnects when you're trying to do something on behalf of the customer. If marketing owns a piece of it, and sales supports a piece of it, but they're not talking, trying to reconcile that is virtually impossible."

Without a centralized owner of revenue systems and processes, RevOps had no ability to enforce alignment. "Again, without any authority to do things in systems or enforce processes that were adopted to be able to support one end-to-end Go-to-Market journey, it just didn't work," Poulin said. His time was spent trying to convince teams to collaborate rather than actually improving operations. "A lot of the time was really just trying to figure out, how do I get these people to talk to each other? How do I get them to realize this is actually in the common good, in the best interest of the customer?" Instead of focusing on efficiency, automation, and scalability, RevOps was reduced to playing mediator between warring departments.

Frustration quickly set in. "That's why I only lasted there a short amount of time," Poulin admitted. The inability to create meaningful change led him to reassess what he needed in a RevOps role moving forward. "One of my criteria for my next job was, Do I own this? Can I actually do something with it? If not, I don't want to be there."

Poulin emphasized that the failure of this RevOps model came down to lack of ownership, misalignment between teams, and a lack of authority to drive real change. "It's not about crazy control," he said. "It's really just like, if you want me to be successful, and you want revenue operations to be successful at this company, these are the things that I have to have." Without ownership of data, systems, and cross-functional alignment, a RevOps function is doomed to fail.

Since Poulin left, this company abandoned the failed model and transitioned to a more traditional RevOps structure, with clear ownership and alignment between sales, marketing, and customer success. "They have moved to a traditional revenue operations model and I think they managed that through a RevOps council, which they didn't have before," Poulin noted.

Poulin's experience at this large tech company highlights several critical mistakes that organizations should avoid when building out RevOps at scale:

1. If RevOps does not own key systems, data, and decision-making processes, it becomes a powerless advisory function instead of a driver of operational efficiency.
2. If Sales and Marketing don't trust each other, RevOps will spend all its time playing referee rather than driving revenue growth.
3. Just because a RevOps model worked at one company doesn't mean it will work somewhere else. RevOps must be tailored to the specific needs and culture of the organization.

4. Defining global processes is meaningless if teams can simply ignore them. RevOps must have the power to enforce adoption and alignment.

5. Revenue operations must be integrated across Sales, Marketing, and Customer Success. If RevOps is isolated, it will struggle to create lasting impact.

6. RevOps cannot be just a consulting function. Leaders must have the ability to make decisions, enforce change, and optimize systems across the revenue engine.

RevOps is a powerful function when implemented correctly, but deeply ineffective when mismanaged. Poulin's experience at this large tech company illustrates what happens when RevOps is stripped of its authority, placed in an isolated role, and expected to drive change without ownership. Fortunately, companies are learning from these mistakes, shifting toward integrated RevOps models that align directly with Go-to-Market functions.

"For RevOps to be successful, I don't necessarily need to own everything," Poulin concluded. "But I do need to have a very strong voice and the ability to drive and influence change. Without that, you're not going to be successful."

Conclusion

A successful revenue engine isn't just about technology or strategy—it starts with people. RevOps succeeds when it brings clarity, structure, and collaboration to an organization, ensuring that sales, marketing, and customer success all operate from the same playbook.

Building a strong RevOps function requires more than just fixing broken processes; it's about creating a foundation that allows teams to scale efficiently. For RevOps leaders, clarity and trust are essential. Sales reps need confidence that territory changes, lead routing, and compensation models are designed with fairness and efficiency in mind. Marketing teams must trust that the data they rely on is accurate and aligned with sales priorities. Customer success must feel empowered to provide feedback that shapes long-term growth strategies. RevOps is the glue that makes all of this possible—but only when it operates with transparency, consistency, and a commitment to continuous improvement.

Ultimately, a high-performing revenue engine is built on a unified culture, where RevOps isn't just a back-office function but a strategic partner driving success at every level. Whether you're in a start-up, a high-growth company, or an enterprise, the right RevOps structure will evolve with you, ensuring that your business remains agile, scalable, and primed for sustained growth.

7

Centralizing the Data in Your Revenue Engine

We all know data silos are bad. When marketing, sales, and customer success teams operate in separate systems with siloed data, the result is a sputtering, not scaling, revenue engine. Disjointed customer experience, inaccurate forecasting, and missed opportunities abound.

Your siloed data doesn't just slow you down; it actively sabotages your revenue potential. Insights from the IDC Global CDO Engagement Survey reveal that data fragmentation is the biggest roadblock to digital transformation.[71] The study found that fragmentation and complexity negatively impact innovation, while data mature organizations generate 250 percent more value from their business operations than less mature organizations.

Centralized data, alternatively, creates growth. Research published by The Customer Data Platform Resource found that centralized data gave 64 percent of companies surveyed greater efficiencies and 57 percent business growth.[72]

How do we achieve a work environment where teams aren't second-guessing lead quality, struggling with outdated customer records, or piecing together insights across disconnected platforms? The answer is found in taking a centralized, scientific approach to data.

The Scientific Approach to Data

As business operations mature, revenue operations teams intuitively understand that the systematic processing of data is key to business functions. In technology, you may call it data analysis and forecasting. In health care, you may call it diagnostics and prognostics. In academics, you may call it analysis and conclusions. Regardless of what you call it, the ability to successfully analyze the past and predict the future is dependent upon clean, honest, transparent data.

Amy's background in academics has informed the way she approaches data as the lifeblood of an organization. Her doctorate in Organizational Communication draws upon sociology, organizational theory, rhetoric, organizational behavior, business, and philosophy to understand organizations as socially constructed dynamic entities with people, processes, and data in pursuit of a collective goal. For an organization to be effective, people, processes, and data must all be aligned holistically toward that goal.

The way we approach data in business should be the same way we approach data scientifically. In fact, the research design process in academic research studies is similar to the way we effectively approach data in a business environment.

First, we identify and design the research problem. "How much of our pipeline will turn into closed won bookings this quarter?" is a common question. Next, we conduct a literature review. We examine industry trends, see what other luminaries are saying about the macroeconomic environment, and identify knowledge gaps that may prevent us from seeing clearly. We formulate a research question or a hypothesis: "Based on our pipeline velocity and win rate, we expect to book 25 percent of our pipeline." We identify the right data collection procedures and collect the data. We identify the reporting and formulas that are applicable to our analysis and report on those. We draw conclusions, predict the future, and identify areas for further research.

This scientific approach to data is very similar, in fact, to what industry veterans Sean Lane and Laura Adint outline as the "data journey" in chapter 12 of *The Revenue Operations Manual*: data collection, reporting, insights, and prediction.[73]

By adopting a scientific approach to data management, users create a unified foundation and a seamless data flow that equips your RevOps team with data-driven insights that support processes, drive GTM strategies, align teams, and bolster operational infrastructure so RevOps can finally operate with clarity, precision, and confidence. Let's look deeper at how we collect and analyze data, then use it to report and forecast.

Data Collection

Too many companies treat data like a junk drawer, stuffed with lead lists, CRM updates, customer interactions, and unstructured insights that no one knows how to use effectively. Marketing has its lead data, sales works with account and operational data, customer success is drowning in customer interactions, and somewhere in the mix, RevOps is trying to align it all. If these data types aren't centralized, your revenue engine doesn't have the fuel it needs to run well.

How can sales close deals faster if their account data is outdated? How can marketing optimize campaigns if they can't see real-time lead behavior? How can customer success drive retention if they don't have access to the full customer journey? Let's first look at different types of data, then how we can build a system to collect it appropriately.

Types of Data

Every piece of data in RevOps is connected, and when it's fragmented, so is your revenue growth. To understand the importance of centralizing data, it's critical to examine the various types of data. **This includes:**

1. **Lead Data:** Information on potential customers entering the funnel.
2. **Opportunity Data:** Insights into active deals and their progression.
3. **Operational Data:** Focuses on the day-to-day transactions and activities of a business.
4. **Customer Data:** Ensures Customer Success alignment.
5. **Sales Enablement Data:** Includes training and competitive insights.
6. **Structured and Unstructured Data:** Structured data is organized, easily searchable, and stored in databases (like opportunity records in a CRM), while unstructured data is more free-form, such as emails, call transcripts, and meeting notes.

Lead Data in Marketing. Marketing teams generate and manage lead data, which serves as the foundation for sales pipeline growth. This data includes:

- **Demographics** (name, company, title, industry, location, etc.)
- **Firmographics** (company size, revenue, funding, etc.)

- **Behavioral data** (website visits, content engagement, ad interactions, event participation, etc.)
- **Attribution data** (how a lead discovered the company and moved through the funnel)

Opportunity Data. Unlike lead data, which focuses on potential customers who've shown interest but aren't really viewed as serious prospects, opportunity data tracks prospects who have progressed further down the sales funnel and appear actively engaged in the sales process.

This data tracks more detailed information about the potential deal, including:

- Estimated deal size
- Number of outreach attempts (phone calls, emails, form fills, etc.,)
- Probability of closing
- Expected close date
- Specific pain points or requirements of the prospect.

Operations and Account Data in Sales. Sales teams rely on both operational and account-level data to prioritize and close deals efficiently. These datasets include:

- **Pipeline and forecast data** (deal stage, expected close date, probability of closing)
- **Account history** (past interactions, deal history, objections, and notes from previous calls)
- **Contact records** (decision-makers, influencers, and stakeholders within an account)
- **Engagement metrics** (emails sent, meetings scheduled, calls made, proposals sent)

A centralized CRM ensures that sales teams can quickly access a holistic view of every prospect and customer, reducing redundant outreach and improving deal velocity.

Customer Data in Customer Success. Once a prospect converts into a customer, the customer success team needs a full view of customer interactions to drive retention and expansion. This data includes:

- **Product usage data** (which features the customer uses, frequency, adoption trends)
- **Support tickets and history** (challenges faced, resolution times, customer feedback)
- **Renewal and churn indicators** (subscription details, engagement trends, contract expiration dates)
- **Expansion opportunities** (upsell/cross-sell potential based on customer behavior)

When customer success teams lack visibility into historical sales interactions or product usage trends, it's difficult to proactively manage churn or identify upsell opportunities. A unified customer data platform enables teams to provide a seamless and personalized customer experience.

Sales Enablement Data. Sales enablement teams provide sales reps with the content, tools, and training needed to close deals effectively. A centralized repository for sales enablement data includes:

- **Content performance** (which sales collateral is most effective in closing deals)
- **Training completion rates** (which sales reps have completed required onboarding/training sessions)

- **Playbook effectiveness** (conversion rates of deals that followed specific sales strategies)
- **Competitive intelligence** (data on competitors' offerings and positioning)

By centralizing sales enablement data, RevOps can ensure that reps have instant access to the right materials at the right time, improving sales efficiency and win rates.

Structured and Unstructured Data in Database Work

Revenue operations often involve managing structured, semi-structured, and unstructured data. Understanding these data types is key to optimizing database architecture and analytics:

Structured data: This refers to highly organized data stored in relational databases, such as CRM records, lead lists, and financial transactions. This type of data is easy to query and analyze.

Semi-structured data: This type of data doesn't conform to a rigid tabular format but contains organizational markers like tags or metadata. Common examples include:

- XML and JSON files: Used for data interchange between systems, these formats encapsulate data within hierarchical tags or key-value pairs, allowing for flexible data modeling.
- Emails: While the body content is unstructured, elements like sender, recipient, and time stamps provide a semi-structured framework.
- HTML documents: Web pages use HTML tags to structure content, blending unstructured text with a semi-structured format.

Unstructured data: This includes data that doesn't fit neatly into database tables, such as email conversations, call transcripts, social media interactions, and customer reviews. Studies show 80 percent of company data is unstructured, which means teams are missing out on valuable insight to drive Go-to-Market.[74]

RevOps teams that unify structured, semi-structured, and unstructured data can generate more predictive insights and automate complex processes like sentiment analysis for customer feedback.

Data Collection Methods

Data collection is one of the most important parts of any business. Because of our digital economy, there are millions of data points that businesses are collecting daily. Data has even been heralded as the new currency upon which the success of modern business is built.[75] Collecting data in a clean, ethical, and usable way is extremely important and has increasingly large consequences when data collection is interrupted or collected in unethical ways. Here are a few types of data collection.

Continuous Data Collection[76]

Much like its name, continuous data collection gathers information on customer behavior or business operations on an ongoing basis. The real-time capabilities make this useful for tracking trends.

- Website Analytics: Tools like Google Analytics continuously track user interactions on websites, providing data on page views, session duration, and user flow.
- CRM Systems: These platforms continuously update customer information, interactions, and sales activities.

- Marketing Automation: These tools continuously collect data on email engagement, campaign performance, and lead behavior.
- Social Media Monitoring: Platforms that track social media interactions, mentions, and engagement metrics in real time.

One-Time Data Collection[77]

One-time data collection gathers information at a specific time for a specific purpose. It is particularly useful for measuring the relevance of a specific topic or validating a hypothesis.

- Surveys and Polls: Collecting customer feedback or market research data at a specific moment
- Focus Groups: Conducting in-depth discussions with a selected group of participants to gather qualitative insights
- Interviews: One-on-one conversations with customers or stakeholders to gather detailed information
- Observations: Watching and recording customer behavior or interactions in a specific setting

First-Party Data Collection[78]

First-party data is the type of data most easily collected, as it comes directly from your audience or customers through owned channels and platforms.

- Website Behavior: Tracking how users interact with your website, including pages visited and actions taken.

- Customer Feedback: Directly soliciting opinions and preferences from customers.
- Purchase History: Recording transactional data from your e-commerce platform or point-of-sale systems.
- Email Engagement: Monitoring how subscribers interact with your email campaigns.
- Mobile App Usage: Tracking user behavior within your company's mobile applications.

Third-Party Data Collection[79]

Third-party data from external sources provides strategic market insight that supplements data missing from first-party data.

- Data Aggregators: Companies that collect and compile data from various sources to create comprehensive datasets.
- Market Research Firms: Organizations that conduct industry-wide studies and provide insights to multiple clients.
- Social Media Platforms: Offering aggregated and anonymized data about user demographics and behaviors.
- Public Records: Government databases and publicly available information sources.

Through different data collection methods, RevOps teams can create a comprehensive view of their customers, market, and business performance. Data collection is so important that some businesses have collected it in ways that have made consumers feel increasingly violated. Because of this, government bodies around the world have created consent and privacy laws aiming to protect individuals and ensure businesses use responsible marketing practices, such as the US CAN-SPAM Act, Canada's Anti-Spam Legislation (CASL), Australia's Spam Act, European Union's General Data Protection Regulation (GDPR), United Kingdom's Privacy and Electronic Communications Regulations (PECR), New Zealand's Unsolicited Electronic Messages Act, and others.

While the exact regulations are beyond the scope of this chapter, suffice it to say that all of these regulations are designed to put guardrails around unsolicited communication and require companies to secure opt-in permissions for consumer protection.

Analyzing Data for Actionable Insights

As the RevOps model continues to evolve, more companies are recognizing that revenue operations isn't just a bridge between marketing, sales, and customer success, it's the connective tissue that brings siloed data together to create a clearer, more complete view of the customer journey from start to finish.

"Companies are starting to understand that if you treat revenue as a science, and approach it like a process engineer would: analyzing each stage and conversion rate across your sales, marketing, and customer success efforts based on underlying data; then layer on the voice of the customer, that's when you can drive meaningful impact and wins across the business," said Katerina Ostrovsky, RevOps leader and data analytics expert, during a *Go To Market Podcast* interview with Amy.[80]

She continued, "The real foundation is the data that lives across all these disparate systems. If you have the right data model to unify it . . . and the BI, analytics, and reporting in place, you can guide where and how to deploy your limited resources. You'll know exactly where to focus to make the biggest impact. That's where RevOps becomes truly strategic! Helping companies make smarter decisions and prioritize what actually moves the needle."

Once data has been organized and collected, intelligent data analysis strategies can surface powerful insights, support better decision-making, and uncover hidden opportunities. Some of the most common and effective data analysis models include[81]:

Descriptive Models

- Summary Statistics—Snapshots of data through means, medians, standard deviations, and distributions.
- Data Visualization—Charts, graphs, and dashboards to illustrate patterns and trends.
- Clustering and Segmentation—Groups data points based on similarities, often used for customer segmentation.

Diagnostic Models

- Correlation and Regression Analysis—Determines relationships between variables and identifies key drivers behind trends.
- Root Cause Analysis—Pinpoints factors influencing a specific outcome.

Predictive Models

- Machine Learning Models—Uses algorithms (e.g., decision trees, random forests, neural networks) to forecast future outcomes.
- Time Series Analysis—Examines historical trends to predict future performance, commonly used in financial forecasting.

- Propensity Modeling—Assesses the likelihood of specific actions, such as customer churn or purchase intent.

Prescriptive Models

- Optimization Models—Suggests the best course of action by analyzing constraints and objectives.
- A/B Testing—Compares different strategies to determine which yields the best results.
- Scenario Analysis—Simulates different business scenarios to assess potential outcomes.

Cognitive and AI-Driven Models

- Natural Language Processing (NLP)—Extracts insights from unstructured data like emails, reviews, and social media.
- Deep Learning—Identifies complex patterns in large datasets, often used for image recognition and fraud detection.

A Data Quality study conducted by Software Development Times found that a mere 16 percent of businesses surveyed have fully integrated data analytics into their strategic decision-making processes.[82] The same study found 34 percent of companies are in the "initial phases of recognizing the importance of data but have not yet fully integrated it into their decision-making processes."

To truly capitalize on these insights, you need seamless data flow, strong governance, and a strategy that prioritizes customer lifetime value.

In the *Go To Market Podcast* hosted by Amy, Prasad Varhabatla, head of RevOps at Philips, delivered some insightful guidance.[83] "You need to start thinking about the customer in terms of what is the full lifetime value of this customer," Prasad said. "Am I there right now? What are the other ways in which I can use the data that I currently have about the customer's preferences, customer's buying patterns, and customer's needs, to maximize the customer lifetime value and also build a great relationship that actually stands the test of time?"

Prasad confirms that if you have customer master data, there has to be one place that feeds everything else. "You can do whatever you need to do to enrich that part, but you have to hold that particular system, that particular process, that particular area accountable, and put governance around it," he said.

For instance, out of the thousands of products your company offers, you know that some of those products or subscriptions may be coming up to end of life or end of service. If you have an automated system that can leverage data properly, you will know well in advance, maybe 15 months or 18 months in advance, that there is an opportunity coming up with this customer where your sales team can flip this particular product that they purchased ten years ago with the latest version of that device.

"There's a lot more you can do, where you can unearth opportunities that you didn't know existed. Get ahead in the conversation. It's a competitive market. It's not that we are the only company who delivers a particular product. Our competitors are also always there at our heels, trying to get the same customer," Prasad said. "Your install base has your future business, if you can use it properly."

When shopping for tools to help optimize data analytics, look for these features:

1. *Data Integration and Connectivity*—The ability to connect seamlessly with various data sources (CRM, ERP, cloud storage, APIs, etc.). Popular brands include MuleSoft, Informatica, Talend, and Fivetran.

2. *Visualization and Reporting*—Intuitive dashboards, charts, and customizable reports to make data insights easy to understand. Tableau, Google, and Microsoft products are great choices.

3. *Scalability and Performance*—The tool should handle large datasets efficiently and grow with your business needs. Top brands include Google, Snowflake, Amazon Redshift, and Databricks.

4. *AI and Automation Capabilities*—Features like predictive analytics, machine learning, and automated data cleansing to enhance decision-making. Brands like Fullcast, Salesforce Einstein, IBM Watson, Google, and Databricks are driving AI innovation in planning and data analytics tools.

"In today's data-driven world, we are all looking to gain efficiency through automation," wrote Amy Calabro Vieira, Vice President of Commercial Operations at Norstealla, in a LinkedIn post. "But when it comes to building a successful data strategy, simply automating tasks can be a recipe for missed opportunities. Data automation should be a tool within your strategy, not the strategy itself."

Reporting

Your data is only as powerful as your ability to use it. A clean dataset without structured reporting is like having a map with no legend—confusing, inefficient, and a wasted opportunity. If your team can't easily access and interpret critical insights, you're not just missing out; you're falling behind. A "reporting essentials" folder isn't just a convenience—it's a strategic necessity. It centralizes must-have reports, eliminates guesswork, and ensures every department operates from the same source of truth.

The most common reports that assist in RevOps strategies help optimize revenue processes, improve forecasting, and align sales, marketing, and customer success. According to Salesforce,[84] here are some of the key reports RevOps teams rely on:

1. *Revenue and Forecasting Reports*
   - Revenue Forecast Report—Predicts future revenue based on pipeline data, historical trends, and market conditions.
   - Sales Pipeline Report—Breaks down open opportunities by stage, deal size, and expected close dates.
   - Bookings vs. Quota Report—Compares actual sales bookings to quota targets for performance tracking.
2. *Sales and Performance Reports*
   - Sales Performance Dashboard—Tracks key metrics like win rates, average deal size, and sales cycle length.
   - Quota Attainment Report—Measures how individual reps and teams are performing against their targets.
   - Lead Conversion Report—Analyzes how leads move through the funnel and where drop-offs occur.
3. *Marketing and Demand Generation Reports*
   - Marketing Attribution Report—Shows which channels and campaigns drive the most revenue.
   - Lead Source Performance Report—Identifies the best-performing lead sources based on conversion rates.
   - Customer Acquisition Cost (CAC) Report—Calculates the cost of acquiring new customers across different channels.

4. *Customer Success and Retention Reports*
   - Churn and Retention Report—Highlights customer retention rates and reasons for churn.
   - Customer Lifetime Value (LTV) Report—Estimates the long-term revenue impact of customers.
   - Net Promoter Score (NPS) and Customer Satisfaction (CSAT) Reports—Measure customer sentiment and loyalty.
5. *Efficiency and Operational Reports*
   - Sales Cycle Analysis Report—Examines the time it takes to close deals and identifies bottlenecks.
   - Rep Productivity Report—Assesses rep activity levels (calls, emails, meetings) versus closed deals.
   - Funnel Velocity Report—Measures how quickly leads progress through the sales funnel.
6. *Financial and Strategic Reports*
   - ARR (Annual Recurring Revenue) and MRR (Monthly Recurring Revenue) Reports—Essential for tracking revenue growth in subscription-based models.
   - Customer Profitability Report—Compares revenue generated by customers to the cost of serving them.
   - Scenario Planning and Growth Projections—Helps model different revenue growth strategies and their impact.

Rather than have teams scrambling through disconnected spreadsheets, reporting with technology tools allows for data to be aggregated, synthesized, analyzed, and displayed to help teams confidently make decisions. "If we assume for a second that people have preferences for different tools—let's say maybe HubSpot does a great job of leads, but Salesforce is great at opportunities—connect the two,"

Prasad said. "There's no religion around tools. If you can afford the tools and you already have the tools and you're still using the tools, connect the tools, it doesn't matter."

These reports are designed to measure performance based on key performance indicators. Reports measuring everything from pipeline velocity to revenue per employee can provide essential business insights critical to running the organization.

Forecasting

Having data-driven tools that can anticipate customer buying behaviors, market shifts, and other critical business variables empowers RevOps teams to be proactive. It's as close as we are going to get to a crystal ball. Because we have addressed forecasting in the previous chapter, we'll just touch on a few points here. Forecasting allows us to use data for the following purpose.

Optimize Predictive Analytics

Predictive analytics is a powerful tool that enables businesses to anticipate future outcomes by analyzing historical data. In RevOps, it plays a crucial role in forecasting sales, understanding customer behavior, and optimizing strategies to drive revenue growth.

Implementing predictive analytics within RevOps offers several advantages, according to SAS[85]:

1. *Accurate sales forecasting*: By examining past sales data and market trends, predictive models can forecast future sales performance, allowing organizations to set realistic targets and allocate resources effectively. We'll dive more into forecasting in the next section.

2. *Enhanced customer insights:* Analyzing customer interactions and purchase histories helps identify patterns, enabling personalized marketing strategies and improved customer retention.

3. *Optimized marketing campaigns:* Predictive analytics can determine customer responses or purchases, as well as promote cross-sell opportunities, helping businesses attract, retain, and grow their most profitable customers.

4. *Improved operational efficiency:* By forecasting demand and managing resources proactively, companies can streamline operations, reduce costs, and enhance overall efficiency.

Despite its benefits, adopting predictive analytics in RevOps comes with challenges. The effectiveness of predictive models heavily depends on the quality of data, according to Charlie Cowen.[86] Inaccurate or incomplete data can lead to misguided decisions. Combining data from various systems can also be complex, requiring robust integration strategies to ensure a unified and accurate dataset.

Another thing to consider is interpreting complex data models necessitates specialized skills. Investing in training programs can bridge this gap and empower teams to leverage predictive analytics effectively.

To maximize the benefits of predictive analytics in RevOps, follow these three steps:

1. *Ensure Data Quality:* Implement rigorous data governance policies to maintain accuracy and consistency across all data sources.

2. *Invest in the Right Tools:* Utilize advanced analytics platforms that can handle large datasets and provide actionable insights.

3. *Continuously Monitor and Refine:* Regularly assess predictive models and refine them based on new data and changing market conditions to maintain their effectiveness.

By embracing predictive analytics, RevOps teams can make informed decisions that drive strategic initiatives and foster sustainable revenue growth.

Almost 60 percent of business leaders report using data analytics to drive business innovation.[87] However, the same study from NewVantage Partners also discovered only two in five organizations are managing data as an asset, and that presumably includes predictive analytics.

This predictive concept of working *on* the business instead of *in* the business is key for Lonny Sternberg's success as a leader in Go-to-Market strategy.

"Working on the business is more proactive," Lonny said. "It's about understanding when to perform an evaluation or an audit of where you are today, and diving deep into the KPIs. The framework I like to use is people, process, systems, and tools—not just people, process, and tech. So when you've done that full evaluation, I think you're prepared to lead that proactive approach and say, 'I understand how to achieve our objectives. I understand we can achieve a gross margin percentage of X, a top-line revenue of Y, and an NPS score of Z, etc.'"

"Then," he added. "You're in a position where you have that framework, that evaluation and you're expertized in the business with the ability to support, 'We have a gap here, or we are really good at this, or I think we need to double down our investment in this other area to achieve some of our goals.'"

Instead of being reactive, constantly fielding requests to "just implement this thing," RevOps teams should be in the driver's seat—mapping every process, tool, and KPI to the customer journey with precision. Using frameworks like the Winning by Design bowtie model, for instance, teams can create an end-to-end blueprint that ensures every system and strategy aligns.[88]

When you know exactly how each step in the journey connects, you're not just executing tasks; you're driving revenue growth with intention. This is the difference between scrambling to keep up and proactively optimizing for success.

Proactive data might set the pace, but ignoring reactive data means flying blind to the deeper truths. When positioned with equal priority, reactive analytics unpacks the "why" behind proactive insights and highlights the hidden factors that impact GTM strategies and RevOps workflow. This information will prove valuable as your company progresses to implementation.

Other Practical Forecasting Applications

AI-driven propensity models use advanced machine learning algorithms to analyze historical data and predict the likelihood of a lead converting into a high-value customer. Lead behavior, demographics, past interactions, and engagement patterns models assign a "propensity score" to each lead, which measures their potential to make a purchase or become a long-term customer. With this information RevOps teams can prioritize leads, tailor outreach, and allocate resources. Top brands to consider include Salesforce, HubSpot, SAS, and IBM.

Scenario planning helps businesses prepare for potential market shifts by creating and analyzing multiple future scenarios. It involves identifying key drivers of change—such as economic factors, technological advances, or regulatory changes—and developing various possible outcomes based on different assumptions.

Proactive strategies help businesses stay resilient and agile. By considering a range of "what-if" scenarios, companies can anticipate risks, identify opportunities, and make informed decisions on how to adapt their strategies. Brands like Oracle, SAP, Kepion, and Anaplan have top scenario planning models.

AI-supported automations can easily analyze customer data, sales history, and behavior patterns, then recommend target leads, ideal outreach strategies, and well-timed follow-up. Automated recommendations help streamline workflows, boost productivity, and ensure that sales teams are always working with the most relevant and timely information. Brands like Salesforce, HubSpot, and Zoho are constantly innovating AI capabilities for data analytics.

The Challenge of Complex Data

Data silos keep critical insights trapped in isolated systems, forcing teams to work with incomplete information. The sheer volume of data is paralyzing, making it nearly impossible to separate meaningful signals from noise.

And let's not forget the chaos of inconsistent data formats—when sales, marketing, and customer success teams each define metrics differently, how can leadership trust the numbers? Worst of all, when the right people can't access the right data at the right time, decisions get delayed, opportunities slip away, and revenue suffers.

Experts like Prasad and Jared Barol, a GTM leader and RevOps advisor, agree that data governance is essential. The second thing is to put some governance around it, so people can't go off the grid and do stuff. Moreover, if they go off the grid and do stuff, you are able to track them, so that you know where they are and how to get that data back.

"There is nothing that the tools of the world today cannot do around the revenue operations and sales operations processes," Prasad said.

Nevertheless, Prasad has heard his share of RevOps teams complain about poor-performing tools. "The tool is not broken," he said. "The way you're using it is broken."

A Word About AI

If we intend to talk about the RevOps scientific method to centralize and leverage complex data, AI must be part of the conversation. An entire library could be devoted to just what we have learned about AI in the past year. Anything we could say about AI will be too little, but it must be mentioned, as a discussion about data without AI will be grossly incomplete.

Traditionally, RevOps teams rely on a cycle of hypothesis, testing, and iteration to refine Go-to-Market strategies, but fragmented data often slows progress. AI can help to reduce these silos by automatically aggregating and normalizing data from multiple sources—CRM systems, marketing platforms, customer success tools, and finance databases—into a single source of truth.

"Isn't that the mantra of RevOps anyway?" Rob Levey, a RevOps leader, said during a *Go To Market Podcast* discussion with Amy.[89] "We get stuck in the CRM, adding fields, we get stuck in Excel sheets, and we never get to do—or we don't spend anywhere near enough time—on the strategic, important stuff where we grow in the business. The more these tools can help us declutter all of the boring, mundane stuff, that leaves us more time for the exciting, impactful business-growing opportunities."

With AI continuously validating assumptions, detecting trends, and optimizing workflows, RevOps teams can move beyond gut-feel decision-making and instead operate with data-backed precision, accelerating revenue growth and operational efficiency. This level of precision is crucial for decision-making, as clean, well-structured data leads to more effective sales strategies, optimized marketing efforts, and better customer experiences. The ability of AI to work effectively depends, however, on how clean the data is. We expect to see a lot more businesses pop up exclusively to manage data hygiene in the future because of the importance of this interplay between data and AI. This is also one reason that some people are considering syncing directly to a data lake and avoiding a CRM like Salesforce altogether.

In this chapter, we've offered a road map that we hope changes your view of data as a strategic asset that extends far beyond contact lists and tracking sales action items. When organizations centralize, standardize, and streamline their data, RevOps teams go from firefighting to forecasting. A single source of truth means faster decisions, better collaboration, and a clearer path to growth. The question isn't whether your data is a challenge—it's whether you're ready to transform it into a strategic advantage.

RevOps Centralized Data Strategy Checklist

☐ **Audit Existing Data Sources**
- Identify all data sources used across marketing, sales, and customer success.
- Assess integration needs and pinpoint data gaps.
- Document data ownership and update frequency for each source.

☐ **Adopt a Centralized CRM or Data Warehouse**
- Select a centralized platform (e.g., Salesforce, HubSpot, Snowflake, or CDP).
- Ensure compatibility with existing systems and scalability for future growth.

- Set up a structured data model to support unified reporting.

☐ **Ensure Data Hygiene and Governance**
- Define and enforce data validation rules to prevent duplicates and inaccuracies.
- Establish clear roles for data management and maintenance.
- Implement a routine data cleansing process to maintain integrity.

☐ **Automate Data Integration**
- Utilize APIs and automation tools to sync data across platforms.
- Minimize manual data entry to reduce errors and inefficiencies.
- Set up automated workflows for real-time data updates.

☐ **Enable Cross-Departmental Access**
- Define role-based permissions to ensure secure access to data.
- Break down silos by allowing visibility across revenue-generating teams.
- Standardize reporting formats to ensure consistency in insights.

☐ **Use AI and Analytics for Insights**
- Implement AI-driven analytics for customer segmentation and forecasting.
- Leverage predictive models to identify revenue opportunities.
- Continuously refine data models to improve accuracy and relevance.

Conclusion

Data is the raw material of long-term revenue success. In this chapter, we've walked through the full data journey that transforms scattered insights into a powerful strategic asset. It begins with the basics: defining and centralizing lead, opportunity, customer, and operational data. Without this foundational step, your revenue engine is running on guesswork instead of grounded strategy.

From there, we explored how data collection evolves through structured, unstructured, and semi-structured formats—each critical for building a full picture of the customer journey. We discussed how to collect data continuously or at specific moments in time and how to integrate third- and first-party sources into a unified system. Then we examined how to analyze that data, not just for dashboards and reports, but for forecasting, scenario modeling, and uncovering revenue opportunities before they surface.

Importantly, we also addressed how to implement these insights through systems that actually work. A centralized data strategy is only as strong as the governance, processes, and tools supporting it. And implementation isn't just a technical task—it's an organizational one, involving cross-functional alignment, clear ownership, and the discipline to maintain your source of truth over time.

When data is fragmented, teams are out of sync, strategy execution lags, and revenue suffers. But when data is unified, structured, and intelligently applied, RevOps becomes a growth engine. Accurate forecasts, higher win rates, improved territory design, and better customer experiences all stem from a clear and disciplined approach to data.

Data alone won't close deals, but it will tell you where your best opportunities lie, which signals matter most, and what's holding your revenue engine back. In the end, success doesn't come from having more data; it comes from using it better. And that's the true power of a centralized RevOps data strategy.

8

Technology Focus

The Tech in Your Revenue Engine

While on vacation in Las Vegas, Ryan's back gave out during an acroyoga session (an ambitious combo of acrobatics and yoga) with his wife. The pain was excruciating, forcing him to seek medical attention in a run-down clinic far from his home. When he finally saw his doctor back in Salt Lake City, he was given a diagnosis that hit much harder than expected: "Your core is weak."

The statement struck a deeper chord. Ryan didn't just hear it as a medical fact—he took it as a metaphor for his life and leadership. It was a turning point. "I realized it wasn't just my physical core that needed work," Ryan recalled. "I needed to strengthen my personal discipline, my habits, and even the core systems of the companies I was building." That realization launched him on a journey of self-improvement, not only for his body and mind but also for the way he viewed technology's role in business.

Ryan committed to a rigorous workout routine, focusing on strengthening his core. He hasn't missed more than three core workouts since that day. He also changed his eating habits, incorporating a lot more vegetables into his diet by having juice delivered to his home weekly. His doctor was able to use his X-rays as an example that surgery was not necessary. Ryan also focused on improving his sleep habits, using an Oura ring to track his sleep patterns and find the right balance of rest.

Just as a strong physical core supports the body, efficient technology serves as the core of a business's revenue engine. Without it, a company risks inefficiency, poor decision-making, and stagnation. But with the right tools and strategies, technology can propel an organization to new heights.

Technology enables companies to act quickly, adapt to change, and operate with precision. Ryan sees AI as a critical component, describing it as the ultimate copilot for revenue leaders. AI can streamline processes that were once labor-intensive. For example, instead of teams spending hours analyzing customer data manually, AI tools can generate insights in seconds, helping companies identify opportunities and act on them before competitors do.

Beyond efficiency, integrated systems have the power to connect sales, marketing, and customer success teams. When everyone operates from the same source of truth, you create alignment, and that's when a company becomes unstoppable. This alignment isn't just about data; it's about creating workflows that are repeatable and scalable—what we are calling the "revenue engine."

The benefits don't stop at internal operations. Technology also plays a crucial role in customer engagement. AI-powered platforms can guide users through complex products, reducing onboarding time and enhancing satisfaction. This is about empowering customers to succeed, fostering loyalty, and turning them into advocates.

Businesses must commit to building a technological foundation that supports their long-term goals. Technology is that core for modern businesses. It enables you to move faster, think smarter, and adapt to whatever comes your way. This means investing in tools that not only solve immediate problems but also position the company for sustainable growth. But you need to be intentional about what technology you bring into your business' "core." For leaders, the lesson is clear: Just as personal growth requires discipline and intentionality, so does the integration of technology into a company's operations.

Done right, technology doesn't just support growth—it drives it. In this chapter, we'll explore the technology that will help you power your RevOps organization, including some core components of your tech stack. Next, we'll dive into ways to evaluate new tools and how AI can help you take RevOps to the next level.

The Tools That Power RevOps

We're spoiled for choice nowadays when it comes to powerful tech solutions that can supercharge our strategies. The right tools can support what you do while also turning complex processes into seamless workflows and fragmented data into actionable insights. For RevOps leaders, this abundance of technology presents an exciting opportunity to build a tech stack that not only meets current needs but also scales effortlessly as the business grows.

"Historically, the intent of most productivity software has been to make jobs easier. In the future, it'll be about replacing tasks as part of a job. Pricing and commercial strategies are already starting to shift (e.g., software costs being considered as a fraction of a salary.) What does this mean?" Rachel Krall, strategy and operations leader, asked via LinkedIn.[90] "First, it's important to start thinking about jobs as a list of tasks, some are more likely to be disrupted than others. Recognize your customers and buyers are also being disrupted. Evolve your internal and external product roadmap to respond—how can you support your teams and customers through this evolution? For example, how can you increase overall technology fluency so that teams can embrace these new technologies to free more time for what they love?"

Back to the Indy 500 analogy from the introduction—winning isn't just about having the fastest driver or even the most-synchronized pit crew; it's about equipping the team with the best tools to gain an edge. In racing, that edge might come from a gravity-reflow system that shaves crucial seconds off pit stops. In RevOps, it's about building a tech stack that keeps your revenue engine running at peak performance. The right tools enable you to execute flawlessly and win big.

Prasad Varahabhatla, a seasoned RevOps leader, offered a striking insight during a recent conversation: "There's no manipulation in Excel that a tool or platform can't do better and faster."[91] He shared a story about organizations struggling with fragmented data—where marketing uses HubSpot, sales relies on Salesforce, and customer success operates on yet another CRM. Instead of empowering collaboration, this siloed approach led to conflict as leaders argued over whose data source was accurate. Prasad's solution was to connect the tools; it doesn't matter if you have preferences for HubSpot or Salesforce—integrate them, define a single source of truth, and hold that accountable. His advice encapsulates the core of a successful tech strategy: simplicity, integration, and alignment.

In this section, we'll dive into the essential components of a modern RevOps tech stack, explore how to make the smartest choices from the plethora of options available, and uncover how AI is redefining the way we plan, execute, and optimize our revenue operations.

Core Components of a RevOps Tech Stack

At its core, a RevOps tech stack must achieve these three primary goals:

1. Unify data
2. Streamline workflows
3. Enable insights that drive better decision-making

By integrating tools designed for specific functions across marketing, sales, and customer success, you create a seamless, high-performance ecosystem.

"The approach we are taking when introducing AI tooling is from a use-case-first perspective," said Matt Piotrowski, an experienced VP of Operations. "We identify use cases that require lots of human effort to drive and/or there is a low change cost (e.g., process/workflow does not exist or is currently not being utilized) and a measurable impact."[92]

Here's an expanded look at the essential tools every RevOps team should consider, how they interact, and the unique value each brings to your operations.

Customer Relationship Management (CRM). A CRM system, such as Salesforce, HubSpot, or Microsoft Dynamics, serves as the heart of any RevOps tech stack. It provides a unified repository for all customer data, enabling a 360-degree view of interactions across marketing, sales, and customer success. Beyond managing contacts and accounts, modern CRMs offer powerful features like automation, pipeline visualization, and real-time reporting.

When properly integrated with other tools, the CRM becomes a single source of truth, ensuring every team operates from accurate and up-to-date data. For instance, marketing automation platforms feed lead data directly into the CRM, while customer success tools update customer health scores, creating a seamless flow of information that aligns all teams around the customer life cycle.

Marketing Automation Platform (MAP). Platforms like Marketo, Pardot, and HubSpot Marketing Hub bring structure and efficiency to your marketing campaigns. These tools automate repetitive tasks like email marketing, lead scoring, and audience segmentation, freeing up time for creative strategy. Marketing teams can design multi-touch campaigns and track engagement across channels while ensuring qualified leads are delivered to sales at the optimal time.

MAPs should integrate tightly with CRMs, enabling automated workflows such as transferring MQLs (marketing-qualified leads) to the appropriate sales reps. This integration ensures that sales teams are equipped with the right information to engage prospects effectively.

"Accurately tracking marketing campaign attribution can be tricky," wrote SaaS Strategist Andrew Sims in a LinkedIn post.[93] "With customers interacting across multiple channels—email, social media, ads, and more—it's tough to pinpoint exactly which effort led to a sale. This can cause confusion around what's really driving growth."

That's why investing in the right tools and processes to track attribution is crucial. When done right, it provides clear insights that help sales and marketing teams focus on the most impactful activities, improving overall performance and ensuring that resources are used wisely.

Sales Performance Management (SPM) Platform. An SPM platform is a vital component of a RevOps tech stack, as it centralizes and automates key processes like territory planning, quota setting, and performance tracking. This integration enhances collaboration across sales, marketing, and customer success teams, ensuring alignment with overarching revenue goals. Fullcast, for example, offers an AI-powered, no-code platform that integrates with CRMs like Salesforce to enable real-time adjustments to sales strategies, ensuring territories and quotas remain balanced and responsive to market dynamics. While this market is still fragmented, the industry is moving toward a comprehensive suite of tools—including capacity planning, lead routing, quota and commission planning, and data hygiene—to empower organizations to synchronize Go-to-Market strategies with execution, fostering increased sales productivity and revenue growth.

Sales Engagement Tools. Sales engagement platforms like Salesloft or Outreach enhance the productivity of sales reps by automating repetitive tasks and providing guided workflows. These tools enable email sequencing, call tracking, and task reminders, helping reps stay focused on building relationships and closing deals.

When synced with a CRM, these tools provide real-time updates on prospect interactions, ensuring everyone from RevOps to sales leaders has visibility into the status of opportunities. For example, if a sales rep schedules a call through Outreach, that interaction is automatically logged in the CRM, maintaining continuity across platforms.

Customer Success Platforms. Customer success platforms like Gainsight and Totango focus on the post-sale experience, ensuring customer satisfaction, retention, and growth. These platforms track metrics like customer health scores, product adoption rates, and support ticket activity. They also offer proactive alerts for renewal opportunities or signs of churn.

Data Analytics and Business Intelligence (BI) Tools. Tools like Tableau, Domo, and Microsoft Power BI aggregate data from multiple systems, transforming it into actionable insights. RevOps teams rely on BI tools to build dashboards that monitor KPIs, identify trends, and support strategic decisions. These tools become even more powerful when connected to the CRM, MAPs, and customer success platforms.

Workflow and Integration Tools. Workflow and integration platforms like Zapier, Workato, and MuleSoft act as the connective tissue of your tech stack, enabling seamless data exchange between tools.

For example, a lead captured through a web form can be automatically routed to the CRM, scored in the MAP, and assigned to a sales rep in the engagement platform—all without manual intervention.

Territory and Quota Management. Specialized tools like Fullcast simplify the complexities of territory planning, account assignment, and quota management. These platforms provide dynamic modeling capabilities, allowing RevOps teams to adapt quickly to changes in head count, market conditions, or strategic priorities.

Fully integrated with the CRM and BI tools, these platforms can ensure alignment between sales goals and operational execution. For instance, when a new sales rep is hired, territory tools can automatically carve out a fair and balanced territory and adjust quotas accordingly.

The true power of a RevOps tech stack lies in how these tools interact. When marketing automation tools deliver qualified leads directly to a CRM, and sales engagement platforms automatically update prospect activity, RevOps gains a clear and complete view of the revenue engine. When customer success platforms feed data back into analytics tools, businesses can measure the full impact of retention efforts on revenue growth.

"The ability to automatically distribute out of territory accounts is a game changer and will save a ton of time while giving all of sales and leadership confidence the process is being managed equitably," said Brennan Petar, a SaaS executive and RevOps advisor to Fullcast.

By connecting these tools through workflow automation platforms and ensuring data consistency, RevOps leaders can create a tech stack that not only works but works together.

What's in the Average RevOps Team's Tech Stack?

In part to understand how modern revenue teams are building and managing their technology stacks, we conducted the 2025 State of RevOps survey. The results, based on responses from ninety-six RevOps professionals, reveal that most organizations are juggling a large number of tools, struggling with adoption, and actively trying to balance innovation with integration.

The average revenue tech stack consists of thirteen tools, spanning CRM, marketing automation, engagement, forecasting, billing, compensation, document management, and more. While this level of tooling reflects the complexity of modern GTM motions, it also introduces risk—especially when teams lack the time or resources to maintain, integrate, and optimize every piece of the stack.

Utilization Gaps Are Widespread. When asked how well-utilized their stacks are, only 10.8 percent of respondents said they are "early adopters" using their tech well. The majority fell into one of two middle categories:

- 35.1 percent said they use most tools fairly well but don't adopt new features quickly.
- 41.9 percent admitted that while some tools are well-utilized, others are still not fully deployed.
- A smaller but notable 12.2 percent of respondents reported having "a lot of underutilized or unused tools."

In fact, the average team estimated that 29 percent of their current tech stack is underutilized or not used at all. That's nearly a third of investment potentially wasted or idle—often due to lack of training, unclear ROI, or poor integration.

When we asked what's standing in the way of better adoption, several common barriers emerged:

- 54.2 percent cited a lack of training and enablement resources.

- 44.4 percent said they have too many tools to learn and use effectively.
- 43.1 percent said they struggle to demonstrate ROI from their tech investments.
- 41.7 percent pointed to poor integration between tools.
- 36.1 percent noted a lack of alignment between teams.

These barriers echo the broader challenges we explored earlier in the chapter: disconnected systems, misaligned processes, and limited visibility across teams.

Nearly 80 percent of companies say they review the effectiveness of their tech stack annually (49.3%) or quarterly (31%). However, just 10 percent review on a monthly basis or more frequently. While annual reviews may be enough for slower-moving organizations, fast-scaling companies can find themselves locked into poor-fit tools—or underutilizing expensive platforms—if they don't revisit tech decisions more regularly.

Inside the Stack: Tools RevOps Teams Are Actually Using. The responses also offer a peek into the most common tools deployed across different RevOps functions:

- *CRMs:* Salesforce dominated CRM usage, with many respondents also leveraging HubSpot and Microsoft Dynamics (mentioned in open responses).
- *Order Management:* 69.4 percent of companies use Salesforce for order management, followed by NetSuite (33.3%) and SAP (9.7%).
- *Billing Systems:* NetSuite leads again here, used by 60.9 percent of respondents, followed by Stripe (10.1%) and Zuora (8.7%).
- *Revenue Recognition:* One-third of respondents (31.7%) reported not using any system for revenue recognition,

while others mentioned SAP (13.3%), Oracle (10%), and Stripe (11.7%).

- *Commissions:* 28.2 percent do not use a dedicated commissions platform. Among those who do, Xactly (22.5%), CaptivateIQ (18.3%), Spiff (15.5%), and QuotaPath (8.5%) were the most common.
- *Territory Management:* A full 57.8 percent of respondents do not use any territory management software. Those that do favor Salesforce Territory Management (15.5%) or Fullcast (11.3%). A notable 14 percent rely on homegrown or cobbled-together solutions.
- *Document Management for Compensation Plans:* Docusign is the clear leader here, used by 83.3 percent of respondents. Adobe Sign and PandaDoc are used by smaller numbers, while Conga Contracts and Nintex had no reported usage.
- *Payroll Systems:* ADP was the most common (46.8%), followed by Workday (9.7%) and TriNet (9.7%).
- *Sales Process Documentation:* Most teams rely on a mix of spreadsheets (54.2%), CRM notes (38.9%), and LMS platforms (37.5%). Notably, 5.6 percent said they don't document their sales process at all.

The data shows that RevOps leaders are managing increasingly complex tech environments, often with limited support. Despite best intentions, many organizations are building tech stacks faster than they can optimize or align them. Without regular audits, cross-functional planning, and a clear strategy for adoption, even the best tools can become liabilities.

To prevent underutilization and reduce technical debt, the best RevOps teams:

- Regularly audit their tech stack for redundancies and inefficiencies.
- Align tool selection with clear business use cases and strategic objectives.
- Invest in enablement, training, and cross-team collaboration.
- Use integration platforms and automation to ensure tools work together.
- Document ownership, workflows, and success metrics for each system.

The goal isn't to have more tools. It's to have the right tools working in harmony. That's what turns your tech stack into the backbone of a modern, scalable revenue engine.

How to Evaluate New Tools While Avoiding Technical Debt

The abundance of tools available to modern organizations is a double-edged sword. While the right solutions can supercharge efficiency, streamline processes, and provide superior insights, a poorly managed tech stack can lead to overlapping functionality, unnecessary expenses, and the creeping specter of technical debt.

The best time to update your tech stack is before major initiatives, such as Go-to-Market planning for a new fiscal year. Regular reassessments, at least annually, help keep your stack optimized and prevent technical debt from accumulating.

Signs it's time to reassess:

- Tool adoption rates are low, or feedback indicates dissatisfaction.
- Manual processes persist despite available automation.

- Data inconsistencies or silos hinder decision-making.
- Costs rise without a corresponding increase in value.

Not every shiny new tool will solve your problems. Avoid solutions that:

- Lack flexibility to scale with your growth.
- Fail to offer robust integration options with your existing stack.
- Provide limited reporting and analytics capabilities.
- Skimp on customer support and training, leaving teams frustrated.

Managing technical debt, the unseen cost of maintaining suboptimal systems, is crucial for ensuring your RevOps tech stack stays agile and scalable. Here's how you can carefully evaluate whether each tool contributes meaningfully to your business goals or creates unnecessary overhead:

- Outline processes and define success criteria.
- Conduct a comprehensive audit.
- Identify and prioritize cross-functional tools.
- Map out tech stack architecture.
- Share documentation for internal validation.
- Plan and execute the transition strategy.

Four Drivers of Tech Stack Decisions. A well-structured RevOps tech stack isn't just about having the latest tools—it's about ensuring every solution directly supports your business objectives. When evaluating and optimizing your tech stack, focus on four core drivers:

1. *Sell More*—Does the technology help your team increase revenue by improving lead conversion, sales velocity, or customer retention?
2. *In Less Time*—Does it streamline workflows, eliminate manual processes, and accelerate deal cycles?
3. *At the Right Price*—Does it enhance pricing strategies, discounting approvals, and deal profitability?
4. *While Lowering Costs*—Does it reduce inefficiencies, eliminate redundant tools, and maximize ROI?

Sales Stack Framework. To ensure your tech stack aligns with these goals, use this Sales Stack Framework, which can be used for any tools in your RevOps tech stack.

1. *Stakeholders—Identify, Engage, and Align:* Tech decisions impact multiple teams—RevOps, Sales, Marketing, Finance, and IT. Align stakeholders early to define goals and ensure cross-functional buy-in.
2. *Technology—Assess Current Stack and Identify Gaps:* Map your existing tech stack to understand what's working, what's redundant, and where gaps exist.

3. *Audit—Evaluate Capabilities and Limitations:* Conduct a structured assessment of your tools to measure adoption, integration, and business impact.

4. *Compare—Match Tech Capabilities to Business Needs:* Ensure each tool addresses an actual capability gap rather than adding unnecessary complexity.

5. *Know—Ask the Right Questions:* Before committing to a new tool, ask:
   - Does it integrate with our existing systems?
   - Will it scale with our business?
   - Does it simplify or complicate workflows?
   - What's the total cost of ownership, including training and maintenance?

By applying this structured approach, you can ensure that every tool in your RevOps tech stack is a strategic asset—not just another addition to an overloaded system.

The AI Advantage for RevOps

We're living in a golden age of technology, where AI is revolutionizing RevOps and offering tools that would have seemed impossible just a few years ago. In the 2025 State of RevOps Survey, we discovered that the RevOps teams have an average of three AI tools in their tech stack, with the most common uses being call transcription, chatbots, lead scoring and lead routing, and sales forecasting.

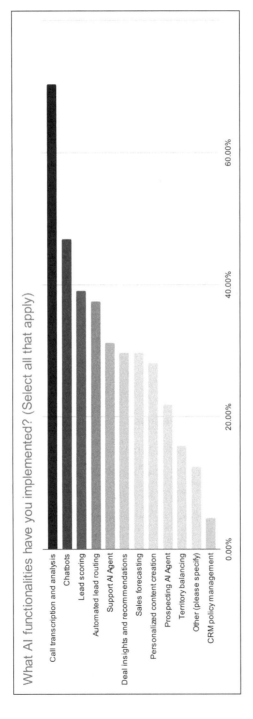

The most common AI tools that RevOps teams are planning on implementing include ones that reveal insights on deals, ones that handle prospecting, and additional sales forecasting capabilities.

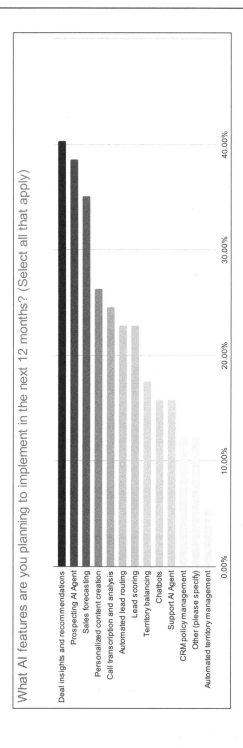

What AI features are you planning to implement in the next 12 months? (Select all that apply)

What we're seeing around AI . . . it's still large and very expensive, maybe even the largest and most expensive science project that we've ever endeavored on in humanity. There's still a lot to be proven," said James Dotter, MX's Chief Business Officer.[94]

For RevOps teams, AI isn't just a nice-to-have anymore. It's essential. The rise of AI-driven tools has opened doors to efficiencies and insights that can transform GTM strategies, driving better alignment, faster execution, and scalable growth.

According to Workato, the use of generative AI in business processes grew by 400 percent in 2023, with nearly half of RevOps teams leading the charge.[95] This surge comes from a recognition of how AI empowers teams to automate repetitive tasks, make smarter decisions, and create more meaningful customer experiences. But the road to AI success isn't without its challenges. Legacy systems, fragmented data, and unclear objectives can slow adoption and limit impact.

"The biggest challenge for RevOps professionals implementing AI is the quality of the underlying data sets," Tessa Whittaker, VP of Revenue Operations, explained in a recent interview with *Miami Local*.[96] "AI is only as effective as the data it's built on, and many companies struggle with incomplete or siloed data. At ZoomInfo, we're incredibly lucky to have the best B2B data available, ensuring our data remains agent-ready and powering efficient, high-impact automation and insights."

That's why preparation matters. Building a strong foundation ensures you're not just adding shiny new tools but creating a cohesive system that drives measurable results. Whether it's automating lead routing, using predictive analytics to forecast with precision, or improving collaboration across sales, marketing, and customer success, AI has the potential to be a game changer for your RevOps teams.

To truly harness the power of AI, you need tools that align with your Go-to-Market strategy and address your specific challenges. Follow this guide when you're looking at a new AI tool to incorporate into your tech stack:

1. **Define Your Strategic Objectives**
   - What challenges are you solving?
   - How will this tool align with your GTM strategy?
   - Can it adapt as your business evolves and your team changes?

2. **Prioritize Data Integration**
   - Does the tool integrate seamlessly with Salesforce?
   - How does it handle data hygiene and deduplication?

3. **Assess AI Capabilities**
   - Can it offer actionable insights, not just data overload?
   - Does it support predictive analytics and proactive recommendations?

4. **Evaluate Usability and Adoption**
   - Is the tool intuitive for your teams to use?
   - What training or support is provided to ensure adoption and buy-in?
   - Can it enhance collaboration across sales and marketing teams?

5. **Measure ROI and Scalability**
   - Does the tool provide real-time reporting on performance and ROI?
   - Can it scale as your organization grows?

6. **Ensure Security and Compliance**
   - How does the tool secure sensitive customer and operational data?
   - Is it compliant with industry standards (e.g., GDPR, CCPA)?

AI is not just about internal efficiency anymore. For customers, AI-powered RevOps tools mean faster responses, more personalized interactions, and an overall better experience. In a world where customer expectations are at an all-time high, AI helps you not only meet but exceed those standards.

Conclusion

A well-structured revenue engine isn't just about having the right people or processes, it requires a strong technological foundation that enables efficiency, agility, and long-term scalability. This chapter explored how companies can leverage technology as the fuel for their revenue engine rather than allowing it to become an expensive burden. When implemented correctly, technology streamlines workflows, unifies data across departments, and enhances decision-making. A thoughtfully designed tech stack can significantly improve sales efficiency, reduce planning time, and align Go-to-Market teams for better collaboration.

However, with an overwhelming number of tools available, organizations must choose their tech wisely. The key to an effective RevOps stack is integration, simplicity, and scalability, ensuring that every tool serves a purpose, eliminates inefficiencies, and enhances cross-functional alignment. Looking ahead, AI will play an even bigger role in RevOps, automating routine tasks, improving forecasting accuracy, and personalizing customer interactions. But AI is only as powerful as the data and processes behind it. Businesses that invest in AI without first ensuring a strong operational foundation risk adding complexity rather than efficiency.

In the end, technology should support and strengthen your revenue engine, not dictate or disrupt it. By carefully selecting, integrating, and optimizing their tech stack, businesses can ensure that their revenue operations remain agile, data-driven, and built to last. Just like a strong core supports an athlete's performance, a well-structured tech stack enables RevOps teams to execute flawlessly, scale efficiently, and drive sustained growth.

9

Optimization and Execution

The Processes in Your Revenue Engine

Every January 31st at Salesforce marked the calm before the storm. On February 1st, the new fiscal year began, and thousands of salespeople needed to be ready with updated territories, compensation plans, and quotas. But what most people don't see is what happened in the six to eight months leading up to that moment. Bala Balabaskaran, who helped lead the planning, called it the "Go for Growth" process, and it was a monumental undertaking that reveals just how difficult it is for large organizations to align strategy with execution at scale.

The "Go for Growth" cycle began quietly in July or August, when cross-functional teams, over four hundred people across the company, began pulling together the data and resources needed to make the upcoming fiscal year successful. The scope was huge. The planning touched every part of the sales engine, from strategic growth targets to the nitty-gritty of territory alignments and compensation modeling. Everything had to be built from the ground up and ready to go by February 1st.

The earliest phase was all about data. Bala described "massive data projects" that could take up to six weeks, just to clean and standardize account, contact, and territory data across Salesforce's sprawling systems. This wasn't just spreadsheet cleanup; it was foundational. Without trusted data, the rest of the plan would crumble.

Once the data was clean, the team could begin planning how Salesforce would grow. This meant defining the company's growth targets, identifying regions or industries to double down on, and modeling how sales capacity needed to shift to meet those goals. Territory modeling came next—assigning accounts, balancing pipeline, removing overlaps, and making sure every rep had the right book of business.

But territory planning was only one piece of a much larger puzzle. The team also had to plan capacity, asking: How many reps do we need? Where? In what roles? How many new hires do we need to onboard to hit our number? That led into role planning, where the team mapped out new functions, redistributed responsibilities, and adjusted team structures to support the model.

The last and perhaps most sensitive part of the plan was compensation modeling. Bala and his team had to design incentive plans that aligned behavior with company goals: plans that would motivate reps, drive the right outcomes, and avoid the kind of internal friction that can derail even the best-laid strategy.

All of this culminated in a coordinated launch on February 1st. But even then, things didn't fully settle until March or April. People had to get used to new territories, new rules, new reporting lines. Adjustments were inevitable. The sheer scale and manual effort of the process meant it always took a few months for the dust to clear.

Even the best sales organizations in the world struggle to operationalize growth. Planning was slow, reactive, and deeply manual.

That insight ultimately inspired his work with Fullcast, where he set out to build something Salesforce didn't have at the time—a system for managing growth planning with the speed, precision, and agility that modern RevOps teams need. That system became the GrowthOps Framework.

This chapter explores how to bring strategy to life through the GrowthOps Framework, a model built to align planning and execution at scale. We'll walk through the core elements of high-performance RevOps execution, from performance-to-plan tracking to process automation, capacity management, revenue enablement, and predictive analytics. Each of these components plays a critical role in building a revenue engine that is not only optimized but also agile, repeatable, and ready to scale. Let's dive in.

The GrowthOps Framework: Turning Strategy into Scalable Execution

The GrowthOps Framework is a set of principles and tools designed to operationalize growth planning across the revenue engine, not just once a year during annual planning, but continuously. It brings together planning, execution, routing, capacity, and enablement into a unified system that can scale.

At its core, GrowthOps is about replacing ad hoc processes with structured, data-driven motion. It integrates systems and teams so that changes—whether to head count, roles, routing rules, or territory design—don't require fire drills or six-week planning sprints. Instead, they happen fluidly, guided by policy and powered by automation.

The GrowthOps Framework structures revenue operations into three key phases (Optimize, Perform, and Grow) ensuring that RevOps teams can systematically scale revenue while maintaining efficiency and predictability.

GrowthOps Framework

	Revenue	Profitability	Predictability
GROW	• Customer Lifetime Value • Effort to Revenue • Rate of Growth • Market Share	• Margin • Pricing • Revenue Productivity • Acquisition Cost Payback	• Forecast • Cash Flow • Capacity & Hiring • Churn
	New Logos	Expansion	Pipeline
PERFORM	• New Account Growth • New Markets	• Usage Growth • New Products • Renewals & Churn • Customer Satisfaction	• Pipeline Efficiency • Pipeline Growth • Marketing Contribution
	Align	Accelerate	Review
OPTIMIZE	• Segmentation & Territories • Coverage Model • Role Design • Process & Policy	• Incentive Comp • Partners & Channel • Workforce Productivity • Infrastructure & Tools • Hiring	• Performance • Data Quality • Compliance • Attainment

1. **Optimize: Building a Scalable Foundation:** Before
   revenue growth can accelerate, the foundation must
   be strong. The **Optimize** phase focuses on refining
   internal processes, ensuring alignment across teams, and
   eliminating inefficiencies. It includes:
   - *Align:* Establishing segmentation, territory
     design, coverage models, role structures, and
     standardized policies to ensure clear ownership and
     accountability.
   - *Accelerate:* Implementing effective compensation
     structures, partner programs, and workforce
     productivity initiatives while optimizing tech
     infrastructure and hiring.
   - *Review:* Maintaining high data quality, compliance,
     and performance visibility to drive accountability
     and informed decision-making.
2. **Perform: Executing with Precision:** Once the
   foundation is in place, the focus shifts to performance,
   ensuring that sales and marketing teams can operate
   efficiently and scale effectively. The **Perform** phase is
   divided into three key areas:
   - *New Logos:* Expanding into new markets and
     acquiring new customers through targeted
     strategies.
   - *Expansion:* Driving usage growth, launching new
     products, increasing renewals, and improving
     customer satisfaction.
   - *Pipeline:* Strengthening pipeline efficiency,
     fueling pipeline growth, and ensuring marketing's
     contribution to revenue is maximized.
3. **Grow: Scaling Revenue with Predictability:**
   Sustainable growth requires a focus on strategic

expansion and profitability. The **Grow** phase ensures that scaling efforts remain efficient and predictable. It includes:

- *Revenue:* Increasing customer lifetime value, improving revenue efficiency, and accelerating market share growth.
- *Profitability:* Optimizing margins, pricing strategies, and revenue productivity while reducing acquisition costs.
- *Predictability:* Enhancing forecasting accuracy, cash flow management, hiring capacity planning, and churn reduction.

By structuring growth planning through these three phases, the GrowthOps Framework ensures that organizations can move beyond reactive processes and drive scalable, data-driven growth. It connects high-level strategy with execution, enabling RevOps teams to manage change seamlessly and proactively.

Unlike traditional RevOps, which often focuses on optimization after the fact, GrowthOps starts upstream. It connects the strategy (where you want to go) with the mechanics that get you there: how leads are routed, how accounts are assigned, how reps are ramped, how capacity is managed, and how team transitions are handled.

Here's how organizations of any size can start using GrowthOps:

1. *Automate routine workflows:* Route leads, assign opportunities, and trigger tasks automatically based on rules. No more manual handoffs or bottlenecks.
2. *Align planning with execution:* Connect annual territory, capacity, and compensation planning directly to the systems your team uses every day.

3. *Standardize processes across teams:* Ensure marketing, sales, customer success, and support all follow the same workflows, definitions, and handoff steps.
4. *Manage capacity in real time:* Monitor how much each rep or team can handle, and adjust routing and assignments automatically as work gets done.
5. *Create consistent onboarding and renewals:* Use task groups and templates to ensure smooth transitions for customers—from closed-won to onboarding to expansion.
6. *Automate account transitions:* When reps leave or territories shift, GrowthOps can trigger checklists and ownership updates to keep everything on track.
7. *Ensure data quality and visibility:* Track data completeness, spot errors, and score the health of your CRM, so everyone works from the same source of truth.
8. *Drive accountability with dashboards:* Equip sales managers and leaders with real-time views of performance, pipeline health, and process compliance.

The Journey to Growth Operations. RevOps maturity is a journey that evolves through four distinct stages: Chaotic, Defined, Optimized, and Agile. As organizations move through these phases, they build a more structured, efficient, and data-driven approach to growth.

The Journey

From Sales Operations to Growth Operations

Chaotic

No Processes
Incomplete Data
No Lead qualification
No Marketing Automation
Manual Comp Calculation
Few Selling Roles

Defined

CRM implemented
Basic Firmographic Data
Minimal Duplicates
Defined Lead qualification
Criteria
Lead sources tracked
Excel based Comp Calculation
Few selling roles

Optimized

CRM Tuned and Optimized
Sales Policies Automated
Minimum data cleaning required
Lead scoring system
Automated qualification Criteria
Territory and Team Modeling
Incentive Compensation
transparency
Automatic Compensation
calculation

Agile

Sales Ops Manages burden on rep
Customer and Opportunity Scoring
Propensity scoring
Lead Prioritization
Rep Level Marketing Tool
Account Based Marketing
Pricing and Incentive Comp
systems time
Compensation Prediction
3rd Party Tools integrated into Sales
Motion

At the Chaotic stage, there is little to no structure in sales operations. Processes are either nonexistent or highly inconsistent, leading to inefficiencies and lost opportunities. Characteristics of this phase include:

- No formal processes or structured workflows
- Incomplete or unreliable data
- Lack of lead qualification and tracking
- No marketing automation, leading to inefficiencies in outreach
- Compensation calculations done manually with little transparency
- Few dedicated selling roles, limiting revenue potential

Organizations in the next stage (Defined) begin to implement basic systems and processes. While still maturing, they are moving toward a more structured approach:

- CRM implementation to centralize customer data
- Basic firmographic data collection to segment leads
- Defined lead qualification criteria to filter out unqualified opportunities
- Lead sources tracked for better attribution and reporting
- Excel-based compensation calculations providing more structure but still requiring manual effort
- Introduction of specialized selling roles to improve focus and efficiency

At the Optimized stage, organizations transition from manual processes to automation, increasing efficiency and accuracy. Growth becomes more predictable as teams leverage structured frameworks:

- CRM fully optimized with automated workflows
- Sales policies automated to reduce administrative work
- Minimal data cleaning required due to better governance
- Lead scoring system implemented to prioritize high-value opportunities
- Automated qualification criteria for consistent lead evaluation
- Territory and team modeling to ensure balanced coverage
- Incentive compensation transparency for fair and strategic rewards
- Automatic compensation calculation reducing manual workload and errors

In the final Agile stage, organizations operate with a high level of efficiency, leveraging advanced analytics and automation to make data-driven decisions. RevOps becomes a strategic advantage, driving sustained growth:

- Sales Ops removes operational burden from sales reps, enabling them to focus on selling
- Customer and opportunity scoring based on behavioral and firmographic data
- Propensity scoring and lead prioritization to optimize outreach efforts
- Rep-level marketing tools to personalize engagement at scale
- Account-based marketing (ABM) aligning sales and marketing efforts
- Automated pricing and incentive compensation systems for real-time adjustments

- Compensation prediction models to forecast earnings and align incentives with strategy
- Seamless integration of third-party tools into sales motions for a connected tech ecosystem

By progressing through these four stages, companies can transform from reactive sales organizations to Agile Growth Operations, where revenue efficiency, predictability, and scalability drive long-term success.

GrowthOps in Practice. In most companies, lead routing is a black box, filled with manual workarounds and exceptions. GrowthOps replaces that chaos with intelligent automation. Whether you're using a simple round-robin method or routing based on the lead's region, status, or relationship history, the system can make dynamic assignments that factor in rep capacity, time zone, login status, vacation schedules, and more.

If someone's out of office, they're automatically removed from the rotation. If a duplicate lead appears within a certain window, it goes right back to the original SDR. No need to reassign manually or worry about dropped leads.

Beyond routing, GrowthOps also handles capacity management in a way that scales. Instead of fixed daily limits, reps can be assigned a quota of leads per day, week, or hour—and as they work those leads, new ones get assigned automatically. New hires can be given a reduced load during ramp-up, while top performers can take on more. If leads sit untouched for too long, they're rerouted to someone else. It's a living system that adjusts in real time.

But it's not just about the front of the funnel. GrowthOps introduces a shared flow for inbound and outbound prospecting, normalizing how leads become opportunities. Both motions result in handoff opportunities that follow a consistent process—from SDR to AE and beyond. This eliminates the disconnect between inbound marketing and outbound sales efforts and ensures a clean transition for the buyer.

"I love SDRs," wrote Tom Germack, Senior Vice President of RevOps at Oracle. "Forward thinking companies are changing their GTM to get prospects info to advance the purchase decision without those awkward phone calls."

Once opportunities are in flight, GrowthOps continues to guide execution with embedded support systems. Reps can request help through Deal Support Requests (DSRs), which are routed to RFP teams, pricing experts, or competitive intel resources. The requests are tracked like cases, so usage and response times can be measured. It's a seamless way to give reps access to critical support without cluttering Slack or inboxes.

One of the most powerful features of GrowthOps is task automation. The framework allows RevOps teams to build playbooks for every stage of the buyer journey. When an opportunity reaches a new stage, a predefined checklist of tasks can be assigned to the AE. Similarly, when an account status changes—say, from active to attrited—automated tasks can be triggered across customer success, finance, and support to ensure everyone knows what to do. This isn't limited to just opportunity workflows. It applies to onboarding, subscription management, partner engagement, and even account transitions. The result is an environment where execution happens consistently, even when roles change or teams scale.

GrowthOps also brings structure to account hierarchy. Using DUNS numbers or domains, it automatically builds parent-child relationships between accounts. From there, white space analysis becomes possible: Which parts of a customer's corporate structure are you engaged with? Where are there no open opportunities? Where is your team active—or conspicuously absent? These insights help build intentional account plans instead of relying on gut instinct.

And no growth engine would be complete without accountability. GrowthOps includes tools to track Data Quality Scores across leads, accounts, and opportunities. It can identify incomplete records and flag owners who need to clean them up. It also scores opportunities for volatility—tracking frequent changes to close dates or deal sizes as a signal for managerial attention.

It all comes together through dashboards and reports built for sales managers and executives. These are connected to real-time data, policies, and activity. With GrowthOps, strategy isn't something you present once a year. It's something you live and adjust daily.

In short, GrowthOps turns your RevOps team from a support function into the operating system for growth. It replaces firefighting with foresight, disconnected systems with orchestration, and guesswork with precision. And most importantly, it ensures that when your fiscal year starts—whether that's February 1st or any other day—your entire team is ready to go.

Elements of Excellent Execution

Execution excellence in RevOps is the foundation of sustained revenue growth and operational efficiency. It hinges on nine critical components: speed, policy automation, consistency, data-driven decision-making, cross-functional alignment, accountability, AI-driven efficiency, established workflows, and security/compliance. When these elements are executed effectively, organizations can ensure seamless execution that aligns with strategic objectives and drives meaningful business outcomes.

Speed and agility. The ability to pivot quickly in response to industry shifts, customer demands, or competitive pressures is vital. Organizations that embrace execution agility can seize new opportunities and mitigate risks before they escalate. However, speed must be intentional. Haphazard execution without structure can lead to misalignment and inefficiency. Successful RevOps teams establish frameworks that allow for rapid decision-making while maintaining control and strategic direction, according to the Revenue Operations Alliance.[97]

Company-wide alignment and transparency are important factors in how speedy your team is. Aligning all client-facing roles, including sales, marketing, and client success, with technology and data provides an end-to-end view of the revenue engine. This visibility ensures that teams can operate with speed and agility, adjusting quickly to changing customer needs and market conditions.

Agility in revenue operations isn't just about reacting quickly—it's about preparing for the moment before it arrives. The best RevOps leaders don't just analyze data; they anticipate shifts and position their teams to capitalize on change. Shawn Killpack, VP of GTM Strategy and Operations at Gong, experienced this first-hand when his company underwent a sudden shift in dynamics, a challenge many faced in the post-COVID years. Fortunately, he had already spent time analyzing data and preparing for potential opportunities.

"People often underestimate the effort that goes into preparing data," Killpack explains. "But when you've done the work in advance, you can act with speed and precision. In this case, because we had the right insights, we quickly shifted resources and seized an opportunity we might have otherwise missed." This ability to recognize patterns, adapt quickly, and execute effectively is what separates a rookie from an all-star in RevOps.

Policy automation. Policy automation ensures compliance and efficiency by embedding business rules directly into RevOps workflows. This eliminates manual errors, enhances execution speed, and enforces standardized processes across teams. Automated policies help maintain consistency in lead routing, quota assignments, and sales operations, ensuring teams can focus on high-value activities rather than administrative tasks.

Consistency and repeatability. Execution is not a one-time event but a continuous process that must be reliable and repeatable. Standardized workflows and best practices enable teams to deliver consistent results, regardless of changes in personnel or market conditions, according to Michael Mapes in *Forbes*.[98] By implementing structured operational frameworks, organizations can eliminate guesswork, reduce errors, and foster long-term stability. Repeatability ensures that successful strategies can be scaled efficiently across the organization, maintaining performance even as the business grows.

Standardizing processes across the buyer's journey is essential for creating a unified experience and maintaining consistency in execution. Without structured processes, companies risk inefficiencies that can put a hamper on their Go-to-Market efforts.

Data-driven decision-making. At the heart of effective execution is data. Organizations that rely on real-time insights and analytics can make informed decisions rather than acting on intuition. Data-driven execution enables teams to identify trends, measure performance, and optimize strategies based on objective metrics. RevOps teams must ensure that execution is continuously guided by insights embedded within systems so that decision-making remains dynamic and responsive to changing business conditions.

"I always say that what sounds good in a laboratory, such as a spreadsheet or an analysis, doesn't always translate to the reality of what happens in the field and how people interact with each other," said Jim Sbarra, global sales strategist. "So that's kind of the piece I brought to the ops and finance teams. Because I work really closely with finance, it's just changing that entire mentality around that."

Some recent trends in RevOps include leveraging call recording and AI-driven insights to enhance decision-making and improve sales outcomes, according to Qobra.[99] Companies that prioritize real-time analytics can fine-tune their strategies in response to customer behaviors and market shifts, ensuring that execution remains effective and data-driven.

Cross-functional alignment. Execution excellence requires seamless collaboration across revenue-generating teams, including sales, marketing, customer success, and finance. When these teams operate in silos, execution becomes fragmented, leading to inefficiencies and miscommunication. RevOps plays a crucial role in ensuring alignment by integrating systems, processes, and objectives across teams. By fostering transparency and shared goals, organizations can prevent bottlenecks and accelerate Go-to-Market efforts.

The pain associated with lack of alignment typically becomes obvious as a business is scaling. Consider the RevOps journey of Mindgram, a mental health and well-being start-up.[100] The company was struggling to scale its marketing, sales, and service teams to meet its ambitious growth goals, including a plan to quadruple website traffic. The company used a singular technology solution (HubSpot in this case) as the single source of truth for crafting unique digital marketing campaigns, streamlining sales processes with automated tasks, and enhancing customer support through a unified interface. Within a year, Mindgram achieved its goal of quadrupling its website traffic, which enabled the company to consistently exceed sales targets, improve customer satisfaction, and strengthen internal operations through automation.

Effective, ethical AI. Artificial intelligence has transformed execution by automating routine tasks, optimizing processes, and providing predictive insights. When this book was published, over 80 percent of businesses were already using AI or plan to.[101] That said, AI should enhance human decision-making rather than replace it. The most effective RevOps teams leverage AI to streamline workflows, remove administrative burdens, and uncover strategic opportunities. When combined with human oversight, AI-powered execution allows organizations to operate at scale while maintaining adaptability.

AI-driven efficiency is helping organizations reduce manual effort, improve sales forecasting, and create more personalized customer interactions. However, maintaining human oversight ensures that AI-driven decisions align with overall business objectives and ethical standards. AI will not be replacing companies en masse; instead, companies that are using AI will replace the companies that are not.

"RevOps and AI can mean lots of things to lots of different people, but if we focus on customer intelligence, before the sales rep even picks up a phone or tries to get into an account, we can give them a detailed book on all of the aspects of that company that they'll need to help penetrate new business, or upsell, and drive a bigger renewal," said RevOps Advisor Rob Levey.

Established workflows. Well-structured workflows are the backbone of execution in RevOps. By mapping out standardized processes, organizations can ensure that execution aligns with business strategy and remains scalable. Optimized workflows, whether in a CRM such as Salesforce or a Marketing Automation Platform such as HubSpot, reduce friction in handoffs between sales, marketing, and customer success, ensuring that customer interactions are seamless and efficient. Automation within workflows further improves execution speed and accuracy.

Security and compliance. Security and compliance are critical in execution to protect customer data, adhere to regulatory requirements, and mitigate risks. RevOps teams must integrate security protocols into their execution frameworks, ensuring that automation and AI-driven processes comply with industry regulations. Companies that fail to prioritize compliance risk reputational damage and financial penalties, making security an essential pillar of execution excellence.

Organizations that master execution excellence in RevOps create a sustainable competitive advantage. By prioritizing speed, policy automation, consistency, data-driven decision-making, cross-functional alignment, accountability, AI-driven efficiency, established workflows, and security and compliance, companies can ensure that execution aligns seamlessly with strategy. The ability to execute effectively is what separates market leaders from those left behind.

How to Be Excellent at Execution

One of the most overlooked challenges in building a high-performing revenue engine is not just what gets executed, but how it gets executed. Execution without structure can be chaotic. But structure without flexibility can stifle innovation. This is where a well-designed operational framework becomes critical: It provides the guardrails and cadence needed to ensure consistent execution across Go-to-Market teams, while also creating the space for strategic agility.

Jared Barol, a RevOps expert, described this tension through a real-world example. At a small business, messaging changes could be made and tested in days, sometimes even hours. But in an enterprise environment, where sales cycles can stretch from nine to eighteen months, rapid shifts in messaging or positioning can create confusion, especially when different stakeholders hear conflicting versions at different stages in the journey. When you're selling to a matrix of buyer personas across multiple departments, operational consistency becomes essential to avoid mixed signals that can derail a deal.

The solution isn't to avoid change. It's to build a framework that allows for structured evolution. That starts with how RevOps is positioned within the organization. Jared argues that RevOps should act as an "independent arbiter of metro-sized truth," a function that sits above departmental biases and reports directly into the CEO or an equally strategic leader. This position gives RevOps the authority and objectivity to align systems, data, and teams without getting pulled into functional silos.

This framing of RevOps as a central nervous system of the business is key to building a scalable ops framework. It's not just about Salesforce administration or technical support for sales and marketing teams. A mature RevOps function touches everything: territory design, messaging governance, forecasting strategy, compensation modeling, even long-term GTM planning.

At its best, RevOps becomes the strategic arm that not only manages execution but also shapes how the organization responds to change. It operationalizes flexibility by defining workflows, building feedback loops, and aligning teams around a consistent set of priorities and performance metrics. In this model, agility means being able to test, iterate, and evolve without compromising the integrity of your revenue engine.

In times when efficiency and performance matter more than ever, companies can't afford to operate without a shared framework. An ops framework grounded in objectivity, data, and structured flexibility ensures that even as market dynamics shift, your execution remains aligned, purposeful, and scalable.

Ten Steps for a Structured, Scalable Sales Process

Once you've established an operational framework to align your Go-to-Market engine, the next step is ensuring that your sales process is just as structured, repeatable, and scalable. According to Jared, this means going beyond basic pipeline stages and developing a comprehensive blueprint for how your team engages customers, from first contact to post-sale follow-up. Here's how Jared does it:

1. **Define Your Target Market and Customer Personas**
   Start by getting laser-focused on who you're selling to.
   - *Identify your Ideal Customer Profile (ICP):* Look at your best current customers and use market data to determine who benefits most from your product or service.
   - *Create detailed buyer personas:* Include job titles, company size, key challenges, decision-making behaviors, and purchase drivers.

   Without this foundation, your messaging and outreach will be too generic to resonate. Tailoring your engagement begins with understanding exactly who you're engaging.

2. **Map the Customer Journey to Your Sales Stages**
   Align your internal process to the way your buyers actually buy.
   - *Customer journey stages:* Awareness → Consideration → Evaluation → Decision
   - *Sales process stages:* Prospecting → Qualification → Needs Assessment → Presentation → Objection Handling → Closing → Post-Sale Follow-Up

   This alignment ensures you're delivering the right message and actions at each moment in the buyer's experience.

3. **Define and Operationalize Each Sales Stage**
   Every stage of the sales process should be clearly defined with specific goals, tools, and tactics:
   1. *Prospecting:* Outreach via networking, referrals, social media, and outbound campaigns.

2. *Lead Qualification:* Apply BANT (Budget, Authority, Need, Timing) or similar criteria.

3. *Needs Assessment:* Use discovery calls to understand pain points and tailor solutions.

4. *Presentation/Demo:* Showcase how your offering solves the customer's specific challenges.

5. *Handling Objections:* Prepare responses to common concerns using case studies, testimonials, or ROI calculators.

6. *Closing the Sale:* Use clear calls-to-action, deal timelines, and mutual action plans.

7. *Post-Sale Follow-Up:* Ensure onboarding, satisfaction, and open doors for referrals or expansion.

4. **Build Supporting Tools and Activities**
Equip your team with what they need to execute effectively.
- Sales scripts and email templates for outreach, demos, and follow-ups.
- Marketing collateral like one-pagers, decks, and case studies aligned to personas and stages.
- Follow-up cadences with defined timelines and outreach strategies.

5. **Implement Tools and Systems for Execution**
Technology should streamline your process, not complicate it.
- CRM software to track interactions, manage deals, and ensure visibility.
- Sales automation tools for tasks like follow-ups, lead scoring, and meeting scheduling.

- Analytics dashboards to track performance metrics like conversion rates and pipeline velocity.

6. **Set KPIs and Track Performance**

You can't improve what you don't measure.
- Define KPIs for each stage of the funnel (e.g., lead-to-opportunity conversion, demo-to-close rate).
- Review performance regularly to identify trends, strengths, and bottlenecks.

7. **Train and Enable Your Sales Team**

Execution is only as strong as your team's understanding and buy-in.
- Provide comprehensive training on product knowledge, messaging, and sales methodology.
- Run regular role-playing sessions to build confidence and sharpen skills.
- Set clear expectations around activity levels, responsibilities, and success metrics.

8. **Pilot, Test, and Refine Your Sales Process**

Don't set it and forget it; sales processes should evolve.
- Pilot your new process with a small group to gather feedback.
- Collect insights from the front lines: what's working, what's not.
- Make improvements based on real performance data.

9. **Document and Institutionalize**
   Build a playbook your entire team can rely on.
   - Create a sales playbook that captures every stage, script, asset, and KPI.
   - Update regularly as strategies evolve and new best practices emerge.

10. **Foster a Culture of Continuous Improvement**
    Make optimization part of your culture.
    - Hold regular team meetings to share wins, troubleshoot challenges, and test new ideas.
    - Stay informed about market shifts and emerging sales techniques.
    - Encourage innovation by giving reps room to experiment with messaging and tactics.

A great sales process isn't static. It's tested, refined, and iterated over time. Run pilots. Gather feedback. Watch the data. RevOps should act as the engine behind this iteration, enabling fast, evidence-based tweaks while keeping the broader system aligned.

The goal isn't perfection. It's progress. A sales process built with intentional design and continuous improvement becomes a key lever for scale. It empowers reps, reduces friction, and ensures your Go-to-Market motion can keep pace with your company's growth. When built in partnership with a strong ops framework, it's the difference between a team that's just working hard and one that's consistently winning.

How to Track Performance

To execute effectively, organizations must track progress against their strategic plans while allowing for real-time adjustments. The integration of execution with planning ensures that teams operate with the most up-to-date data. Without a structured approach to performance tracking, companies risk falling behind their objectives and failing to identify early warning signs that could impact their revenue.

This section explores four key aspects of performance tracking: defining key metrics and KPIs, leveraging real-time dashboards, using forecasting for course correction, and establishing a review cadence to ensure accountability.

Key metrics and KPIs. Defining success based on measurable outcomes rather than static projections is critical for effective performance tracking. Key KPI serve as benchmarks that help organizations assess whether their execution aligns with their strategic objectives. According to 6sense, companies should tailor KPIs to their specific business goals, such as Annual Recurring Revenue (ARR), Customer Retention Rate (CRR), and Customer Lifetime Value (CLV).[102]

ARR measures the predictable revenue from ongoing subscriptions, providing a baseline for growth, while CRR assesses the percentage of customers who renew contracts, indicating customer satisfaction and loyalty. CLV estimates the total revenue a customer is expected to generate over their lifetime, guiding strategies for upselling and customer retention.

Tailoring KPIs effectively is all about being able to show that RevOps investments are having an impact on the bottom line. Take the example of Data Flow Technologies, a SaaS company providing easy-to-use data workflow solutions for multiple industry verticals, including finance, health care, and e-commerce. Like many similar companies, Data Flow Technologies' default KPIs were focused on ARR and CRR, plus monthly active users and net promoter score (NPS). The company invited a research team to tailor and adapt these KPIs for measuring the effectiveness of a series of planned improvements to its data workflows.[103] The research team drilled down into the KPIs for three specific quarters, during which the company rolled out one new workflow enhancement at the beginning of each quarter. The researchers were able to produce a powerful KPI graph that showed dramatic, quantifiable gains in user acquisition growth and retention rates, all coinciding with the unveiling of each of the three new workflow enhancements.

Real-time dashboards. Real-time dashboards offer immediate visibility into performance metrics, allowing organizations to monitor KPIs such as sales figures, website traffic, and inventory levels. This instant access enables quick adjustments to strategies, enhancing operational efficiency. By integrating data from multiple sources, dashboards create a centralized view of progress toward key goals, helping teams identify bottlenecks and optimize processes promptly. Implementing real-time dashboards can significantly shorten decision-making cycles, providing a competitive advantage.

Forecasting and course correction. Moving beyond static planning, businesses should embrace dynamic forecasting models to anticipate market trends and customer behaviors. And less than half of sales leaders and sellers feel confident about their forecasts, so it's important to get it right.

Predictive analytics and AI-driven forecasting enable organizations to adjust strategies proactively, ensuring alignment with revenue goals. For example, forecasting revenue in the sales pipeline helps management plan for the future by estimating cash flows, allowing for timely course corrections.

Review cadence. Establishing a structured rhythm for evaluating execution against objectives ensures that performance tracking is an ongoing process. Regular performance reviews (weekly, monthly, or quarterly) enable organizations to assess progress, realign execution with strategy, and drive accountability at all levels. This consistent review cadence allows teams to adapt to market fluctuations and optimize their operations continuously.

Performance tracking is essential for maintaining alignment between strategy and execution. By defining clear KPIs, leveraging real-time dashboards, utilizing forecasting for proactive adjustments, and establishing a structured review cadence, organizations can drive sustainable growth and operational excellence. Embedding these principles into the RevOps execution framework ensures agility and competitiveness in an increasingly data-driven business environment.

Streamlining Processes for Maximum Efficiency

When businesses execute on a RevOps strategy, they commonly are looking to streamline and automate core operational workflows. In fact, this goal is often businesses' main motivation for investing in RevOps. The goal of refining and automating processes via a RevOps-powered strategy is to eliminate unnecessary steps, reduce manual effort, and enhance overall productivity. Organizations that commit to efficiency improvements under RevOps typically experience measurable gains in revenue growth, faster decision-making, and improved team collaboration.

Identify and eliminate bottlenecks. Operational bottlenecks are common in traditional Go-to-Market organizations, especially when departments work in silos and processes are built around outdated systems or disconnected tools. These slowdowns often reveal themselves in frustrating ways—sales reps wasting time manually entering data after every call, leads sitting idle in a CRM waiting to be routed, or customer handoffs that fall through the cracks because no one knows who owns what. These inefficiencies don't just slow execution—they create confusion, misalignment, and missed revenue opportunities.

RevOps helps eliminate these friction points by building unified processes and shared systems that replace manual work with automation and cross-functional coordination. When marketing and sales disagree on what qualifies as a good lead, RevOps steps in to define shared criteria and implement lead scoring that aligns both teams. When a rep leaves or territories are realigned, RevOps ensures account ownership updates automatically—so deals don't get lost in the shuffle. Instead of each team tracking performance in a different system with different metrics, RevOps creates a single source of truth, where dashboards and KPIs reflect shared goals.

The most common bottlenecks, like slow lead follow-up, clunky handoffs between roles, inconsistent definitions, and redundant reporting, are symptoms of structural gaps. RevOps addresses those gaps by connecting systems, aligning teams, and enforcing standards. It replaces reactionary workflows with proactive design, so that operations run smoothly even as the business scales. Identifying bottlenecks through audits, shadowing, or performance data is only the first step. The real value comes when RevOps steps in to resolve them—not just once, but permanently.

Leverage automation. For RevOps, automation tools like Zapier play a crucial role in reducing bottlenecks and ensuring smooth execution across teams.[104] Tasks such as lead routing, quota assignments, deal approvals, and contract processing can be automated to remove manual touchpoints and accelerate workflows.

For instance, intelligent lead routing ensures that leads are automatically assigned to the most appropriate sales rep based on predefined criteria like industry, company size, and previous engagement history. Instead of manually distributing leads, automation ensures that sales reps receive leads instantly, reducing delays and improving response time.

Similarly, automated quota management tools help RevOps teams dynamically adjust sales targets based on real-time data, reducing the need for constant manual recalibration. Approval workflows, which are often a significant cause of execution delays, can be automated to ensure that contracts, pricing approvals, and discount requests move through the organization seamlessly without unnecessary roadblocks.

AI-powered decision-making for process optimization. Beyond simple automation, AI-powered solutions can optimize execution by predicting outcomes and recommending the best course of action.[105] AI-driven forecasting models analyze historical data to identify patterns in revenue generation, helping sales leaders adjust their strategies proactively.

According to Alta, AI can also enhance predictive lead scoring, allowing RevOps teams to focus on high-intent leads rather than wasting time on prospects that are unlikely to convert.[106] By analyzing customer behavior, purchase history, and engagement metrics, AI can assign scores to leads, prioritizing those that are most likely to result in closed deals.

Another AI-driven efficiency gain that the Revenue Operations Alliance has noticed comes from conversational AI and chatbots, which handle initial customer inquiries, qualification, and scheduling, freeing up human reps to focus on high-value interactions.[107] AI chatbots can guide prospects through initial product inquiries, answer frequently asked questions, and even schedule demos based on a sales rep's availability.

Collaboration and workflow standardization. While technology plays a crucial role in streamlining execution, workflow standardization and cross-functional alignment are equally important. Organizations need clear standard operating procedures (SOPs) that define how different teams interact, ensuring that execution remains consistent across the entire revenue funnel.

For example, a RevOps team may define an end-to-end sales-to-customer-success handoff process, ensuring that when a deal is closed, the customer success team immediately receives all necessary details about the new client's needs and expectations. This prevents confusion and ensures a seamless transition for the customer.

Workflow automation tools like Trello, Asana, and Monday.com help teams visualize their execution processes, assign tasks, and track progress in real time. Integrating these tools with CRM platforms ensures that all relevant stakeholders have visibility into ongoing revenue operations, reducing execution gaps and unnecessary back-and-forth communication.

By continuously analyzing these metrics and leveraging AI-driven insights, companies can refine their execution strategies and ensure sustained efficiency improvements. Organizations that invest in process optimization gain a competitive advantage, allowing them to execute with speed, precision, and agility.

Revenue Enablement

Revenue enablement is a strategic approach that equips all revenue-generating teams with the tools, resources, and information they need to effectively engage with prospects and customers at every stage of their buying journey. This holistic strategy ensures that every customer-facing function is aligned and empowered to drive revenue growth.

Traditionally, sales enablement has focused on providing sales teams with the necessary support to close deals. Revenue enablement expands this scope to include all departments that influence revenue generation. By supporting sales, marketing, customer success, and other customer-facing channels, organizations can deliver consistent, relevant, and personalized customer experiences. This unified approach by Seismic breaks down silos across teams and technology, streamlines workflows, and ultimately boosts customer satisfaction and revenue.[108]

There are four main parts of an effective revenue enablement strategy: identifying gaps, establishing a framework, providing relevant content and training, and leveraging technology.

Assess the current state and identify gaps. Begin by evaluating your organization's current enablement maturity. Examine how effectively your teams support prospects and customers across every interaction point. Identify strengths, weaknesses, and opportunities for growth by asking questions such as:

- Are our processes as efficient as they could be?
- What silos exist across teams?
- What barriers hinder revenue-generating behaviors?
- How do we measure performance?

This analysis will provide insights into areas that need improvement and help in crafting a more effective enablement strategy.

Establish a revenue enablement framework. Develop a framework that aligns all revenue-generating teams around common goals. Steps to implement this framework include:

1. *Create a dedicated revenue enablement team:* Assemble a team comprising members from sales, marketing, and customer service. Clearly define their roles and responsibilities in supporting revenue goals.
2. *Align goals and metrics:* Ensure that all teams are working toward shared objectives and utilize common performance metrics to track progress.
3. *Implement consistent processes:* Standardize workflows across departments to ensure a seamless customer experience.

By establishing this framework, organizations can enhance team collaboration, streamline processes, and drive revenue growth.

Provide relevant content and training. Equip all customer-facing teams with the necessary content and training to engage effectively with prospects and customers. This includes:

1. High-quality materials that address customer needs and pain points at various stages of the buying journey.
2. Training sessions to ensure teams can effectively utilize the content and tools provided.

By providing relevant resources and training, teams can deliver consistent and effective messaging to customers.

Leverage technology and analytics. Utilize technology to streamline workflows and gain insights into performance. This involves implementing enablement platforms that centralize resources, track engagement, and provide analytics. It also includes analyzing data regularly to identify areas for improvement and make informed decisions. Leveraging technology and analytics enables organizations to optimize their enablement strategies and drive continuous improvement.

Predictive Analytics

Predictive analytics involves utilizing historical data, statistical algorithms, and machine learning techniques to forecast future outcomes.[109] In RevOps, predictive analytics empowers organizations to anticipate market trends, understand customer behaviors, and optimize sales strategies, thereby facilitating proactive decision-making and strategic planning.

Predictive analytics has already proven its value for a range of business use cases. For example, every year, insurance providers face a critical challenge: how to balance offering competitive policies while maintaining profitability. Predictive analytics has become an essential tool in addressing this issue, allowing insurers to assess risk more accurately and optimize their coverage strategies, according to Qlik.[110] By leveraging advanced analytical models, insurance companies can meticulously evaluate policy applications, comparing new applicants to profiles of existing policyholders with similar coverage. This data-driven approach enables insurers to estimate the likelihood of future claims with a high degree of accuracy. Instead of relying solely on broad risk categories or historical averages, predictive models take into account various factors, such as medical history, driving records, and behavioral data, to personalize coverage options. This method allows companies to offer more tailored policies, setting fairer premiums while ensuring financial sustainability.

Predictive analytics for sales forecasting. Predictive analytics can leverage historical data, statistical algorithms, and machine learning to anticipate future trends and customer behaviors. By analyzing patterns and past performance, Charlie Cowen writes that RevOps teams can make data-driven decisions that improve forecasting, optimize sales strategies, and enhance customer engagement.[111] This proactive approach enables organizations to shift from reactive decision-making to strategic planning, improving efficiency and revenue generation. With the increasing availability of AI-driven insights, predictive analytics is becoming a critical component in staying ahead of market changes and optimizing revenue streams.

One of the primary advantages of predictive analytics in RevOps is accurate sales forecasting. Traditional sales predictions often rely on intuition or outdated historical trends, leading to missed revenue opportunities or overestimated targets. Predictive models, however, analyze multiple variables, such as customer engagement, market fluctuations, and historical deal cycles to generate highly accurate forecasts. Companies that implement predictive analytics in sales planning experience better resource allocation, improved quota setting, and a more predictable revenue flow. This ensures that sales teams focus on the right prospects while optimizing pipeline management to increase close rates and revenue consistency.

Predictive analytics for the entire customer life cycle. Beyond forecasting, predictive analytics enhances customer insights by helping businesses understand buying behaviors and personalize interactions. Customer data, including previous purchases, online activity, and engagement metrics, can be processed through AI models to determine the likelihood of conversion, retention, or churn.

This allows RevOps teams to tailor marketing efforts, create targeted outreach strategies, and allocate sales resources to high-value accounts more effectively. Personalization, driven by predictive analytics, strengthens customer relationships and increases long-term value, ensuring that engagement efforts are aligned with customer needs.

Predictive analytics for mitigating risks. Risk mitigation is another crucial benefit of predictive analytics. Businesses operate in a volatile market where factors such as economic downturns, shifting consumer preferences, and competitor movements can impact revenue streams. By utilizing predictive models, organizations can anticipate risks, such as customer churn, pricing sensitivity, and declining demand, before they become significant issues.

Proactive decision-making, backed by real-time analytics, enables RevOps leaders to implement strategic countermeasures, ensuring business continuity and stability. Companies that leverage predictive analytics to detect early warning signals can optimize revenue operations by reducing churn and maintaining customer loyalty.

Challenges with predictive analytics. Despite its advantages, implementing predictive analytics presents several challenges. One of the most significant hurdles that researchers in the *International Journal of Scholarly Research in Science and Technology* are noticing is data quality.[112] Predictive models rely on vast amounts of structured and unstructured data, and inaccurate or incomplete datasets can lead to misleading forecasts and poor decision-making.

Organizations must ensure data integrity by maintaining clean, well-organized databases and integrating sources effectively. Additionally, predictive analytics tools need seamless integration with existing CRM, marketing automation, and business intelligence platforms. A lack of integration can result in fragmented insights, limiting the effectiveness of predictive strategies. Companies must invest in robust data infrastructure and cross-functional alignment to maximize the value of predictive analytics in RevOps.

Another challenge is the interpretability of complex predictive models. Advanced machine learning techniques can generate highly accurate forecasts, but if business leaders and sales teams do not understand how these models work, adoption may be slow. Transparent AI models and clear visualization tools are necessary to ensure that predictive analytics drives meaningful business decisions rather than becoming an abstract data exercise. Providing training and education on how to interpret predictive insights can enhance adoption and ensure that revenue teams trust and act upon the recommendations made by AI-powered models.

As RevOps continues to evolve, predictive analytics will become an essential driver of revenue growth and operational efficiency. Organizations that embrace predictive analytics gain a competitive edge by making smarter, data-driven decisions that optimize sales performance, customer engagement, and risk management.

Although challenges exist in data quality, system integration, and interpretability, businesses that invest in the right technology and strategies can unlock significant value from predictive insights. By proactively leveraging data to guide revenue strategies, organizations can improve forecasting accuracy, enhance customer relationships, and build more resilient revenue operations.

Conclusion

This chapter explored how the GrowthOps Framework transforms execution from a reactive, fragmented process into a structured, scalable engine for growth. GrowthOps connects strategy to execution through automation, real-time data, and standardized processes, ensuring your team isn't just planning for growth but operationalizing it every day.

We broke down the core components that make GrowthOps work: fast and consistent execution, policy-driven automation, data-informed decisions, and true cross-functional alignment. We examined how performance-to-plan tracking keeps strategy and execution in sync, how streamlined workflows eliminate bottlenecks, and how revenue enablement empowers every customer-facing role with the right tools and insights. We also explored the role of predictive analytics in helping organizations shift from reactive firefighting to proactive, data-led strategy.

Execution is where strategy either succeeds or stalls. With GrowthOps, RevOps becomes the control tower of the revenue engine—building agility, enforcing consistency, and driving accountability at scale. When these capabilities are embedded into your day-to-day operations, your entire Go-to-Market engine moves faster, smarter, and in lockstep toward growth.

10

Revenue Impact

The GrowthOps Framework

When Bala Balabaskaran first joined Salesforce, he quickly learned that bad data isn't just an inconvenience; it's a silent killer of revenue productivity. At the time, he was tasked with helping to scale sales planning operations, but the biggest obstacle wasn't strategy, tools, or head count—it was dirty data.

CRM systems were riddled with inaccuracies like duplicate accounts, outdated contacts, misclassified industries, and inconsistent data formats. Sales reps wasted hours chasing leads that were no longer valid, manually scrubbing spreadsheets instead of selling. Marketing teams launched campaigns using segmentation criteria that were completely unreliable. Forecasting became an exercise in frustration. Leaders were making revenue projections based on data that was already stale the moment it was entered.

At one point, Bala witnessed firsthand how flawed data quality could derail an entire sales cycle: A team of SDRs had been calling into what they believed were high-value target accounts, only to

251

discover that a significant portion of those accounts were either out of business or had been misclassified in the CRM. Reps spent weeks navigating dead-end conversations, leading to a 30 percent drop in productivity across the team. The cost of inaction wasn't just wasted time—it was real dollars lost in missed pipeline opportunities.

Bala has worked with organizations where the cost of inaction was painfully obvious. In one instance, an enterprise sales team lost nearly a quarter of their selling time due to bad data—time that could have been spent closing deals. He's also seen companies pull SDRs off selling entirely to clean data, essentially sacrificing revenue-generating activities to fix a problem that should have been prevented in the first place.

And yet, the cost of over-fixing data can be just as bad. Bala has seen organizations spend millions on massive data cleanup projects that ultimately failed because they weren't tied to a clear business objective. This is why RevOps leaders must take a pragmatic approach to data governance—one that balances two competing interests: Bad data costs money, but good data doesn't come free either. In fact, studies show the impact of bad data on US businesses may reach up to $3 trillion.[113] Simultaneously, the cost of quality data increases almost exponentially, with one analyst estimating that if 90 percent data quality costs index 100 to deliver, then 95 percent would cost 10 to 100 times more than index 100.[114] The companies that win aren't the ones with the cleanest data. They're the ones that know when to fix data, when to let it go, and how to ensure every data investment delivers maximum return.

In this chapter, we'll explore how to build a data-driven revenue engine by focusing on what truly matters—not perfect data, but data that is clean enough, current enough, and structured enough to drive better decisions, more accurate forecasts, and ultimately, higher revenue. We'll start with Bala's Fit-for-Purpose Framework for guiding data governance, then transition to exploring how to establish a data-driven culture that aligns RevOps, sales, and marketing. Next, we'll look at the key revenue metrics that actually matter, best practices for data collection and governance, how to use predictive analytics and AI-driven forecasting, and how to evaluate the ROI of data investments and avoid wasteful efforts that don't drive measurable impact.

The Fit-for-Purpose Framework

After years of managing data challenges at scale, Bala developed a set of core principles to guide his approach to data governance, known as the Fit-for-Purpose Framework. This simple but powerful approach to data governance can help reframe the entire conversation around data quality within an organization. Instead of letting perfection become the enemy of the good or ignoring data quality more than the organization should, teams instead focusing on answering three overarching questions:

1. What are we actually using this data for?
2. How accurate does it need to be to serve that purpose?
3. What is the cost of keeping this data clean—and is it worth the investment?

There are multiple considerations that go into deciding the level of data quality necessary to drive decision-making and the company's bottom line. These dimensions, which come from research from Gartner, include:

- *Validity:* Are the values acceptable for their intended use?
- *Accuracy:* How close to the truth is the data, and how precise is it?

- *Completeness:* How much missing data or white space is there?
- *Integrity:* Are relationships between data points correctly defined?
- *Staleness:* How quickly does the data become outdated?
- *Compliance:* Is the data compliant with regulations and internal rules?

Too often, companies invest massive amounts of time and resources cleaning data for the sake of cleaning it—without truly understanding the ROI of that effort. Bala recalls one conversation with a sales ops team that demanded perfectly accurate revenue numbers for every prospect. But Bala ran the numbers and found that achieving that level of accuracy was costing $30,000 a year in data purchases and maintenance.

The moment the team saw the cost, it changed the trajectory of the conversation. "Maybe it doesn't need to be $30,000 accurate," Bala recalled them saying. "Maybe we can live with $10,000 accuracy." This shift in mindset was critical. Instead of treating data as an abstract problem that simply needed fixing, it became clear that data is an investment—one that must be weighed against business impact.

In this way, the three overarching questions that guide the Fit-for-Purpose Framework can be recast and adapted to the situation at hand. When focusing on the ROI of improving data quality, the questions of the Fit-for-Purpose Framework can be tweaked as follows:

1. What happens if we don't fix this data?
2. How much productivity will be lost if bad data continues to circulate?
3. Is the cost of cleaning and maintaining this data lower than the cost of ignoring it?

Addressing the ROI of sustaining data quality. The real challenge isn't just cleaning up data—it's making sure every dollar spent on data management delivers measurable returns.

All data starts its journey toward becoming bad the moment it is entered. Just like food has an expiration date, data inevitably goes stale over time. Employee counts change, companies get acquired, contacts move to new roles or leave their organizations entirely.

Many RevOps teams assume that purchasing data from a top-tier provider will solve their problems, but you must be wary of false security. There's no such thing as a perfect data provider. Every vendor is slightly behind reality. The real question isn't whether your data is perfect—it's whether it's "good enough" for the purpose you're using it for.

For example, if an SDR team is using firmographic data to prioritize outbound efforts, they may not need absolute precision in employee count. A rough estimate—accurate within a reasonable margin—might be enough to prioritize outreach. However, if the same data is being used to determine territory coverage or quota allocation, then even small inaccuracies could have major downstream consequences.

This is where Bala has found that companies often go wrong. They apply the same data quality standards across every use case instead of tailoring their approach to what really matters. The reality is that some data needs to be pristine, and some data just needs to be "good enough."

Establishing a Data-Driven Culture

We've already spoken a lot about the importance of data in chapter 7. In this section, we'll explore how establishing a data-driven culture ensures that data is not merely an operational by-product but a core component guiding every facet of the organization. A data-driven culture spans how the company prioritizes investing in data quality, as well as how the company uses data to drive decision-making. It's not always an easy task to create a data-driven culture. According to research from Wavestone, over 57 percent of companies struggle to build a data-driven culture.[115]

To foster a data-centric environment, the *MIT Sloan Management Review* recommends that organizations focus on four key areas[116]:

1. **Active leadership engagement.** Leaders must go beyond merely endorsing data initiatives; they need to be deeply involved in articulating the strategic importance of data. This involves clearly communicating the organization's data-driven objectives and ensuring that data utilization becomes an integral part of every employee's role, not just the IT or data teams. Leaders should exemplify data usage in their daily activities, meetings, and reviews, promoting a culture of curiosity and encouraging employees to question existing processes and propose innovative solutions.

2. **Employee empowerment.** Building a data-driven culture requires empowering all employees with access to quality data and the skills to analyze it effectively. This empowerment operates on three levels:
   - Ensure that high-quality data is easily accessible to the right individuals at the right time through robust platforms and governance policies.
   - Provide training that enhances critical thinking, data interpretation, and the ability to derive actionable insights, beyond just tool-specific skills.
   - Invest in the necessary hardware and software to facilitate seamless data operations at both organizational and individual levels.

3. **Cross-functional collaboration.** Effective collaboration between business and technology teams is crucial for successful data-centric culture-building. However, communication barriers, often due to jargon or oversimplification, can hinder this collaboration. Enhancing data literacy across all teams can mitigate these challenges, enabling members to share insights and engage in informed, data-driven discussions.

    For example, Gulf Bank, a leading Kuwait-based financial institution, invested in building a data-driven culture by rolling out a Data Ambassador program that trains non-data science teams in how to use data and analytics tools.[117] In its first year, 140 employees who completed the program were awarded the title of Data Ambassador. The training program has helped connect non–data scientists to their data science colleagues and promoted cross-functional collaboration, especially as technology increasingly blurs the lines between the IT and business sides of banking.

4. **Recognizing data-driven value.** To truly embed a data-driven culture within the fabric of the organization, companies should focus on achieving measurable business outcomes from their data investments, including:
    - Setting specific KPIs that capture the success of data projects and ensuring stakeholder alignment on these targets.
    - Implementing procedures to gather necessary data before launching projects to ensure sufficient information is available for analysis.

- Celebrating achievements by acknowledging the contributions of key stakeholders, which motivates teams and inspires the organization to pursue further data-driven innovation.

For example, when a cold chain logistics company introduced a machine learning–based appointment scheduling system that reduced turnaround times by 16 percent and saved $1.2 million annually in penalties, leadership celebrated by recognizing the team in internal newsletters and town hall meetings.[118] Meanwhile, the marketing team converted the story into a video case study that was shared on social media and through webinars.

As involved as it is to build a data-driven culture, it's an equally involved commitment to sustain it. Leaders must consistently support investments in technology, upskilling, and collaboration, measuring success, and celebrating milestones to sustain momentum and encourage continuous innovation.

Establishing Data Collection and Analysis Processes

For RevOps teams, structured data collection and analysis processes are essential for informed decision-making and strategic planning. By focusing on high-quality, strategically relevant data and leveraging advanced analytics tools, organizations can make informed, data-driven decisions that drive revenue growth. The following are key steps every RevOps leader should be taking to design robust data processes that support and enable data-driven decision-making:

Aligning on revenue goals. An organization's first step to creating data-driven is to align sales, marketing, and customer success teams around unified revenue goals. When different parts of the organization understand what the organization—as opposed to just their own team—is working toward, they realize that they cannot be investing in data initiatives that are not aligned with the organization's revenue goals. RevOps leaders can achieve this alignment by routinely bringing together cross-functional teams via cross-departmental meetings and having introspective conversations about the organization's revenue goals and the critical role that data plays in supporting and enabling these revenue goals.

Establishing consistent procedures and governance policies. All departments across an organization need to agree to consistent procedures for data entry and management. This standardization minimizes discrepancies and ensures that data is accurate and reliable. These requirements should span standardized data fields and standardized data entry protocols. Gartner recommends organizations also should develop and enforce data governance policies to maintain data integrity and compliance with standardized protocols.[119] This includes defining data ownership, establishing protocols for data entry, and setting guidelines for data privacy and security. Regular audits should focus on reviewing data for accuracy and completeness

Investing in integrated data solutions. To ensure data standardization and promote cross-functional collaboration, companies need to invest in an integrated technology solution that centralizes data collection. Platforms should combine CRM, marketing automation, and customer support systems to facilitate seamless data flow between departments. Once data has been centralized, these data management solutions will utilize powerful data analytics tools to identify trends and patterns that inform strategic decisions.[120] Continuous monitoring of these metrics enables RevOps teams to make proactive adjustments to Go-to-Market strategies, ensuring alignment with evolving business objectives and market conditions.

Moreover, RevOps leaders should schedule time for cross-functional teams to discuss what the data reveals. The next section of this chapter provides more detail about how to analyze data in ways that drive long-term decision-making.

"At most companies, reps manually update lead and contact status fields. Say I'm an SDR or a sales rep. When I start working on a new lead, I'll manually mark the contact as assigned. If the prospect replies and we start a conversation, I'll change the status to in progress. When I land the deal, I'll manually update the field to closed. But here's the problem: the data is only as good as the salesperson inputting the information. Inevitably, there are going to be mistakes," Feras Abdel, RevOps director, wrote in his blog series, *You Know They Aren't Right and You Run Them Anyway.*[121]

"Reps are busy. They're spinning a bunch of plates at any one time. If a hot prospect calls, they're going to skip over administrative tasks like manual data entry to answer. It's a slippery slope. As soon as the data is unreliable, it's worthless and reps stop using the field entirely. From a revenue operations perspective, that's a huge headache. We can't report effectively. Because we can't use the data, we lose functionality in our sales engagement platform (SEP). And there's opacity in our lead generation, meaning we lose a lens to evaluate strategies and tactics. The good news is that all this is fixable. The status quo is to have sales reps manually manage everything. They update the status field and take action. Our new approach flips that entirely. Under our new workflow, reps take an action and that automatically changes the lead status."

Proactively and routinely cleaning data. As hard as a company works to ensure all data being entered is clean, data inevitably becomes outdated, inconsistent, or incomplete. Rather than only cleaning data after errors are discovered, it's critical to have a plan in place for periodically doing routine data maintenance; automation can play a key role in streamlining this time-consuming but necessary work. The cadence of routine data cleaning will be shaped by the cadence of data-driven decision-making within the organization. In other words, if RevOps leaders discover in the process of trying to use data to generate revenue-related insights that the data needs to be cleaned first, the organization isn't doing data maintenance on a routine enough cycle. For example, Bala recalls discovering data quality issues between a client's CRM and internal systems that then took a month and a half just to fix—a costly setback because the data quality issue was only discovered in the course of the company mining this data to inform a strategic business decision.

Key Metrics for Measuring Success

What are the right metrics to track when it comes to data? Many organizations fall into the trap of measuring everything simply because they can, leading to analysis paralysis and wasted resources. Instead of collecting vast amounts of data without a clear strategy, RevOps teams should focus on key performance indicators (KPIs) that directly impact revenue growth and operational efficiency.

Bala recommends that RevOps teams create and then commit to regularly reviewing and refining a core set of KPIs that align with evolving business objectives. Under the Fit-for-Purpose Framework that guides data management practices, Bala recommends focusing on fit-for-purpose metrics—in other words, metrics that get used to make strategic decisions that drive growth.

While identifying fit-for-purpose metrics may seem like it should be intuitive, that's actually not the case because of a phenomenon known as survivorship bias. In the context of KPI setting, survivorship bias refers to a company's tendency to gravitate toward KPIs that it knows it can measure—rather than taking the extra step of figuring out what's important to measure and then figuring out how.

Taft Love, founder of the consulting firm Iceberg RevOps, shared during a conversation with Fullcast's Tyler Simons that the most effective way to avoid KPI survivorship bias is to fundamentally rethink the KPI conversations happening at the C-suite level.[122] Taft encourages RevOps leaders to articulate in plain English what are the questions that the C-suite wants to know about the company's performance—regardless of whether the company has existing data reporting infrastructure in place to answer these questions. "Whether or not they can answer them today is irrelevant, and there's a chance we won't be able to answer all of them," Taft shared. "But it helps me understand how they think about running their business."

So, how do fit-for-purpose metrics translate to influencing what KPIs a company actually measures? Take Taft's example of two sales reps who each send out one thousand emails and each get four meetings. Sales Rep A gets meetings with three midsize companies and one Fortune 500 company, while Sales Rep B gets meetings with four different divisions of a single midsize company. If one of the company's KPIs is the number of meetings that sales reps get, both reps would hit the same KPI target, even though Sales Rep A is likely to have a much more significant bottom-line revenue impact than Sales Rep B. That's why it's so critical to be aware of survivorship bias with existing KPIs; it's this self-awareness that opens the door to critical, introspective conversations about how to identify KPIs that are truly fit-for-purpose.

Below are the essential KPIs every data-driven RevOps team should monitor to assess success and optimize their strategies.

1. *Annual Recurring Revenue (ARR):* This metric represents the consistent revenue generated annually from subscriptions or contracts, providing insight into the

company's growth trajectory. Monitoring ARR helps organizations assess their financial health and scalability.

2. *Conversion Rate:* This KPI measures the percentage of leads that become paying customers, reflecting the effectiveness of sales and marketing strategies. For example, if you have two hundred leads and five become customers, your conversion rate is 2.5 percent. Analyzing this metric helps identify areas for improvement in the sales funnel.

3. *Net Revenue Retention (NRR) Rate:* NRR captures the percentage of recurring revenue retained from existing customers over a specific period, including upsells and accounting for downgrades and churn. A high NRR indicates strong customer satisfaction and effective account management. According to Bain & Company, a 5 percent increase in customer retention can boost profits by over 25 percent.[123]

4. *Customer Lifetime Value (CLV):* CLV estimates the total revenue a business can expect from a single customer account throughout the entire relationship. Understanding CLV helps in making informed decisions about customer acquisition and retention strategies. For instance, if a customer spends $10,000 per purchase, buys twice a year, and stays for five years, their CLV is $100,000.

5. *Sales Pipeline Velocity:* This metric measures the speed at which leads move through the sales pipeline, ultimately resulting in revenue. It provides insights into the efficiency of the sales process and helps identify bottlenecks. Improving pipeline velocity can lead to faster revenue generation.

6. *Customer Acquisition Cost (CAC):* CAC calculates the average expense of acquiring a new customer, including costs related to marketing, sales, and other associated expenses. Balancing CAC with CLV is essential to ensure profitability. A lower CAC indicates more efficient customer acquisition strategies.

7. *Churn Rate:* This KPI measures the percentage of customers who discontinue their relationship with the company over a specific period. A high churn rate can indicate issues with customer satisfaction or product value, necessitating strategic interventions to improve retention.

By focusing on these KPIs and ensuring their alignment with strategic objectives, organizations can make informed decisions that drive growth and efficiency. Regularly reviewing these metrics allows for timely adjustments in strategies, ensuring sustained success in a dynamic business environment.

Data-Driven Decision-Making

Data-driven decision-making (DDDM) has become a cornerstone for organizations striving to enhance accuracy, minimize biases, and align strategies with real-world market dynamics.[124] This approach entails basing strategic choices on empirical data analysis and interpretation rather than solely on intuition or anecdotal evidence. Within the realm of RevOps, DDDM plays a pivotal role in harmonizing sales, marketing, and customer success efforts to foster revenue growth.

To effectively embed DDDM within RevOps, organizations should concentrate on three critical areas:

1. **Comprehensive Data Collection and Integration.** The initial step involves gathering pertinent data from a multitude of sources, including Customer Relationship Management (CRM) systems, marketing platforms, and customer feedback channels. This encompasses sales figures, marketing campaign outcomes, customer interactions, and support tickets.

   Integrating this diverse data provides a holistic view of the customer journey, enabling more informed and nuanced decisions. Data analytics serves as a fundamental pillar in modern RevOps, guiding decision-making and informing strategy with unwavering objectivity.

2. **Advanced Data Analysis and Interpretation.** Employing sophisticated analytics tools allows organizations to delve deeper into the collected data, identifying intricate trends and patterns that inform strategic decisions. For instance, predictive analytics can forecast future sales performance by analyzing historical data and prevailing trends, enabling companies to plan their market presence, allocate resources efficiently, and set realistic financial targets, according to the Revenue Operations Alliance.[125] We'll talk more about the nuts and bolts of forecasting in the next section of this chapter.

3. **Continuous Monitoring and Strategic Adjustment.** Regularly reviewing key performance indicators (KPIs) ensures that strategies remain aligned with evolving business objectives. This continuous monitoring allows RevOps teams to promptly identify emerging trends

and potential issues, facilitating proactive adjustments to strategies. Embracing data-driven metrics provides companies with a holistic view of customer data and insights, leading to improved customer experiences and increased revenue.

DDDM Challenges. While DDDM offers numerous benefits, organizations may encounter several challenges. Inaccurate or incomplete data can lead to misguided decisions. For instance, if data is outdated, duplicated, or inconsistent, the resulting insights may be flawed, leading to poor decision-making. Ensuring data quality requires regular audits, validation processes, and the implementation of data governance policies, writes Ramesh Panuganty from MachEye.[126]

Disparate data systems across various departments can hinder the integration process, leading to fragmented insights. When data is stored in isolated silos, it becomes challenging to obtain a comprehensive view of the organization's operations. Integrating data from various sources is essential to provide decision-makers with a unified view and comprehensive information.

CRO versus Head of Revops: Leverage RevOps Expertise

A lack of expertise in data analysis can impede the effective interpretation of data. Even with high-quality data, if team members lack the skills and the time to focus to analyze and interpret it, the organization cannot fully leverage its data assets.

For instance, the CRO is a revenue-driving force, no doubt. But when it comes to interpreting data for the daily grind of RevOps? That's the Head of RevOps' strong point. The CRO sees the big picture, but the Head of RevOps is the one digging into the data, spotting inefficiencies, and making real-time adjustments that keep revenue teams firing on all cylinders.

"While a RevOps leader is laser-focused on optimizing revenue functions, a COO is responsible for aligning all aspects of operations—from logistics to human resources to product delivery," said Cody Guymon, a Go-to-Market advisor and RevOps expert.[127] "In this trusted advisor role, your value extends beyond just reporting numbers. You become a strategic partner who anticipates challenges, identifies opportunities, and provides solutions backed by data."

Although their title may not always reflect their function, studies referenced by the Revenue Operations Alliance show that 23 percent of RevOps pros have been working in revenue operations for over a decade.[128] They thrive in the data-driven, cross-functional world, ensuring all revenue teams are in sync and delivering results.

"A successful RevOps leader's ability to integrate systems and drive efficiency makes them the glue that holds everything together—key traits that make them stand out when looking for a COO role," Cody said. "RevOps leaders are like the architects of revenue generation, working across sales, marketing, and customer success to optimize processes and ensure smooth data flow."

Shifting to a data-driven culture may face internal resistance. Employees accustomed to traditional decision-making processes might be hesitant to adopt data-centric approaches. Overcoming this resistance requires strong leadership, clear communication of the benefits of DDDM, and involving employees in the transition process to foster buy-in and acceptance.

Collecting and utilizing vast amounts of data raise concerns about data privacy and security. Organizations must ensure compliance with data protection regulations and implement robust security measures to protect sensitive information. Failure to do so can lead to legal repercussions and damage to the organization's reputation.

Finally, ensuring that data-driven decision-making processes are unbiased and fair is a significant challenge. Organizations must be vigilant to prevent biases in data collection and analysis that could lead to unfair or discriminatory outcomes. Implementing ethical guidelines and conducting regular reviews of decision-making processes can help mitigate this risk.

Addressing these challenges requires a comprehensive approach that includes investing in the right tools and infrastructure, fostering a data-centric culture, ensuring data quality, and implementing robust data governance policies. By proactively managing these challenges, organizations can fully realize the benefits of data-driven decision-making.

Data-driven decision-making is a powerful approach that enables organizations to make informed, objective, and strategic choices. By effectively collecting, integrating, and analyzing data, businesses can enhance their decision-making processes, leading to improved performance and a competitive advantage. Embracing DDDM within RevOps ensures that sales, marketing, and customer success strategies are aligned with empirical insights, driving sustainable revenue growth.

Revenue Forecasting

With all of the tools and solutions out there now, it has never been easier for businesses to use data to accurately forecast their revenue. Predicting future earnings is essential for setting growth targets, allocating resources, and making strategic decisions. It involves analyzing historical data, market trends, and current sales pipelines to predict future earnings. However, despite advancements in technology, many companies still struggle with inaccurate forecasts due to poor data quality, lack of integration between systems, and outdated forecasting methods.

Reliable revenue forecasts start with a strong, well-managed pipeline. "Pipeline is one of the most important things I focus on because if you have an adequate pipeline, your sales life is better, and you feel more confident," said Andrew Conley, SVP of Revenue at Guideline. "You have multiple ways to hit your number, but you also have peace in how you communicate with customers. There's no weird urgency to close deals unnaturally or push deals that aren't ready to be moved." When pipeline health is prioritized, sales teams can operate with clarity and confidence, ensuring that forecasts aren't built on last-minute deal scrambling but on a steady, predictable flow of opportunities.

One significant challenge is the presence of inaccurate or incomplete data, which can lead to misguided decisions. Disparate data systems further complicate the integration process, making it difficult to obtain a unified view of the business. Additionally, a lack of expertise in data analysis can hinder the effective interpretation of data, emphasizing the need for investment in training programs to bridge this gap. Transitioning to a data-driven culture may also face internal resistance, requiring deliberate change management strategies. Forecasting solutions require pristine data to generate reliable predictions, and operations teams must work diligently to ensure data integrity. Without clean data, forecasts become unreliable, leading to potential missteps in strategy.

To overcome these challenges, businesses should adopt best practices in revenue forecasting as laid out by CaptivateIQ.[129] Regularly updating forecasts based on new data ensures they remain relevant amid changing market conditions. Incorporating cross-functional expertise can enhance the comprehensiveness of forecasts, as different departments offer valuable insights. Investing in modern technology, such as advanced analytics tools, can streamline the forecasting process and improve accuracy.

Planning and forecasting should be continuous processes rather than annual events. Bala has observed that companies are shifting away from traditional annual planning cycles, opting instead for ongoing adjustments to their Go-to-Market strategies. This approach allows businesses to remain agile and responsive to evolving market conditions, ensuring that their operational plans are always aligned with current realities. By integrating continuous planning with high-quality data management, organizations can enhance their forecasting accuracy and maintain strategic agility in dynamic markets.

To improve revenue forecasting, companies must invest in high-quality data, integrate their systems, and foster a culture that embraces analytics. By doing so, they can transform their forecasts from educated guesses into strategic assets that drive smarter business decisions.

Conclusion

In this chapter, we explored the pivotal role of data in driving revenue growth and operational efficiency in RevOps. Bala Balabaskaran's experiences at Salesforce highlighted how poor data quality can cripple productivity and cost businesses significant revenue. The Fit-for-Purpose Framework emphasized that data doesn't need to be perfect—it just needs to be accurate enough for its intended use. By focusing on validity, accuracy, completeness, and ROI-driven decision-making, RevOps teams can prevent wasted resources and ensure reliable insights.

We examined how to establish a data-driven culture, where leadership engagement, employee empowerment, and cross-functional collaboration make data a strategic asset rather than an IT afterthought. A structured data collection and analysis process ensures data is integrated, governed, and visualized effectively to drive smarter decisions.

Key metrics like ARR, NRR, and CLV help organizations measure success. However, its effectiveness hinges on data quality and continuous refinement. We also explored revenue forecasting, where shifting from rigid annual planning to dynamic, real-time adjustments allows businesses to stay agile and responsive.

Part 3

Performance for Sustainable Growth

11

High-Performance Growth Maturity Model

The mission to land a man on the moon wasn't just a triumph of engineering but also of operational alignment. Teams across engineering, manufacturing, computing, and Mission Control operated with one unified goal: making the impossible possible. A man walking on the moon wasn't achieved overnight. In the early years, NASA faced siloed research centers, communication breakdowns, and misaligned processes. Each team worked with its own priorities until leadership realized that success depended on cohesion and shared accountability.

In 1963, NASA underwent a major transformation.[130] Administrator James E. Webb and Associate Administrator Robert Seamans spearheaded a restructuring initiative to boost efficiency and oversight within the agency. Key centers like the Manned Spacecraft Center, Marshall Space Flight Center, and Launch Operations Center were realigned to report directly to George Mueller, the newly appointed Associate Administrator for the Office of Manned Space Flight. Mueller introduced rigorous management systems, including configuration control and "all-up" testing, which streamlined operations and played a pivotal role in achieving the audacious goal of landing on the moon before the decade's end.

Similarly, Joseph Francis Shea, as manager of the Apollo Spacecraft Program Office, was a champion for engineering discipline and configuration management. He introduced systematic design reviews and rigorous change control processes, ensuring that any modifications to the spacecraft were meticulously evaluated before implementation. These management practices were instrumental in coordinating the efforts of numerous teams and contractors, ultimately leading to the triumphant success of the Apollo program.

Finally, in 1969, history was made when astronauts Neil Armstrong and Edwin "Buzz" Aldrin became the first humans to walk on the moon.

NASA's journey from disjointed operations to unified mission success serves as a powerful analogy for the stages of RevOps maturity. Just as NASA identified inefficiencies, streamlined communication, and aligned its teams around a shared goal, organizations today must navigate their own paths to meet their own moon-sized goals. The RevOps Maturity Model provides a framework to guide this iterative transformation, helping businesses assess their current capabilities and then develop multiphase plans for incrementally achieving greater operational alignment and efficiency across revenue-generating teams. By understanding these stages of RevOps maturity, organizations can optimally position themselves for rapid, outsize success with RevOps, just as NASA did with Apollo.

While the previous chapters in this book were about establishing a foundation for what an optimized RevOps system should look like, this chapter transitions into the nitty-gritty nuts and bolts of how to incrementally work toward RevOps maturity.

In this chapter, we'll explore the three stages of RevOps maturity in detail. We'll examine the key components and challenges of each stage. We'll guide you through assessing your organization's position on the maturity journey and taking actionable steps to unlock your full RevOps potential. Finally, we'll explore how the Maturity Model can be applied to companies of different industries, business models, sizes, and stages of the business.

Aspirations Toward Maturity

Every forward-thinking business leader recognizes intuitively that working toward more mature, articulated, proven practices is an essential goal. The reason is simple: Organizations that don't invest in becoming more mature versions of themselves are destined to fail. RevOps maturity provides a road map to achieve this transformation iteratively, helping organizations become more data-driven, accountable, and aligned around the customer. Over 80 percent of executives interviewed in one study are redefining their commercial architecture, consolidating sales operations, and adding specialized roles to support engagement across the customer life cycle.[131] CRO roles have more than doubled to over 9,000 in the past three years, while companies increasingly adopt titles like Chief Growth Officer, Chief Commercial Officer, and Chief Customer Officer to oversee unified revenue teams. However, titles alone are insufficient. More than 80 percent of growth leaders emphasize that top-down leadership from the CEO is critical for enabling the transformation of commercial models to unify sales, marketing, and customer success.

Maturity aspirations don't automatically turn into maturity successes. On the journey to RevOps maturity, Forrester notes most businesses lack a structured method for designing their RevOps functions, leading to ill-conceived structures that impact long-term sustainability of RevOps strategy.[132] Take the story of Mari Manglaras, a mainframe and web engineer, who pivoted to a career integrating sales and operations to optimize revenue generation. In other words, she was doing RevOps before there was RevOps. In her first two months as a sales rep, she failed miserably at meeting quotas. But she listened and learned every day, figuring out on her own how all of the chess pieces fit together, as she explained to Amy during a recent podcast interview.[133] She studied the talk tracks of sales reps, what customer engagement tactics to deploy and when, how a different deft touch might be required for a different industry vertical. By her third month, Mari's own understanding of RevOps had matured: She hit 1,000 percent of her goal. Needless to say, she was quickly promoted to sales and operations management, making her responsible for evolving the RevOps maturity of the entire organization and helping the sales team always hit 200 percent of its goal.

"No other team could touch us," she said.

As her organization's RevOps leader, Mari couldn't follow a structured RevOps maturity pathway. That's because she started investing in RevOps maturity before her organization could even define what RevOps was. All she had was her own intuition to go on. Fortunately, RevOps leaders today don't need to forge a maturity pathway on their own. The RevOps Maturity Model provides a structured framework for assessing an organization's current RevOps capabilities, pinpointing where the organization is weak, and developing clear, articulated plans for incrementally advancing discrete elements of the organization's RevOps capabilities. The model establishes three overarching stages of RevOps maturity—Developing, Intermediate, and Advanced—that collectively capture the range of incremental improvements needed to progress from basic operational functionality to advanced strategic alignment.

Three Stages of RevOps Maturity

The RevOps Maturity Model progresses through three primary stages—Developing, Intermediate, and Advanced—each representing a milestone in an organization's operational alignment and efficiency. At every stage, certain key components define success and provide a road map for growth and transformation.

Developing Stage. In the Developing stage, organizations are just beginning to address the challenges of siloed teams and fragmented operations. Leadership alignment is often limited, with sales, marketing, and customer success working independently toward goals that are not unified or clearly defined. Processes tend to be inconsistent and undocumented, leading to miscommunication and inefficiencies. Systems and tools are typically disconnected, creating redundancies and limiting the ability to generate actionable insights. The focus at this stage is on identifying pain points, creating basic alignment, and laying the foundation for more structured operations.

In the early days of Fullcast, Bala had developed a strong product, but there was no pipeline when Ryan came on as CEO, requiring an immediate effort to generate one. This demonstrates a Developing Stage challenge, where product development is prioritized, but sales and marketing operations are not yet integrated or aligned. It is important to be explicit about the company's direction and where it is headed. If weeks go by without this direction, it could cause problems when it comes time to raise money.

Intermediate Stage. As organizations progress to the Intermediate stage, they begin to streamline their operations and foster cross-functional collaboration. Leadership teams align more closely on shared goals and metrics, with a growing recognition of the need for integrated strategies across all revenue-generating functions. Processes become more standardized and optimized to enhance efficiency and reduce friction in the customer life cycle.

Teams start to grow in complexity, with specialized roles emerging to handle increasingly sophisticated operational needs. Systems and tools are integrated to provide a unified view of performance, enabling more accurate forecasting and data-driven decision-making. Data quality improves significantly, with governance practices and real-time reporting becoming central to operations. This stage is marked by a shift from reactive problem-solving to proactive planning and execution.

Advanced Stage. At the Advanced stage, organizations operate as cohesive, data-driven entities. Leadership alignment is fully realized, with RevOps playing a strategic role in guiding decision-making at the highest levels. Processes are fully integrated and continuously refined to adapt to changing market conditions and customer needs. Teams are well-structured and specialized, functioning as strategic partners across the organization.

Sophisticated systems and tools, often powered by AI and machine learning, provide predictive insights that drive proactive decision-making. Data becomes a core asset, enabling precise forecasting, personalized customer experiences, and innovative strategies that differentiate the organization in the marketplace. At this stage, RevOps is no longer just an operational function but a critical driver of strategic growth and competitive advantage.

The journey to RevOps maturity is not a rat race. Faster is not always better, and the right pace for one business is not necessarily the right pace for another. In fact, businesses commonly scale RevOps incorrectly. They tend to overinvest in technology solutions, creating redundant functionality that becomes costly and time-intensive to maintain over time. Simultaneously, businesses tend to underinvest in their RevOps implementation team, magnifying the organization's inability to maintain more technology and more complex workflows. Thus, the most judicious approach to achieving RevOps maturity is to move incrementally and deliberately through the stages of RevOps maturity. It's the best chance an organization has at sustainable, long-term RevOps success.

The Six Dimensions of RevOps Maturity

The RevOps Maturity Model is a strategic framework that helps businesses assess their operational efficiency, identify areas for improvement, and plan for sustainable growth. By leveraging this model, businesses can evaluate their current operational efficiency, pinpoint areas for improvement, and strategically plan for sustainable growth.

The RevOps Maturity Model, as laid out by Ben Mohlie from Hyperscayle, categorizes maturity into six critical dimensions: leadership alignment, process definition, team structure, systems and tools, data foundation, and customer-centric execution.[134] These categories provide a structured pathway for organizations to assess and elevate their RevOps capabilities.

Leadership Alignment. Leadership alignment is a critical component of RevOps maturity. Organizations must ensure that leadership teams share common goals and metrics, aligning GTM strategies effectively. As alignment improves, executives unite under a comprehensive RevOps strategy that drives accountability and long-term success.

RevOps success begins with leadership alignment. At early stages, leaders might operate independently with limited collaboration. As maturity increases, leadership aligns on shared goals, metrics, and a unified strategy. Fully mature organizations embed RevOps as a central function driving accountability and ensuring GTM cohesion at the executive level.

Sales, marketing, and customer success leadership align their vision with company-wide goals and RevOps strategies. This includes establishing shared KPIs ensuring accountability for demand generation and alignment on shared goals, such as revenue targets, pipeline health, and customer retention.

Process Definition. Processes must be clearly defined to enable efficient collaboration and scalability. Undocumented and inconsistent processes lead to inefficiencies and miscommunication. Organizations should aim to standardize and optimize their processes to align with the customer journey, delivering exceptional experiences.[135] A well-defined process foundation is crucial for identifying operational gaps and ensuring smooth transitions throughout the customer life cycle.

Processes evolve from fragmented and inconsistent workflows to fully integrated, automated systems aligned with the customer life cycle. Processes are designed and refined to support the customer life cycle, focusing on reducing friction, enhancing engagement, and increasing customer satisfaction. For example, automated workflows might ensure timely follow-ups or proactive issue resolution. RevOps ensures seamless coordination across departments and identifies inefficiencies to optimize operations. Mature organizations implement sales playbooks, standardized opportunity stages, and clear handoff protocols between sales, marketing, and customer success.

Team Structure. RevOps teams evolve in structure and complexity as organizations grow. Initially, teams may consist of a small group managing basic operations. However, as complexity increases, the introduction of specialized roles and a structured hierarchy becomes necessary. A fully developed team operates as a strategic partner to leadership, with a VP or equivalent leader managing a robust team of specialists and analysts. The team structure must scale in parallel with the company's GTM motion to avoid bottlenecks and inefficiencies.

RevOps teams also may expand to include roles focused on customer experience, such as Customer Insights Analysts or CX

Strategists. Collaboration between sales, marketing, and customer success teams becomes seamless, with shared accountability for customer outcomes.

Systems and Tools. Systems and tools are critical for supporting RevOps functions. Early-stage organizations often rely on disconnected systems, leading to inefficiencies and tech debt. As organizations grow, integrating core systems like CRMs and marketing automation platforms becomes essential. At higher levels of maturity, businesses leverage sophisticated, centralized platforms powered by AI and machine learning to provide predictive insights and enable proactive decision-making, according to Gartner.[136] However, overinvesting in tools without ensuring alignment with business needs can create additional challenges.

For example, technology adoption begins with basic tools like email marketing platforms and evolves to include sophisticated marketing automation, ABM platforms, and analytics tools. Fully mature teams leverage AI for campaign personalization, predictive analytics for audience targeting, and tools to measure multi-touch attribution.

Data Foundation. Data serves as the backbone of a successful RevOps strategy. Poor data quality and manual reporting are common challenges that hinder decision-making, according to a Fullcast interview with Matt Haller, an experienced Sales Ops leader.[137] Implementing standardized data governance and real-time reporting capabilities can address these issues. Advanced organizations achieve a single source of truth, with analytics and predictive models driving decision-making across the customer life cycle. Insights derived from accurate data empower organizations to make informed, strategic decisions.

Data governance evolves to prioritize customer data accuracy, privacy, and accessibility. Predictive analytics and AI are leveraged to anticipate customer needs, tailor experiences, and proactively address potential churn risks. Successful organizations rely on real-time analytics to monitor pipeline health, track performance, and inform decision-making. Predictive analytics helps sales teams prioritize opportunities and forecast revenue with greater precision.

Customer-Centric Execution. Sales teams focus on building trust and delivering value to customers. Customer feedback and needs inform sales strategies, while personalized interactions and seamless handoffs between departments enhance the customer experience. This stage focuses on ensuring that the customer experience is seamless, personalized, and continuously optimized at every touchpoint.[138]

"Understanding evolving customer buying and usage patterns is critical to building an efficient business. Buyer research, self-serve needs, and product-led growth/sales led growth expectations have significantly changed," said Mudit Garg, SVP and GTM Operator.[139] "Enterprise data can be a mess, but an AI-friendly data architecture can simplify the customer journey and create a 360-degree view of the customer."

Marketing prioritizes creating exceptional customer experiences. Campaigns are tailored to customer personas and pain points, delivering value at every touchpoint. Feedback loops with sales and customer success ensure marketing strategies stay aligned with customer needs. Sales teams focus on building trust and delivering value to customers. Customer feedback and needs inform sales strategies, while personalized interactions and seamless handoffs between departments enhance the customer experience. A mature sales function ensures every interaction reinforces customer loyalty and satisfaction.

***

Organizations progress through the RevOps Maturity Model by investing strategically across these six dimensions. The framework serves as a guide for assessing current capabilities, identifying gaps, and implementing improvements. A mature RevOps function drives efficiency, accountability, and growth, ensuring that all GTM efforts align with business objectives and customer needs.

Self-Assessment: Where Are You on the Journey?

A key step in leveraging the RevOps Maturity Model is understanding where your organization currently stands. Self-assessment, when done honestly and completely, uncovers opportunities for growth and aligning your RevOps strategy with your business objectives. By evaluating performance across the six dimensions of RevOps maturity, you can create a targeted road map for improvement.

Organizations rarely operate at the same maturity level across all dimensions. For example, a company may excel in leadership alignment, with executives united under a shared vision, but struggle with fragmented systems that limit cross-functional collaboration. This variability is why a holistic view is critical. Assessing each dimension separately helps you pinpoint specific gaps while ensuring your strategy accounts for the interplay between them.

Questions to Guide Your Assessment. To accurately evaluate your current state, ask targeted questions within each dimension:

- Are leadership teams aligned on shared goals and metrics?
    - o Are there shared KPIs across sales, marketing, and customer success teams that are reviewed regularly by leadership?
    - o How often does leadership revisit and refine the RevOps strategy based on business performance and market conditions?
    - o Is there clear accountability for each leader's role in supporting the RevOps function?

- o Are cross-functional meetings held to ensure alignment and collaboration on GTM strategies?
- o Are there structured mechanisms (e.g., OKRs or quarterly business reviews) to measure alignment across teams?

- Are your processes defined, standardized, and optimized?
  - o Have all key processes been documented, and are they accessible to relevant teams?
  - o Are there established workflows for onboarding, lead routing, and opportunity management?
  - o How frequently are processes reviewed and optimized based on operational performance?
  - o Are processes designed to adapt to changing customer behaviors and market dynamics?
  - o Are there clear guidelines for handoffs between marketing, sales, and customer success teams?
  - o How well do your processes account for and mitigate common bottlenecks or delays in the sales funnel?
  - o Do processes seamlessly align with the customer journey, or are there bottlenecks causing friction?

- Does your RevOps team have the expertise and resources to support your GTM motion?
  - o Are roles clearly defined, and do they enable cross-functional collaboration?
  - o Are there gaps in skill sets within the RevOps team that hinder operational effectiveness?
  - o How well does the RevOps team collaborate with other departments to align priorities?

- Are roles within the team specialized (e.g., analysts, systems administrators, strategists), or are responsibilities overlapping?
  - Do team members have the training and resources necessary to stay updated on RevOps best practices?
  - How effectively does the team balance tactical execution with strategic initiatives?

- Are your systems and tools aligned with business needs?
  - Are your current tools integrated to provide a unified view of operations?
  - How often do you audit your tech stack to identify redundancies or gaps?
  - Are tools being fully utilized, or are there features that remain underused?
  - Does your tech stack align with your organization's size, growth stage, and GTM complexity?
  - How efficiently do tools enable data sharing and collaboration across teams?
  - Are there clear ownership and governance practices in place for each tool in your stack?

- Is your data accurate, accessible, and actionable?
  - Is there a standardized approach to data entry and management to ensure consistency?
  - How often do you conduct data audits to clean and validate your datasets?
  - Are there systems in place to ensure compliance with data privacy regulations (e.g., GDPR, CCPA)?
  - Can teams easily access data to inform decision-making without reliance on manual reports?

- o Are predictive models or analytics tools being used to generate actionable insights?
- o How effectively does your data strategy support long-term planning and forecasting?

- How well does your RevOps strategy align with customer needs?
  - o Are you delivering value at every touchpoint, and do feedback loops inform your operations?
  - o How effectively does your RevOps strategy address pain points at each stage of the customer journey?
  - o Are there mechanisms to gather and act on customer feedback in real time?
  - o How personalized and consistent are interactions across marketing, sales, and customer success?
  - o Are SLAs in place to ensure timely and seamless handoffs between teams?
  - o How well do you leverage data to predict and address customer needs proactively?
  - o Are customer retention, upsell, and advocacy metrics actively monitored and tied to RevOps KPIs?

Scoring Your Maturity. For a structured self-assessment, consider scoring each dimension on this scale by Six & Flow[140]:

- **Poor:** Processes are ad hoc, and collaboration is limited. Data is siloed, and leadership alignment is weak.
- **Average:** Some alignment exists, but it is inconsistent. Processes and systems are in place but not optimized.
- **Good:** Clear improvements are visible. Teams collaborate effectively, and systems are integrated to support operations.

- **Excellent:** Full alignment, integration, and optimization are achieved. RevOps drives efficiency and delivers measurable impact across all dimensions.

Once you've completed your assessment, focus on the areas with the greatest potential impact. For example, if your systems and tools are well-integrated but your processes are inconsistent, prioritize standardizing workflows to unlock efficiencies. Or if leadership alignment is weak, invest in fostering executive collaboration and creating shared goals.

Self-assessment is not a one-time exercise. As your organization evolves, so too will your RevOps needs. Schedule regular assessments to ensure your strategy adapts to changing market conditions, business objectives, and customer expectations. By continuously evaluating your maturity and addressing gaps, you can build a resilient RevOps function that drives sustainable growth.

Assessing Your Organization by Industry, Business Model, and Size

As organizations progress along the RevOps Maturity Model, one key differentiator between early-stage and mature RevOps functions is the ability to balance strategy, operations, and tactical execution. A high-performing RevOps team isn't just focused on long-term planning; it ensures day-to-day execution remains strong while staying connected to frontline realities.

As RevOps leader Balaji Krish explains in an episode of the *Go To Market Podcast* with Amy Cook, "Only 40 percent of our ops should be strategy. The other 60 percent is operational and tactical. You'll never learn those operational, tactical things if you're not in touch with what's going on."[141] RevOps leaders must adopt both zoomed-in and zoomed-out perspectives—developing high-level strategies while maintaining a firm grasp on execution. Without this balance, organizations risk misalignment between leadership's vision and on-the-ground realities.

At the highest level of maturity, RevOps functions operate as a well-integrated system, seamlessly connecting strategic goals with operational execution. By maintaining this 40-40-20 balance (40% strategy, 40% operations, 20% tactical), mature RevOps teams ensure that strategy is grounded in real-world insights, operations are scalable, and tactical execution remains agile.

No two organizations are the same, and the way a company approaches RevOps maturity should reflect its unique characteristics. Industry dynamics, business model complexities, and organizational size all play significant roles in shaping the path to operational excellence. By considering these factors, organizations can craft RevOps strategies that align with their specific challenges and opportunities.

Industry. Different industries face distinct operational requirements and customer expectations, which directly impact RevOps priorities.

- **Technology (B2B SaaS):** In the highly competitive SaaS sector,[142] rapid scalability and customer retention are critical. For example, a SaaS company offering cloud-based collaboration tools may prioritize advanced data analytics to track customer usage patterns and predict churn. RevOps processes would focus on ensuring seamless onboarding, automated renewal reminders, and robust feedback loops to improve customer satisfaction.
- **Retail and E-Commerce:** For a direct-to-consumer (DTC) retail brand, RevOps efforts might center on real-time inventory visibility and streamlining order

fulfillment processes.[143] Technology investments could include CRM tools integrated with inventory systems and predictive analytics to optimize product recommendations.

- **Manufacturing:** Manufacturers often deal with long sales cycles and complex supply chains.[144] A heavy machinery manufacturer, for instance, might focus on improving RevOps by integrating sales and channel partner data into centralized platforms to provide better demand forecasts and enhance partner collaboration.

Business Model. The complexity of a company's business model also shapes its RevOps strategy, especially in managing the customer life cycle.

- **B2B:** A business-to-business software firm with a high annual contract value (ACV) would focus on account-based marketing (ABM) and tailored RevOps processes for enterprise clients. For example, a cybersecurity company may invest in systems that align marketing automation with sales outreach to identify and nurture key stakeholders in target accounts.
- **B2C:** A consumer-facing subscription service, such as a streaming platform, may focus its RevOps efforts on automating customer engagement and retention workflows. AI-driven insights could be used to predict customer churn and send personalized offers to retain users.
- **Hybrid Models:** Companies with both B2B and B2C elements, such as a software provider selling enterprise solutions alongside consumer licenses, need dual strategies.[145] RevOps for B2B operations would focus on account-based

approaches, while B2C efforts might emphasize automated customer segmentation and self-service tools.

Size. Organizational size significantly influences RevOps maturity, determining the complexity of operations and the level of resources available for investment.

- **Small Businesses and Start-Ups:** Early-stage companies often operate with limited resources, requiring lean RevOps strategies. For example, a start-up in its Series A stage might use basic CRM tools like HubSpot for lead management while relying on a small team to handle marketing and sales operations. The focus would be on building foundational processes and achieving initial alignment across departments.
- **Mid-Market Companies:** As companies grow, the need for integrated systems and formalized processes increases. A midsize company with $50 million in annual revenue may adopt advanced sales engagement platforms and data centralization tools like Salesforce to streamline operations and gain insights into customer behavior.
- **Enterprises:** Large organizations face challenges related to scale and complexity. For instance, a global enterprise in the pharmaceutical sector may use AI-driven analytics to manage massive datasets across multiple regions and business units. Their RevOps efforts would focus on optimizing cross-functional collaboration, ensuring compliance with regulatory standards, and leveraging predictive models for strategic planning.

Tailoring RevOps strategies based on industry, business model, and size ensures that resources are allocated effectively and efforts are aligned with organizational goals, writes Venkat Viswanathan in *Forbes*.[146] By assessing these factors, organizations can identify industry-specific challenges, adjust processes and tools to accommodate the nuances of their business model, and scale operations strategically based on company size. By aligning RevOps efforts with these dimensions, businesses can address unique operational needs while setting themselves up for sustainable growth and competitive advantage.

Conclusion

This chapter detailed the RevOps Maturity Model as a framework to help organizations achieve operational excellence. By breaking down maturity into six critical dimensions—leadership alignment, process definition, team structure, systems and tools, data foundation, and customer-centric execution—we outlined the steps businesses can take to progress from basic functionality to strategic cohesion.

We then explored the importance of aligning leadership around shared goals and metrics, standardizing and optimizing processes, and building a RevOps team structure that scales with organizational complexity. We also discussed the critical role of integrated systems, accurate data, and customer-focused strategies in driving efficiency, accountability, and growth.

By leveraging self-assessment and tailoring strategies to their unique industry, business model, and size, organizations can identify gaps, prioritize improvements, and create a road map for sustained success. The RevOps Maturity Model empowers businesses to align their operations with strategic objectives, ensuring long-term competitiveness and growth.

We broke down how the RevOps Maturity Model can be used for companies in different industries, business models, and size. Finally, we spent some time exploring how the RevOps Maturity Model progresses from developing, intermediate, and advanced phases along the company's journey.

12

The Pit Crew

Building a Successful Team

Ryan has a unique spreadsheet that he always keeps updated. It's not a list of investors or customer accounts; it's a list of people he's met over the years, people he's worked with, people he's watched from afar and thought, "I want to work with them someday." It's not just a list of names. It's part of a long-term strategy of building a team that can take your RevOps team to success.

When he stepped in as CEO of Fullcast, he didn't need to scramble to figure out who to hire. He already knew. He knew exactly who he was going to call and when. He had a plan—not just for the first hires, but for who to bring in at different stages of growth. Because building a great company isn't just about the product or the market—it's about the people.

Ryan's approach to team-building is not to worry about selling. Worry about delivering. If you do great work, if you keep your word, if you make sure that when people bet on you, they win, then the best talent will want to follow you. That's why when he

reached out to his former colleagues, some of whom could have easily been CEOs in their own right, they didn't hesitate. They weren't
just following a title or a paycheck; they were following someone
they trusted.

Because Amy had the history and trust built with Ryan, she
decided to join him at Fullcast as Chief Marketing Officer. She had
seen firsthand that when Ryan committed to something, he followed
through. That's the kind of leadership people want to rally behind.

Building a great team isn't just about hiring smart people. It's
about hiring complementary people. Ryan understood his own
strengths, but more importantly, he understood his weaknesses.
He wasn't interested in being the smartest person in the room; he
wanted to surround himself with people who could push him, challenge him, and take the company further than he could on his own.

Relationships compound, just like money. The people you invest
in today could become your cofounders, your executives, your biggest advocates down the road. But that only happens if you put in
the work before you need them. The best leaders don't just hire people. They build alliances. They create environments where top talent
wants to come back, time and time again. That's how you build a
company that doesn't just succeed in the short term—but wins for
the long haul.

That's why Ryan keeps that spreadsheet. That's why he spends
time understanding his team's strengths, weaknesses, and long-term
goals. Because when you need to build a RevOps team that can take
your company to the next level, you don't want to start from scratch.
You want to be ready.

Success depends on how you structure, develop, and empower
your team. A RevOps leader doesn't just need skilled operators;
they need a group of strategic thinkers who can execute, adapt, and
scale with the business. In this chapter, we'll break down the essential components of building a RevOps team that thrives. We'll talk

about developing and retaining top RevOps talent, the personal career path for finding success in RevOps, and expanding your network and influence as a RevOps leader. By the end of this chapter, you'll have a framework for not only hiring the right people but also developing, retaining, and leading a team that can take your company to new heights. Let's get started.

Hiring and Retaining Top RevOps Talent

If you're a new RevOps leader or a CEO, one of the first tasks on your hands may be figuring out who to hire and how to retain your best employees. This task is challenging, especially considering that 70 percent of the global workforce comprises passive candidates who are not actively seeking new opportunities, according to LinkedIn statistics.[147] As in any top-performing team, retaining top RevOps talent is as crucial as hiring them.

While bringing skilled professionals on board sets the foundation, keeping them ensures sustained growth and operational excellence. High turnover can disrupt processes and erode institutional knowledge. And it can be costly too. According to research, the average cost to replace an employee is approximately six to nine months of their salary.[148] For RevOps roles, which require specialized knowledge, this figure can be even higher.

To effectively build a high-performing RevOps team, organizations must implement strategic approaches to identify, attract, and retain the best talent. These include hiring for potential, being proactive, creating clear career paths, investing in your people, and more.

Hire for Potential, Not Just Experience. Unlike traditional functions like sales or finance, RevOps is a relatively new discipline, and hiring based solely on years of experience can be misleading. The best RevOps professionals often come from nontraditional backgrounds—engineering, CRM administration, sales enablement, or consulting—because they bring problem-solving skills, adaptability, and a deep understanding of Go-to-Market operations. A great RevOps hire isn't just someone who knows how to build reports or manage tech stacks; they must also:

- Be agile and flexible, able to adapt to shifting GTM strategies.
- Have a problem-solving mindset, capable of breaking down challenges and applying frameworks to find solutions.
- Understand the business holistically, not just their specific function.
- Be able to hold their ground when working with sales, marketing, and finance leaders who all have competing priorities.

For example, a RevOps leader looking to hire an operations analyst might not limit their search to someone with direct RevOps experience. Instead, they could consider a former engineer with a deep understanding of systems, integrations, and automation—someone who can quickly implement and optimize new tools while also thinking strategically about how processes fit together.

Be Proactive in Recruiting Candidates. With only 30 percent of the global workforce actually actively seeking jobs, organizations cannot rely solely on traditional job postings to attract top RevOps talent. Proactive recruitment strategies are essential.[149]

To successfully attract and hire these individuals, organizations must take a proactive approach to recruitment. Here are some key strategies to engage passive RevOps candidates effectively:

- Tap into RevOps-specific communities such as Modern Sales Pros, Pavilion, and RevOps Co-op to connect with potential hires.
- Encourage employee referrals by incentivizing team members to recommend qualified candidates from their own networks.
- Build relationships with industry influencers who can introduce you to top talent. Many RevOps leaders engage with thought leaders and peers for advice and networking.
- Connect with potential hires early, before they're actively job searching to build rapport and establish trust.
- Attend and sponsor key RevOps and industry events.
- Ensure a strong Glassdoor and LinkedIn presence, as many passive candidates will research a company's reputation before considering an opportunity.
- Like Ryan, you can also keep your own database of high-potential RevOps professionals so that when a role opens, you have a curated list of qualified candidates to contact.

By proactively engaging with passive candidates through networking, events, and personalized outreach, companies can significantly expand their talent pipeline and attract the best RevOps professionals even before they start looking for new opportunities.

Create Clear Career Paths. One of the biggest gaps in RevOps today is the lack of well-defined career paths. In sales, the trajectory is clear: SDR $\rightarrow$ AE $\rightarrow$ Sales Manager $\rightarrow$ VP of Sales. But in RevOps, professionals often find themselves wondering: Do I move into marketing ops? Sales ops? Customer success? Should I aim for a leadership role? Can I reach the executive level from RevOps?

This uncertainty leads to high attrition. In fact, 83 percent of RevOps professionals are looking to take the next step in their careers, often because they don't see a clear future within their current organization. To retain top talent, RevOps leaders must:

1. *Define clear milestones for growth.* Employees need to know exactly what it takes to move from RevOps Analyst to Manager to Director and beyond.
2. *Connect their work to meaningful impact.* RevOps professionals don't want to be measured on vague metrics like "adoption of Salesforce." Instead, tie their success to revenue efficiency, deal velocity, or pipeline acceleration.
3. *Support different career trajectories.* Not every RevOps professional wants to manage people. Some prefer a technical path, mastering systems and automation. Others thrive in strategic roles, influencing GTM strategy. Recognizing these paths and supporting them is critical.

For example, one RevOps leader shared how they supported an employee who had no interest in people management but wanted to deepen their expertise in CRM architecture. Instead of forcing them into a leadership role, they built a growth plan focused on advanced certifications, strategic projects, and industry networking, eventually positioning them as an internal expert and driving greater value for the business.

Invest in People, Not Just Tools. Companies often default to investing in new technology to solve operational challenges, but RevOps is a people-first function. A cutting-edge RevOps tech stack is useless without skilled professionals who can architect, optimize, and adapt it to business needs.

Retention starts with giving employees:

- Fair compensation that reflects their impact.
- A defined path to success with clear goals and milestones.
- Opportunities for advancement—even if it means helping them grow into a role outside the company.

Top talent will stay where they can grow. If you commit to their success—even if it means preparing them for an opportunity outside your company—you build trust, loyalty, and a stronger network of future A-players.

Cultivate a Strong Employer Brand. A strong employer brand is crucial for attracting and retaining top talent. In fact, 89 percent of human resources leaders agree that a strong employer brand gives them a competitive advantage when it comes to attracting talent,[150] and companies with a strong employer brand are twice as likely to attract qualified candidates.[151] Consider these strategies to build a strong employer brand from Lis Anderson in *Forbes*[152]:

1. *Clearly communicate your mission, values, and culture.* This transparency helps potential candidates understand the organization's core principles and assess alignment with their personal values.
2. *Showcase the work environment.* Providing insights into the daily work life, team dynamics, and office culture can give candidates a realistic preview of what to expect.
3. *Recognize and reward employee achievements.* Acknowledging and celebrating successes fosters a positive work environment and enhances the company's reputation as a desirable place to work.

By implementing these strategies, organizations can enhance their employer brand, making them more appealing to top-tier talent and improving overall employee satisfaction and retention.

The Flywheel Effect: How Great Teams Attract Great Talent. Finally, the best way to attract top RevOps professionals is to take care of the ones you already have. A-players attract other A-players. If your current team feels empowered, engaged, and valued, they'll naturally become advocates—referring high-quality candidates and building a strong culture.

The best RevOps teams are built not just by hiring the right people but by creating an environment where they can thrive, grow, and contribute strategically. Companies that do this will not only solve their talent crisis but also position RevOps as a key driver of business success.

Supporting the Professional Development of RevOps Team Members

Although it may seem obvious, a RevOps leader can never afford to forget where they came from. Every member of a RevOps team is on a career journey similar to the one that has earned someone the title of RevOps leader. RevOps leaders need to demonstrate emotional intelligence as they are coaching, mentoring, and training their team to success, whether the goal is to support a team member in one day becoming a RevOps leader, or to find any number of other potential career paths that are optimal for a particular RevOps team member.

Because RevOps is still a relatively new discipline, RevOps team members are not necessarily going to be on the same trajectory or have the same career experiences as the RevOps leader had. Indeed, there is no single, predefined trajectory for professionals looking to enter or grow within the field. Many start their journey in different functional areas—some coming from CRM administration or business intelligence, others from sales or marketing operations. Over time, people tend to become RevOps leaders based on their ability to integrate technology, processes, and data to optimize revenue generation.

"I have a deeply held belief that when you help people have more options, choices, paths to walk down or doors to open, they tend to make good decisions about which doors to walk through," said Ben Davis, CXO of the Year in 2019 in *Utah Business*.[153]

Given that many RevOps leaders have never held other, lower levels of jobs on a RevOps team, it's important for RevOps leaders to be aware of where different levels of RevOps team members are at on their career journey.

"Always be learning. It's not going to be the same annual turn every year," Cody Guymon, a RevOps leader, said during an episode of the *Go To Market Podcast*.[154] "And my biggest thing is, listen to sales reps. Listen to the sales leaders because they're on the front lines. They understand what's happening in the moment, so they're going to know if there's momentum in a certain vertical or not, and what sales methodology is really landing and what messaging is landing in the market. Just stay curious."

Let's explore the qualities that are typically associated with RevOps team members at the early-career, mid-career, and senior-career levels:

Early-Career RevOps Roles. Those who are just starting in RevOps are focused on mastering the tools and processes that enable efficient revenue operations.[155] Many professionals enter the field through roles such as data analysts, CRM administrators, or revenue coordinators. These positions require strong analytical skills, attention to detail, and the ability to manage and interpret large datasets that drive revenue decision-making.

A key aspect of early-career success in RevOps is understanding the systems that underpin GTM execution. This means developing proficiency in platforms like Salesforce, HubSpot, or other CRM systems while also learning about automation, reporting, and workflow optimization. Many new RevOps professionals find themselves troubleshooting data discrepancies, maintaining system integrity, and supporting sales and marketing teams with operational tasks.

However, succeeding at this stage requires more than just technical expertise. RevOps professionals must begin developing cross-functional communication skills, as they will need to collaborate with teams across the organization. Those who excel at translating complex data into actionable insights will quickly distinguish themselves and set the stage for career progression.

Mid-Career RevOps Roles. As professionals advance in RevOps, they transition from being individual contributors to owning larger strategic initiatives.[156] Common mid-career roles include RevOps Manager, Strategy Lead, or Systems Architect. At this level, responsibilities shift from day-to-day execution to designing and optimizing revenue processes, forecasting revenue trends, and managing a company's tech stack for scalability.

One of the biggest shifts at this stage is the move from being reactive to proactive. Instead of simply responding to operational needs, mid-career RevOps professionals must anticipate challenges, identify inefficiencies, and implement solutions before they become problems. This requires a deep understanding of the organization's revenue model and the ability to align data, processes, and technology with long-term business objectives.

Developing a strategic mindset is critical to success at this level. Mid-career professionals must learn how to evaluate revenue performance holistically, integrating insights from sales, marketing, and customer success teams to optimize the entire customer journey. Understanding concepts like pipeline velocity, churn reduction, and territory design becomes essential for making data-driven recommendations to leadership.

In addition to technical expertise, mid-career RevOps professionals must begin cultivating leadership skills. This includes managing direct reports, influencing cross-functional stakeholders, and demonstrating the ability to own and drive business outcomes. Those who excel in these areas will be well-positioned to move into senior leadership roles.

Senior-Level RevOps Roles. At the highest levels of RevOps, professionals move into leadership roles such as Head of RevOps, Vice President of Revenue Operations, or even CRO. These roles require a deep understanding of business strategy, financial management, and organizational leadership. At this stage, RevOps is no longer just about optimizing processes—it's about shaping the company's overall revenue strategy.

Senior RevOps leaders play a crucial role in aligning GTM teams with company-wide goals. They partner with executives, board members, and investors to drive growth, improve profitability, and scale revenue operations efficiently. The ability to navigate organizational change, implement strategic initiatives, and communicate the financial impact of operational decisions is what separates top RevOps leaders from their peers.

At this level, professionals must be able to tie operational improvements to key financial metrics such as gross margin, customer lifetime value, and ARR growth. Strong business acumen is essential, as RevOps leaders are expected to contribute to high-level discussions on revenue planning, market expansion, and competitive positioning.

As RevOps becomes increasingly embedded in executive decision-making, those in leadership roles must also develop strong change management skills. Implementing new processes and technologies at scale requires the ability to influence stakeholders, gain buy-in from leadership, and manage resistance to change.

Moving from Tactical Execution to Strategic Leadership. One of the biggest changes that RevOps team members go through as they move into RevOps leadership roles is transitioning from a tactical, execution-focused role to a strategic leadership position.[157] Early-career RevOps practitioners often get caught up in day-to-day problem-solving—fixing data inconsistencies, managing automation, and ensuring sales teams have the resources they need. However, moving up the career ladder requires shifting focus to big-picture thinking and long-term revenue impact.

Thus, RevOps leaders should be looking for opportunities to train the next generation of RevOps leaders as business leaders, as opposed to just operational experts. Instead of just reporting on performance, future RevOps leaders need to be able to provide strategic insights that help drive business decisions, including learning to anticipate revenue challenges, forecast outcomes, and recommend data-driven solutions.

As RevOps leaders develop a deeper understanding of Go-to-Market strategy, analytics, and cross-functional alignment, they're positioning themselves as the next generation of CROs. Instead of being seen as back-office operators, they're stepping into roles that directly drive revenue strategy and business outcomes.

"I expect in the next ten years that all these VPs of RevOps will become CROs, and we'll have this wave of very technical and operations-minded CROs," said Jen Igartua, CEO of Go Nimbly.

How AI and Automation Are Reshaping RevOps Careers. The rise of AI-driven automation is transforming RevOps, shifting the role from operational task management to strategic revenue optimization, according to Wandee Lee on Handoffs.org.[158] Automation is reducing the time spent on manual data entry, lead routing, and forecasting, allowing RevOps teams to focus on higher-value activities such as predictive analytics, customer segmentation, and revenue intelligence.

Thus, another key aspect of RevOps professional development should focus on encouraging RevOps team members to embrace AI tools and automation strategies. Learning how to leverage AI for pipeline analysis, account scoring, and performance benchmarking will be critical for helping RevOps team members to stay ahead in an increasingly data-driven industry.

Getting Better at Building RevOps Teams over Time

Like any business leader, RevOps leaders get better at building resilient, high-performing RevOps teams over time. To continuously hone these team-building skills, Revops leaders should invest in a number of specific activities, including:

Networking. RevOps leaders should build a well-cultivated RevOps network that provides access to diverse perspectives, best practices, and emerging trends, all of which are essential in a field that thrives on cross-functional alignment. Engaging with professionals across various disciplines gives RevOps leaders the best chance at gathering the insights they need to streamline processes and drive revenue growth.

One study that explored the long-term effects of networking on career success found that networking behaviors, such as engaging with colleagues outside of work, maintaining connections with former professional contacts, and attending industry conferences, directly contribute to career growth.[159]

Bridging operations and strategy. To build high-performing RevOps teams, RevOps leaders must bridge the gap between operations and strategy, translating data into insights that drive business decisions. They need to earn the trust of revenue teams by demonstrating not just efficiency, but revenue impact. They must also be able to articulate a compelling vision for RevOps that goes beyond tactical execution and highlights its role as a growth enabler.

Positioning RevOps Teams as a Key Decision-Maker in GTM Strategy. RevOps leaders must work to position their teams as essential contributors to Go-to-Market strategy.[160] Instead of simply responding to operational needs, they should actively align the team's work to support pipeline planning, quota setting, and resource allocation discussions. RevOps leaders also should lead their team in implementing AI-driven forecasting models, optimizing account-based marketing strategies, or redesigning sales compensation structures—all areas that demonstrate the value of RevOps beyond tactical execution. Finally, RevOps leaders should expand their team's proficiency beyond technology and process optimization, including understanding profit and loss (P&L) statements, revenue forecasting, and competitive analysis

The C-suite is more likely to support RevOps leaders in building their teams when they see clear evidence of their bottom-line impact. For instance, RevOps leaders should lead their team in demonstrating how a data-driven approach led to a 15 percent increase in sales efficiency. This not only secures ongoing support from leadership but also motivates the RevOps team by highlighting their contributions to the company's success.

An Experience in Building a High-Impact RevOps Team from the Ground Up

Whitney Merrill, an experienced Go-to-Market leader, offers a powerful example of how to strategically build a RevOps function that drives long-term success.[161] His journey into RevOps was rooted in sales, but as he gained deeper exposure to revenue processes and technology, he saw an opportunity to bring structure, efficiency, and strategy to revenue operations.

Merrill's pivotal RevOps experience began when he was working at a major technology company undergoing massive transformation.

The company had ten separate Salesforce instances, each managed independently across different teams, leading to operational inefficiencies and siloed data. This fragmentation was not sustainable, especially as the business was simultaneously shifting from a point-solution model to a subscription-based offering. This type of transition required tight integration between sales, marketing, and customer care—otherwise, the company risked a chaotic and unscalable Go-to-Market strategy.

Recognizing the urgency of the situation, Merrill approached the company's Chief Sales and Strategy Officer (CSSO) with a bold proposition: integrate revenue operations across marketing, customer care, and sales to create a unified RevOps strategy. He understood that RevOps needed to be at the center of this business transformation and saw an opportunity to modernize how revenue teams operated.

Instead of waiting for leadership to dictate a solution, Merrill took the initiative. He assembled a small but highly focused RevOps team, bringing together:

1. Trainers to ensure consistent enablement across Go-to-Market teams.
2. New business development reps to create a seamless customer acquisition strategy.
3. Sales engineers to optimize technical sales processes and align them with customer needs.

This small, cross-functional team didn't just optimize sales processes—it rebuilt the foundation of revenue operations for the entire business.

Initially, Merrill and his team focused on consolidating the ten Salesforce instances into a more centralized system. This was no small feat. Merging multiple CRM instances meant aligning disparate data sources, standardizing sales processes, and ensuring seamless integration across marketing and customer care. This integration created one source of truth for revenue data, improving forecasting accuracy, sales efficiency, and executive decision-making.

But this wasn't just a technology project—it was a business transformation initiative. The company's shift from a point solution to a subscription-based model required an entirely new approach to sales and customer engagement. Instead of treating deals as one-time transactions, the focus had to shift toward long-term customer value, retention, and expansion. Merrill's RevOps team played a crucial role in redefining sales motions, optimizing renewal processes, and aligning incentives to support this new revenue model.

Over time, this team grew in scope and influence, eventually running all revenue operations across sales, marketing, and customer care. They also handled the organization's revenue planning process, ensuring predictable and scalable growth. Finally, they managed renewal operations, solidifying the company's transition to a subscription-based business.

By embedding RevOps deeply into the organization's Go-to-Market strategy, Merrill's RevOps team ensured that it was seen not as an administrative function but as a revenue-driving engine that played a central role in business growth. His journey into RevOps was a deliberate move to turn revenue operations into a competitive advantage for the company. Through strategic thinking, cross-functional collaboration, and deep operational expertise, Merrill increased his influence by building a high-impact RevOps function that scaled alongside the company's evolving business model.

There are several specific lessons we can learn from Merrill's approach to building a RevOps team from the ground up:

- *Start Small But Think Big*: Merrill didn't wait for an executive mandate to build RevOps. He identified a critical business need, put together a lean but impactful team, and demonstrated value before scaling up.

- *Integrate Across Functions*: RevOps is not just about sales. By aligning sales, marketing, and customer care, Merrill's team ensured a seamless customer journey and data consistency, essential for transitioning to a subscription model.
- *Prioritize Systems and Scalability:* Tackling Salesforce integration early helped create one source of truth for revenue operations. This avoided operational silos and gave leadership better visibility into revenue performance.
- *Own Revenue Planning:* By managing the organization's revenue planning and renewal strategy, Merrill's RevOps team positioned itself as a business-critical function, not just a support role.

The most impactful RevOps teams don't just support revenue operations; they drive revenue strategy. By embedding RevOps deeply into Go-to-Market strategy and making it a core pillar of revenue planning, leaders can ensure that RevOps is seen as an engine for growth rather than an administrative function.

Merrill's journey also highlights the importance of strategic foresight. The shift from a point solution to a subscription model was a fundamental business transformation, requiring not just new processes, but an entirely new operational mindset. RevOps, when executed effectively, enables an organization to scale, adapt, and thrive in changing market conditions.

For RevOps professionals looking to expand their impact, Merrill's example is clear: Find the critical revenue bottlenecks, build cross-functional alignment, and proactively own revenue strategy. That's how RevOps leaders move from operational execution to strategic business leadership.

Conclusion

Building a successful RevOps team requires strategic hiring, intentional development, and strong leadership. We started with hiring and retaining top RevOps talent, highlighting the need for proactive recruitment, competitive compensation, and a strong employer brand to attract and keep top performers. Retention is just as critical as hiring, with strategies like professional development, collaboration, and recognition ensuring long-term success.

Next, we mapped out the RevOps career path, showing how professionals move from tactical execution to strategic leadership. AI and automation are reshaping the role, and data-driven decision-making and cross-functional influence are essential for career advancement.

Expanding your network and influence is key to securing executive buy-in and elevating RevOps as a strategic function. Leaders who deliver data-driven insights, communicate effectively, and showcase measurable success position themselves as indispensable advisors in their organizations.

Finally, we examined Whitney Merrill's real-world example, demonstrating how a small but strategically structured RevOps team can drive business transformation, not just operational efficiency. His experience underscores that RevOps is not just a support function—it's a revenue engine.

By mastering these principles, RevOps leaders can build teams that scale, adapt, and drive lasting business success. Next, we'll explore how to build a successful revenue engine for the long term.

13

Going the Distance

Building a Successful Revenue Engine for the Long Term

Ryan has a list of multiple businesses that, on paper, should have been incredibly successful. They had great products, loyal customers, and strong initial traction. Yet, despite all of that, they still failed. Why? Their CEOs were so focused on running the businesses from day to day that they never sold the big vision to investors or built an engine that could sustain long-term growth.

Venture capitalists don't invest in companies just because they're solid businesses. They invest because they see a clear path to massive returns. Investors don't care about whether a business will reach $5 million, $10 million, or even $25 million in annual recurring revenue (ARR). They want to know whether it has the potential to become a billion-dollar company or larger.

If a founder only focuses on the big vision, investors will question if there's a realistic plan to achieve it. If they get too caught up in execution, investors will doubt whether the business has enough scale potential to matter. The best leaders, whether they're founders, revenue leaders, or RevOps professionals, know how to balance both.

The statistics on start-up failures tell a clear story:

- Ten percent of start-ups fail in the first year.[162]
- Only two in five start-ups ever become profitable.[163]
- One-third of start-ups break even, while another third continue to lose money.

Ryan's insight applies to more than just fundraising; it's the key to building a revenue engine that lasts. Too many companies build Go-to-Market models optimized for the moment, rather than for long-term adaptability. As a result, their revenue engine works for one stage of growth but collapses when the company reaches its next phase.

Many organizations start with a strong motion that works well in a controlled environment, but as they scale, they fail to adapt to changing market conditions, new customer expectations, and shifting competitive landscapes. Without a clear plan for evolution, what once worked will eventually break. Organizations that are forward thinking, however, are able to adapt to market conditions, anticipate consumer behavior, and take advantage of opportunities as they arise. This perspective is encapsulated in Wayne Gretzky's famous quote: "I skate to where the puck is going to be, not where it has been."

"Understanding how your customers buy, understanding what your sales process is has to be documented first before you can delve into service," Dennis Dube, VP of Revenue Operations, said.[164] "So now that I understand how a customer buys my product or service, where are the areas that make sense for me to capture their feedback? As much or more than anything, going back to those three elements of the survey: fatigue, connection, intention, I think you have to make sure that your organization is ready to do something with it. Because if you ask for feedback and don't do anything with it, it damages your brand far more than never asking for feedback in the first place."

Building a revenue engine that works next year, five years from now, and beyond requires more than just a great initial strategy. It requires a system for continuous improvement, cross-functional alignment, and structured agility.

Mike Rizzo, a GTM advisor, founder, and CEO of marketingops. com, describes building RevOps with revenue-centric functionality and focus like this: "You work with structural product engineers that know the makeup of how to put something together concretely, and you hire developers who understand the art of the possible, who work with project managers to figure out what to build. You have a vision, and you need support to execute that product. You hire these people for their expertise," Mike said.

"The same is true for your Go-to-Market technology. You need somebody who knows the art of the possible, and you need someone with the ideas to translate business needs and your GTM aspirations into actionable technology and execution."

This chapter focuses on how to build a truly sustainable revenue engine over the long term—a future-proofed solution that is poised to keep winning in the next phase of growth, the next economic cycle, and the next shift in buyer behavior. First, we'll explore the continuous improvement cycle that ensures your revenue engine never stops evolving. You'll learn how to implement a feedback-action loop that allows your revenue teams to make ongoing, data-driven adjustments—instead of waiting for a major overhaul when something breaks. Next, we'll dive into creating cross-departmental feedback loops.

From there, we'll shift into agility—specifically, how to adjust your revenue engine without causing chaos. We'll also discuss how to adapt to change without disrupting the business. This includes strategies for recognizing early warning signs, making controlled strategic pivots, and ensuring that small experiments don't throw off revenue operations. Finally, we'll examine when and how to evaluate and evolve your tech stack, make strategic tech investments, and ensure your tools support—not dictate—your revenue strategy. By the end of this chapter, you'll have a framework for continuous revenue evolution—one that allows your business to scale, adapt, and thrive long after the initial strategy is set in place.

The Continuous Improvement Cycle: The Kaizen Philosophy

A durable RevOps function thrives on continuous optimization, not one-time fixes. This philosophy is deeply rooted in the concept of continuous improvement, a cornerstone of successful organizations worldwide. Continuous improvement in RevOps focuses on refining processes, enhancing collaboration, and optimizing strategies to drive revenue growth.

It includes fostering a culture where every team member is empowered to identify inefficiencies and contribute to solutions, ensuring the organization remains agile and responsive to market dynamics. Let's dive deeper into how you can achieve continuous improvement.

The term "Kaizen" (改善) is a business philosophy that originates from Japan, combining "kai" (改) meaning "change" and "zen" (善) meaning "good," thus translating to "change for the better" or "continuous improvement."[165] This philosophy emphasizes that small, incremental changes can lead to significant improvements over time.

This mindset has been embraced by organizations worldwide, with Toyota being one of the most well-known adopters. Kaizen is woven into Toyota's core values, guiding its production system by empowering employees to identify inefficiencies and propose solutions.[166] This commitment to continuous improvement has helped Toyota maintain its reputation for quality and operational excellence.

Masaaki Imai, founder of the Kaizen Institute, identified several key principles that businesses must follow in order to achieve Kaizen[167]:

1. Know your customer.
2. Optimize processes for continuous workflow.
3. Observe challenges firsthand.
4. Empower active participation of all team members.
5. Be transparent with communication.

While these principles can help Toyota become the top producer of cars worldwide by sales volume, they are equally valuable in RevOps, where efficiency, collaboration, and continuous improvement drive sustainable revenue growth.[168]

Know your customer. In RevOps, knowing your customer means ensuring that every revenue team—Sales, Marketing, and Customer Success—is aligned around a clear, data-driven understanding of the ideal customer profile (ICP). Many organizations make the mistake of defining their ICP once and never revisiting it, but customer behavior, market dynamics, and competitive landscapes are constantly evolving.

RevOps teams should continuously refine their customer insights, analyze conversion trends, and adjust targeting strategies to reflect real-time data. This proactive approach not only improves lead quality but also ensures that marketing campaigns, sales efforts, and customer success initiatives are all tailored to attract and retain high-value customers.

Optimize processes for continuous workflow. Another key principle, optimizing processes for continuous workflow, is at the heart of RevOps. Even though you may not be making tweaks to a factory line to speed up production, RevOps leaders must ensure that their revenue engine operates smoothly, without unnecessary friction.

This means automating repetitive tasks, refining lead routing to avoid bottlenecks, and ensuring that data flows seamlessly across CRM, marketing automation, and sales engagement platforms. A continuous workflow allows revenue teams to focus on high-impact activities—such as selling, engaging customers, and closing deals— rather than wasting time on manual processes or outdated systems.

"As SaaS and other software solutions have evolved, we now have a generation of RevOps professionals in the workforce who are very tech-savvy," said Keith Lutz, Tech Executive. "They have a deep understanding of their business processes, markets, and customers. In many ways, they are technologists themselves. Whether it's someone just entering the RevOps field or a veteran with a decade of experience, they have become incredibly tech-savvy and possess an in-depth knowledge of their industry and tech stack."

Observe challenges firsthand. Many revenue teams operate based on assumptions rather than direct observation, leading to misaligned strategies and wasted effort. A RevOps team that follows the Kaizen methodology doesn't just rely on static reports or gut instinct. They embed themselves in the process, listening to sales calls, reviewing customer interactions, and analyzing churn trends to understand where breakdowns occur.

By consistently monitoring key revenue metrics and conducting win/loss analyses, RevOps leaders can identify inefficiencies and make targeted improvements before they become major roadblocks.

Empower active participation of all team members. A defining feature of Kaizen is its inclusive approach to innovation—any employee, at any level, can propose and implement improvements.

The philosophy is rooted in the belief that everyone plays a role in the company's success and should be actively engaged in making the business better, every day.

Too often, RevOps is seen as a back-office function that dictates processes rather than an active, collaborative force that engages with frontline teams. Every team member—from SDRs to sales executives to customer success managers—should have a voice in improving processes.

"In a company, we all understand each other's roles, but in the spirit of collaboration, we shouldn't operate within a rigid chain of command. Instead, we foster a collaborative and open environment where everyone is encouraged to contribute to any conversation or discussion, regardless of their position," Keith explained.

Quarterly revenue retrospectives, open feedback loops, and structured RevOps workshops allow employees to share insights on what's working and what's not. When frontline teams are empowered to contribute to process improvements, they take greater ownership of their roles, leading to higher engagement, better execution, and a more adaptable revenue engine.

Be transparent with communication. Finally, transparency in communication is what enables all of these improvements to take root. RevOps functions as the central hub that connects data, strategy, and execution across the organization.

Without clear, real-time communication, insights remain siloed, and teams struggle to adapt quickly. The Kaizen approach to transparency in RevOps means creating shared dashboards that provide visibility into performance metrics, hosting cross-functional revenue meetings where blockers and opportunities are openly discussed, and ensuring that changes to GTM strategies are well-documented and widely understood. When communication is open and proactive, teams can quickly align around new strategies and execute with confidence.

By integrating these Kaizen principles, RevOps leaders can create a self-improving revenue engine—one that continuously refines itself, scales efficiently, and adapts to shifting business conditions.

Creating Cross-Departmental Feedback Loops

Creating cross-departmental feedback loops is essential for continuous improvement. The following are key strategies for fostering the feedback mechanisms necessary to enhance efficiency, drive innovation, and achieve sustainable revenue growth.

For Michael McKinnon, an expert in data analytics and CRM, cross-training among teams with a focus on building a specialized knowledge base is an effective way to ensure seamless, collaborative operations and prepares the company for revenue growth.

"That's the great thing about having RevOps is because you really have to understand both sales and marketing," McKinnon said, during an episode of the *CMO Huddles Hub* podcast.[169] "If I lose my marketing person, I work with the CMO to hire another marketing person that understands marketing tech, and they're part of that. And if I lose my SalesOps person, I'll work with the sales leaders to hire that specific school of sales. They are all called revenue operations and analytics, but they do have specialties within that group."

Break Down Silos. The silo mentality in business, where departments operate in isolation, can significantly hinder long-term revenue growth. When sales, marketing, customer success, and finance teams function independently, it leads to misaligned strategies, redundant efforts, and missed opportunities. For instance, marketing might launch campaigns without consulting sales, leading to leads that don't align with sales strategies. Similarly, customer success may not communicate client feedback to product development, resulting in missed opportunities for product enhancements.

A study published by the *Harvard Business Review* found that companies that foster cross-departmental collaboration experience higher customer loyalty and improved profit margins compared to those operating in silos.[170] Additionally, sales professionals who proactively collaborated across departments—despite their organization's existing silos—demonstrated higher learning agility and greater sales performance, outperforming those who operated independently.

Here are research-backed steps identified by the *Harvard Business Review* for dismantling silos at your organization[171]:

1. Hire and develop employees that excel at collaboration between teams to bridge departments.
2. Encourage employees to ask questions and reach across the departmental aisles.
3. Help employees see different perspectives from different departments.
4. Broaden your employees' vision by bringing diverse groups together and urging team members to explore distant networks.

Additionally, aligning incentives across teams ensures that all teams are motivated to work together. For instance, integrating performance-based bonuses that reflect the success of collaborative efforts can drive teams to align their strategies and work cohesively. According to a survey by revenue-management consulting firm Alexander Group, 28 percent of over three hundred companies reported integrating incentive-based pay structures into newly created roles.[172]

Build a Culture That Proactively Solicits Feedback. Establishing a culture where feedback is actively sought and utilized is vital for continuous improvement. The adage "what gets measured gets improved" holds true. Regular interdepartmental meetings provide a platform for teams to share insights, discuss challenges, and align strategies. For example, scheduling biweekly check-ins between sales and marketing can ensure that both teams are synchronized in their efforts. In fact, 87 percent of sales and marketing leaders agree that collaboration between their two departments promotes critical business growth.[173] Additionally, utilizing shared dashboards and collaborative tools allows for real-time data sharing and transparency. When all teams have access to the same information, it facilitates informed decision-making and fosters trust.

Review Progress in Regular Check-Ins. Instituting regular revenue review sessions enables teams to reflect on their performance, identify successes, and pinpoint areas needing improvement. These sessions encourage open dialogue and collective problem-solving. In Ryan's company, he conducts weekly Open Management Meetings with the entire company to review revenue targets and progress toward them. This practice ensures that all team members are aligned with the company's objectives and are aware of their contributions to overarching goals.

Structured financial review meetings have been shown to significantly impact organizational performance. According to Milestone Inc., companies that hold monthly financial review meetings benefit from better KPI management, improved team alignment, and more informed decision-making. These meetings provide a framework for reviewing financial results compared to operating plans, identifying issues, and developing action plans to move the business forward.

Likewise, conducting postmortems on unsuccessful initiatives offers invaluable insights. By analyzing lost deals, churned customers, or failed marketing campaigns, teams can understand what went wrong and how to prevent similar issues in the future.[174] This reflective process is crucial for continuous improvement and organizational learning. The insights gleaned from a postmortem can then be applied to update processes, staffing, tools, and infrastructure.

For example, if a customer churns due to unmet expectations, a postmortem involving customer success, sales, and product development teams can uncover gaps in communication or product features, leading to actionable improvements.

How to Create Stability with Room for Agility

A successful revenue engine isn't just about consistency and predictability—it must also be flexible enough to adapt to changing market conditions without causing operational chaos. A comprehensive survey by McKinsey & Company, involving over two thousand global respondents, revealed that organizations undergoing highly successful agile transformations experienced approximately 30 percent improvements in efficiency, customer satisfaction, employee engagement, and operational performance.[175] These organizations also became five to ten times faster and significantly enhanced their innovation capabilities. Notably, companies that achieved such transformations were three times more likely to become top-quartile performers among their peers.

Too often, businesses either over-index on stability, becoming rigid and unable to pivot when necessary, or embrace agility so much that they lose structure, leading to inefficiency and confusion. The key to sustainable revenue growth is finding the right balance between stability and agility, ensuring core revenue operations remain strong while allowing room for innovation and strategic pivots.

The Risks of Overreliance on Stability or Agility. When stability is prioritized at the expense of agility, companies become slow to respond to market shifts, emerging competitors, or changes in buyer behavior. This is in part why 88 percent of Fortune 500 companies from 1955 no longer exist today—they failed to evolve with their industries.

On the other hand, too much agility without foundational stability leads to unpredictable execution, lack of alignment across departments, and inefficient use of resources. Companies that pivot too frequently often experience declining employee morale, higher churn rates, and poor financial forecasting due to a lack of strategic continuity. The goal is to blend structure with adaptability—a model that allows businesses to remain resilient in uncertain environments while still being responsive to opportunities and threats.

A Three-Layer Model for GTM Stability and Agility. To create a revenue engine that can scale while remaining adaptable, companies should implement a three-layer Go-to-Market framework like this one from McKinsey & Company that balances structure and flexibility[176]:

1. *Core Operations (Stable Backbone):* This foundational layer encompasses essential processes, governance structures, and technologies that ensure consistency and reliability. Maintaining a stable backbone allows organizations to support dynamic teams effectively.

2. *Adaptive Processes (Dynamic Capabilities):* Building upon the stable core, this layer introduces flexible processes that can be adjusted in response to market shifts. Agile organizations often operate as networks of high-performing teams, each focused on specific business-oriented outcomes.

3. *Innovative Initiatives (Experimental Edge):* The outermost layer encourages experimentation and innovation. By fostering a culture that supports testing new ideas and learning from failures, organizations can stay ahead of industry disruptions.

Spark, a leading telecom operator in New Zealand, exemplifies the successful application of this balanced approach.[177] In 2018, Spark initiated an agile transformation to enhance customer centricity, employee engagement, and operational efficiency. By restructuring into a network of cross-functional teams supported by a stable backbone, Spark achieved a 30–40 percent reduction in customer complaints, attained a market-leading net promoter score (NPS), and accelerated the launch of new services. This transformation not only increased market share but also positioned Spark as a digital services provider rather than a traditional telecom company.

The most successful revenue engines aren't just well-structured—they're adaptable. By implementing a three-layer approach to revenue operations, companies can maintain a strong foundation while leaving room for innovation and strategic shifts. This ensures that they don't just survive market changes but thrive in them.

A rigid Go-to-Market strategy is a liability in today's fast-changing economy, while an overly fluid approach leads to inconsistency and inefficiency. The key to long-term success lies in building a revenue engine that is both durable and dynamic, balancing stability with agility at every stage of growth.

How to Adapt to Changing Marketplace Conditions

Organizations often grapple with the challenge of adapting to market shifts without disrupting their core operations. A significant number of companies find it difficult to respond swiftly to these changes, leading to potential declines in performance and competitiveness. A study highlighted that a staggering 90 percent of organizations struggle to adapt quickly to market changes, with only a fraction (10%) claiming effective responsiveness within their operations.

This lack of strategic agility can be attributed to several factors:

- *Inertia Due to Success:* Companies that have historically been successful may develop rigid processes and mindsets, making them resistant to change. This phenomenon, known as the Icarus Paradox in the *Harvard Business Review*, suggests that a company's greatest strengths can become its weaknesses when market conditions evolve.[178]
- *Overconfidence and Complacency:* Success can breed overconfidence, leading companies to underestimate emerging competitors or shifts in consumer behavior. This complacency can result in a failure to innovate or adapt strategies accordingly.

The Three-Step Model for Navigating Change in RevOps. To effectively manage change without disrupting business operations, organizations should consider implementing the following three-step model:

1. *Identifying Early Warning Signs*
   - Regularly monitor industry reports, consumer behavior analyses, and economic indicators to anticipate shifts. For instance, the rise of electric vehicles (EVs) has significantly impacted traditional automotive markets, compelling companies to adapt or risk obsolescence.[179]
   - Keep a close eye on competitors' moves, such as new product launches, pricing strategies, or technological advancements. Failure to do so can result in missed opportunities or threats going unnoticed.

- Community-led digital groups are emerging as a powerful real-time barometer for companies to track shifting market conditions. These online communities—whether on LinkedIn, Slack, Reddit, or industry-specific forums—serve as organic hubs where customers, partners, and industry experts actively discuss trends, challenges, and emerging needs.

Unlike traditional market research, which can be slow and expensive, Jared Robin, cofounder of RevGenius, points out that these digital conversations offer immediate, unfiltered insights that reflect evolving buyer sentiment and competitive shifts.[180]

"The difference in the nuance between community-led and audience-led is that audience-led is more a demand movement. It doesn't mean your audience, followers, and subscribers can't talk to each other. But, it's a centralized spot for creating content in many formats, webinars, or podcasts to attract your ICP to listen and partake," Jared said in the interview with Amy. Companies that engage with and analyze these groups can spot early signals of change, refine their messaging, and adapt their Go-to-Market strategies with agility.

2. *Controlled Experimentation*
   - Before a full-scale rollout, test new strategies or products in controlled environments. This approach allows for the assessment of potential impacts without jeopardizing existing revenue streams.
   - Implement processes that gather feedback from these tests to refine and improve strategies

continually. Agile methodologies, which emphasize iterative development and responsiveness, can be particularly effective in this context.

3. *Scaling Validated Changes*
    *   Utilize data from controlled experiments to inform broader implementation. This ensures that changes are based on evidence rather than assumptions.
    *   Introduce validated changes incrementally to allow the organization and its customers to adjust smoothly, minimizing potential disruptions.

Building a Foundation with Technology:
Software-Defined Operations in RevOps

Technology serves as the cornerstone for aligning strategic intent with operational execution. A software-defined operations framework enables organizations to bridge the gap between planning and execution, ensuring that strategic shifts are immediately reflected in day-to-day operations.

Software-defined operations take inspiration from DevOps principles, where infrastructure is managed programmatically through software-defined networks (SDN) and software-defined data centers (SDDC). Applying this approach to RevOps allows companies to automate and enforce policies that govern data quality, sales execution, compliance, and customer interactions. Instead of relying on manual updates and reactive adjustments, organizations can define their operational intent in the form of policies that execute automatically through APIs and integrations.

The ability to react to market conditions in real time is the difference between a well-run, competitive organization and one that struggles with inefficiency and misalignment. A software-defined approach ensures that RevOps teams no longer rely on ad hoc processes, IT bottlenecks, or inconsistent execution—instead, policies can be set, monitored, and enforced with minimal human intervention.

What Is a Policy in RevOps? A policy in RevOps is a deliberate set of principles that guide decision-making and ensure consistency across the organization. Policies act as a governance mechanism that connects strategy with execution, preventing revenue teams from operating in silos or making misaligned decisions.

Policies function in three ways:

1. *Policy Setting:* Defining the strategic intent and establishing operational procedures.
2. *Policy Control:* Evaluating performance against defined policies and identifying areas for improvement.
3. *Policy Action:* Taking automated or manual corrective actions based on policy evaluations.

By shifting from reactive operations to policy-driven execution, organizations gain repeatability, risk reduction, and greater alignment between revenue teams.

In RevOps, software-defined policies provide structure and consistency in areas that typically suffer from inefficiencies, data silos, and manual interventions. The most critical policy areas include:

- *Data Policies:* Ensure CRM data is accurate, valid, reliable, timely, and complete to prevent bad data from undermining decision-making.
- *Customer Interaction Life Cycle Policies:* Define the stages of customer engagement, including campaigns, leads, opportunities, contracts, and renewals, ensuring clean data handoffs at every stage.

- *Sales Resource Life Cycle Policies:* Automate responses to sales rep departures, role transitions, and account assignments, preventing deals from being lost due to personnel changes.
- *Compliance Policies:* Enforce regulations such as GDPR, ASC 606, and trade restrictions to ensure legal and financial integrity.
- *Coverage Policies:* Manage territory assignments, lead routing, and account ownership through automated rules that dynamically adjust to changes in the Go-to-Market model.

By integrating these policies into a software-defined framework, companies eliminate manual decision-making bottlenecks and ensure revenue operations run smoothly at scale.

How Technology Enables Policy. To operationalize policies effectively, a software-defined RevOps platform must include:

- *Policy Definition Tools:* These allow revenue leaders to create machine-readable policies that define how the business should operate.
- *Policy Evaluation Engines:* These continuously monitor data and operations, identifying compliance gaps, inefficiencies, or misaligned execution.
- *Policy Action Engines:* These trigger automated workflows or alerts, ensuring that non-compliance issues are corrected without manual intervention.

For example, if a company updates its territory design in the Go-to-Market strategy, a software-defined system would automatically adjust CRM assignments, sales quotas, and commission structures—without waiting for IT teams, data uploads, or manual changes.

This level of automation ensures that changes to the business strategy are immediately reflected in execution, creating a real-time alignment between leadership and revenue teams.

The Future of RevOps Is Automated. A software-defined RevOps model is the next evolution in revenue operations, providing organizations with the ability to execute strategies with precision and scale operations efficiently. In an era where real-time adaptability determines market leadership, companies that embrace policy-driven automation will outperform competitors that rely on outdated, manual processes.

By shifting to a policy-based, software-defined RevOps framework, organizations can ensure that every aspect of revenue operations—from data management to sales execution to compliance—operates with consistency, efficiency, and agility.

Evolving the Tech Stack for the RevOps Engine

In RevOps, each tool and system in the revenue engine needs to align with strategic objectives and deliver tangible value. However, the average organization has at least ten information management systems.[181] It's not surprising that 56 percent of RevOps leaders view tool consolidation as a priority.[182]

The allure of the latest technology trends can lead organizations into the trap of "shiny object syndrome," where investments are made in new tools without a clear understanding of their applicability or ROI.

Recognizing When to Evaluate Your Tech Stack. Regular assessment of your technology stack is essential to ensure it continues to meet the organization's needs. Key indicators that it may be time to evaluate and potentially update your tech stack include:

- *Performance Bottlenecks:* Frequent system crashes, slow response times, or unexplained slowdowns can indicate that your current technology is struggling to handle operational demands.[183]
- *Scalability Issues:* As your business grows, your technology should seamlessly scale to accommodate increased workloads. If your systems are unable to handle higher volumes without compromising performance, it may be time for an upgrade.
- *Integration Challenges:* Difficulty in integrating new tools or systems with your existing technology can lead to data silos and inefficiencies, hindering overall productivity.

Evaluating and Implementing New Technology. To maintain an effective tech stack, it's advisable to establish a regular review cadence. Depending on the complexity and scale of your operations, conducting tech stack evaluations annually or biannually can help identify areas for improvement and ensure alignment with evolving business objectives. Additionally, trigger-based reviews should be conducted in response to significant organizational changes, such as mergers, market expansions, or shifts in strategic direction.

When considering the adoption of new technology, it's crucial to conduct a thorough evaluation to ensure it complements existing RevOps processes without causing disruption. This involves assessing the tool's scalability, integration capabilities, user-friendliness, and support infrastructure. Engaging stakeholders from various departments during the evaluation process can provide diverse perspectives and help identify early challenges early on.

When to Adopt a RevOps Platform. You may be just starting to build your RevOps tech stack or you may have already accumulated multiple point tools. In either case, when is it time to adopt a RevOps or Territory Management platform? We are not advising that you eliminate point tools completely. In some cases a best-of-breed solution can help you meet your goals better than what is offered in a platform. To determine what will drive your team's efficiency, here are some considerations.

The first step to choosing your tech stack is to map out your end-to-end lead-to-renewal process, from the first moment a lead enters your CRM to the renewal and upsell motions. Your RevOps tech stack should support the complexity of your GTM strategy as seamlessly as possible.

Your CRM is the foundation of your tech stack, but for RevOps efficiency your technology also needs to support crucial GTM planning (territory, quota, and capacity planning) and operations activities (lead routing, data hygiene, forecasting, and incentive compensation.)

Once you have your process mapped, do a deep dive assessment with your team or observe their work in action. The results will give you a good indication of whether your tech stack is hindering efficiency. If so, it may be time to consolidate these functions to a RevOps or Territory Management platform. Here are some important questions to consider:

- How well does your technology handle important GTM workflows?
- Are there gaps or breakdowns that take time and resources to address?
- Are you able to react with agility when GTM resources or strategies change mid-cycle?
- Is your plan often out of sync with execution? For example, if your territories change midyear due to a reorganization, are you able to quickly adapt routing, quotas and compensation issues?

- How well does each technology integrate with your CRM?
- Are you constantly importing and exporting data into spreadsheets?
- Are there potential version control issues?
- Are there any feature redundancies in the tools in your stack?
- Are there additional capabilities that you are paying for but not using?
- Does your team often question which tool provides the best source of truth?
- Can any tools be removed without impacting the buyer's journey or adding more time-consuming tasks to your team?
- Are any tools being used by different revenue functions in silos with little visibility to others?

Companies that maximize efficiency and business agility will win the next business cycle. If your team is bogged down updating systems and code, consolidating your tech stack will create efficiencies that benefit your organization and your customers.

While technology is a critical component of successful RevOps, it's imperative to approach tech investments strategically. By regularly evaluating your tech stack, aligning tools with business objectives, and avoiding unnecessary complexity, your organization can leverage technology to drive sustainable growth and operational excellence.

The RevOps Operating System

Building a revenue engine that stands the test of time requires more than just a solid initial strategy—it demands a system designed for continuous improvement, alignment, and adaptability. As organizations scale, they must navigate increasing complexity in customer journeys, digital engagement channels, and data-driven decision-making. This is where the FACTOR Framework becomes essential.

Just as a company wouldn't rely on outdated financial systems to manage its balance sheet, it can't afford to operate its revenue engine on disconnected tools, spreadsheets, and ad hoc processes. The modern revenue engine needs a cohesive, data-driven system that integrates planning, execution, and optimization into a single operational model.

In the past, revenue growth was largely driven by traditional sales and marketing tactics—field sales reps meeting customers in person, marketing campaigns focused on broad-based brand awareness, and predictable sales cycles driven by human interaction. But today, buyer behavior has fundamentally changed.

Customers increasingly prefer self-directed digital buying experiences, where they research solutions, engage with content, and make purchasing decisions online—often before ever speaking to a sales rep. This shift has forced businesses to reallocate growth resources, prioritizing owned digital channels, data-driven engagement, and automation over traditional sales and marketing methods.

According to research from the Wharton School of Business, this evolution has transformed Go-to-Market strategies in 97 percent of organizations.[184] Companies now invest more in commercial technology, automation, and customer data platforms than in traditional sales and marketing expenses. In fact, digital selling infrastructure and data have become some of the most valuable financial assets on a company's balance sheet—sometimes even more valuable than the products themselves.

This shift has also increased cost and complexity. According to numbers from the Revenue Enablement Institute, the average organization now uses over twenty different digital marketing, sales, and service channels to engage customers, requiring sophisticated orchestration.[185] Additionally, companies are spending more than ever on enabling frontline revenue teams with technology, often exceeding $10,000 per sales rep per year on tools, automation, and AI-powered insights.

Despite these investments, many companies still struggle to drive consistent, scalable revenue growth. The reason? They lack a centralized, structured system for managing their revenue engine effectively.

A GTM Operating System provides the missing framework for sustainable growth. Just like an operating system in a computer, it acts as the foundation that integrates and orchestrates all the moving parts of revenue operations (people, processes, data, and technology) into a cohesive, high-performing system.

A well-designed GTM OS:

- *Aligns Teams and Strategy:* Breaks down silos between Sales, Marketing, Customer Success, and Finance, ensuring all revenue functions work toward common goals.
- *Automates Revenue Processes:* Eliminates manual inefficiencies in territory planning, lead routing, forecasting, and compensation management.
- *Optimizes Data and Insights:* Ensures accurate, real-time visibility into performance metrics and revenue-driving activities.
- *Enables Agility and Scalability:* Allows businesses to adapt quickly to market changes without disrupting execution.

With a GTM OS in place, revenue teams no longer operate in silos— instead, they function as a unified growth engine, where data flows seamlessly, processes are automated, and strategic decisions are made based on real-time insights rather than gut instinct. The businesses that thrive in the next decade will be the ones that treat revenue growth as a system, not a series of disconnected tactics. In the same way that finance, supply chain, and IT functions have evolved into structured, technology-enabled disciplines, RevOps must become a data-driven, technology-powered system that enables sustained growth.

A GTM Operating System is essential for future-proofing revenue operations. It provides the structure, automation, and intelligence needed to navigate complexity, optimize performance, and scale efficiently. By streamlining processes and eliminating inefficiencies, a GTM OS ensures that companies can adapt to change without losing momentum.

When paired with the FACTOR Framework, a structured blueprint for organizing efforts, prioritizing time, and laying the foundation for long-term success, it becomes even more powerful. The FACTOR Framework brings clarity to execution, helping teams focus on what drives real impact rather than getting lost in day-to-day operational chaos.

As companies evolve, the real question isn't whether they need a GTM OS but how quickly they can implement one to stay ahead in a rapidly changing market. Businesses that delay risk falling behind as competitors leverage automation and data-driven decision-making to accelerate growth.

Case Study: Using Sales-Stage Conversion Data to Drive Incremental Change and Double-Digit Gains

When it comes to making meaningful improvements in revenue operations, it's often less about sweeping change and more about smart, focused problem-solving, coupled with process realignment and sales enablement.

Katerina Ostrovsky, a seasoned RevOps leader, shared a powerful example of how key metrics analysis and cross-functional collaboration can unlock significant performance gains.[186] While leading a global RevOps team, Katerina noticed a sharp drop in conversion rates at the negotiation stage of the sales funnel. Rather than assuming the issue stemmed from sales performance, she and her team took a data-informed approach to diagnose the root cause.

By analyzing sales stage conversion data and reviewing hundreds of customer conversations (aided by AI), Katerina uncovered a consistent pattern of confusion, hesitation, and dissatisfaction late in the sales process. The problem wasn't poor negotiation skills, it was the result of misalignment and unresolved concerns that had built up earlier in the buyer journey.

Katerina then partnered with legal, finance, and marketing to restructure the early-stage sales process, ensuring that key concerns were addressed proactively. The goal wasn't to overhaul everything overnight, but to surface friction points earlier, equip reps to address objections more effectively, and build trust and clarity throughout the customer journey.

The result? A double-digit improvement in conversion rates at the negotiation stage! Without retraining the entire sales team or reworking pricing.

"When we really listened and dug into what was behind the drop in conversion, we realized it wasn't about negotiation skills . . . it was about when and how we were handling key prospect objections," Katerina explained. "Once we re-aligned the process and messaging earlier in the journey, the friction at the end disappeared."

The outcome: improved win rates and happier customers: a win-win.

Conclusion

A successful revenue engine is never static. It is a system that evolves over time, continuously improving, adapting to market shifts, and aligning teams around a shared vision. This chapter has explored the key elements required to build a revenue engine that not only drives short-term success but also sustains growth for years to come.

At the core of long-term revenue success is continuous improvement. Companies that treat revenue operations as a fixed structure quickly find themselves outdated. Instead, businesses must embrace the philosophy of Kaizen—making small, ongoing refinements that compound into significant advantages. Organizations that prioritize optimization, efficiency, and collaboration position themselves for long-term stability and scalability.

A critical component of sustainability is cross-functional collaboration. Siloed teams are one of the biggest obstacles to sustained revenue growth. By creating feedback loops across Sales, Marketing, Customer Success, and Finance, companies ensure that decisions are data-driven and aligned with broader business objectives. Regular revenue retrospectives, postmortems on lost deals, and shared performance metrics create a culture of transparency and adaptability, where teams work together to refine strategies in real time.

Agility is another cornerstone of a resilient revenue engine—but agility must be structured, not chaotic. Companies that overcorrect or pivot too frequently often create instability, while those that fail to adapt risk being left behind. A balanced approach, with a stable operational foundation complemented by the flexibility to experiment, allows businesses to make strategic adjustments without disrupting revenue streams. This structured adaptability ensures that the company remains competitive in an ever-changing market.

Technology plays a vital role in supporting, rather than dictating, revenue strategy. Many companies fall into the trap of shiny object syndrome, investing in tools that overcomplicate workflows rather than streamline them. A software-defined approach to RevOps ensures that technology enables efficient execution, aligns with business needs, and prevents tech bloat. By continuously evaluating and refining the tech stack, companies can improve efficiency while maintaining a scalable, cost-effective infrastructure.

Ultimately, a long-lasting revenue engine is one that evolves with the business. Companies that embrace continuous improvement, foster collaboration, balance stability with agility, and use technology strategically will outperform those that remain rigid or reactive. The key to success is not just having a great Go-to-Market strategy today—it's building a system that can scale, adapt, and thrive through every phase of growth, every market shift, and every economic cycle.

14

Speed Bumps and Potholes

Navigating Common Challenges

Knowing the principles of RevOps is crucial, but it is only half the battle. The real test of RevOps mastery comes when things don't go as planned. Market conditions shift, competitors evolve, and internal dynamics change.

"It's not an easy time to be a sales leader," wrote Anjai "AJ" Gandhi, Cofounder of the Go To Market Leader Society and Chief Growth Officer at Marlin Equity Partners, in a LinkedIn post. "(1) Growth expectations are high, (2) budgets are tight, (3) buyers are conservative, (4) AI disruption is a pro and a con and (5) macroeconomics and geo-politics are challenging."

The companies that succeed aren't necessarily the ones with the best initial strategy—they're the ones that adjust fastest when things don't go as planned. Few businesses have faced a challenge as sudden and existential as Airbnb did in early 2020.

At the start of the year, Airbnb was riding high. The company had revolutionized the travel industry, offering people an alternative to traditional hotels, and demand was soaring. Millions of travelers around the world were booking short-term stays, and the company was gearing up for one of the most anticipated IPOs in years. But then, within a matter of weeks, everything changed. The COVID-19 pandemic brought travel to a grinding halt. Countries closed their borders, cities went into lockdown, and nearly overnight, Airbnb's core business model collapsed.

Revenue plummeted by 72 percent.[187] The company lost more than a billion dollars in canceled reservations, and hosts who relied on Airbnb for income found themselves without guests or revenue. Faced with an immediate crisis, Airbnb had to make tough decisions. The company laid off nearly 25 percent of its workforce, cut nonessential programs, and shelved major expansion plans.[188] At that moment, many assumed Airbnb wouldn't survive. With travel demand wiped out, the company had no clear path forward.

But instead of waiting for travel to return, Airbnb rapidly and decisively pivoted its Go-to-Market strategy.

The company recognized that with offices closed indefinitely, remote work was becoming a long-term reality, and people were no longer tied to a single location. Some were looking for temporary places to stay while escaping crowded cities, while others were embracing the flexibility of working from anywhere. Thus, Airbnb shifted its focus from short-term travel to long-term stays.[189]

The platform was quickly adjusted to highlight extended bookings, and new features were added to cater to remote workers looking for comfortable, well-equipped spaces. Messaging changed as well. Instead of emphasizing vacations and weekend getaways, Airbnb's marketing team pivoted to promote the idea of "living anywhere."[190] At the same time, Airbnb introduced a series of health and safety protocols to reassure both guests and hosts that Airbnb properties were safe to stay in during the pandemic.

This complete transformation of the company's Go-to-Market strategy was the company's response to a long-term business plan that no longer made sense. Airbnb effectively used real-time data to adjust in the moment, ensuring that execution aligned with new realities. By mid-2020, long-term stays of twenty-eight days or more became the fastest-growing segment of the business. While competitors in the hospitality industry were struggling with empty hotels and massive losses, Airbnb had successfully repositioned itself to meet the needs of a new type of traveler. By September 2024, long-term stays accounted for approximately 17 to 18 percent of Airbnb's business, up from 13 to 14 percent before the pandemic.

In December 2020, just months after its near-collapse, Airbnb launched its long-awaited IPO. Investors, recognizing the company's ability to pivot under pressure, responded with overwhelming enthusiasm. Airbnb's stock soared, giving the company a valuation of over $100 billion—higher than Hilton, Marriott, and Hyatt combined. What had looked like a death sentence in March 2020 had turned into a great comeback story.

Airbnb's survival wasn't about luck. It was about navigating a consequential problem with speed and agility. When the company quickly realigned its Go-to-Market execution, without waiting for the next annual planning cycle, it wasn't simply a top-down executive decision; it required realignment across marketing, sales, customer success, and product teams to ensure that messaging, operations, and service delivery all worked in sync.

While the COVID-19 pandemic is certainly not a common problem that we hope businesses will have to face again, this level of adaptability is exactly what modern revenue teams need to master. RevOps exists because businesses can't afford to operate in silos or rely on rigid, long-term plans that don't account for inevitable disruptions. Markets shift. Customers change. Competitors innovate. The companies that win are the ones that integrate their strategy with execution, ensure cross-team alignment, and use data to make fast, informed decisions.

"If we thoughtfully approach challenges as growth opportunities—for ourselves, our teams, and our companies—we can emerge from them not only surviving, but thriving," wrote Laura Hayes, an expert in RevOps, customer support, sales ops, and IT, in a LinkedIn post.[191]

This is the final chapter of The RevOps Advantage, and if you've made it this far, you should already have a solid grasp on RevOps and its power to transform how businesses plan, execute, and scale their Go-to-Market strategy. You should understand why alignment across sales, marketing, and customer success is crucial, how data-driven decision-making fuels growth, and why agility is the key to long-term success.

"It all boils down to communication. Going that extra mile, making sure everyone understands what we're doing, why we're doing it and how it benefits our customers," said Sara Colton, an experienced SVP of Revenue Operations.[192]

In this chapter, we'll explore the most common challenges that RevOps leaders must overcome, from combating resistance to change to breaking down silos to managing data accessibility and scaling operations effectively. We'll also dive into real-world business problems—like mergers and acquisitions, competitive shifts, and market volatility—and discuss how a strong RevOps framework allows companies to navigate these challenges with confidence.

"Some of the best advice I have received is that more often than not, moving forward with small imperfections is better than waiting for every last detail to be perfect," Lauren Zion, VP of Business Operations, said during a LiveIntent interview.[193] "It boils down to the fact that in order to know if you've succeeded or failed, you have to first do something."

Every company will face unexpected disruptions. Will your revenue teams be agile enough to navigate these problems? Let's dive in.

Challenge #1: Unifying the Revenue Team—Sales, Marketing, and Customer Success

Unifying the revenue team is essential for driving consistent growth and delivering a seamless customer experience. In fact, if you take anything from this book, we hope it's recognizing the power of multiple departments working collaboratively to tackle shared revenue goals. When these departments operate in silos, it leads to misalignment, inefficiencies, missed opportunities, inconsistent customer interactions, and ultimately, revenue leakage. According to a study by the Aberdeen Group, companies with strong sales and marketing alignment grow 32 percent faster.[194] Similarly, a report by HubSpot indicates that misalignment between RevOps teams can cost B2B companies 10 percent or more of revenue annually.[195]

"Put your people first and everything else will fall into place: I lead a lean team responsible for delivering a very complex transformation road map; when our projects require us to dig deep, it comes down to the people. We've had each other's backs every step of the way and we truly care about one another's personal and professional wellbeing . . . when you have that, any problem no matter how complex can be solved, together," Nicole Farina, Senior Director, GTM strategy and transformation, said via LinkedIn.[196]

To overcome the perpetual challenge of cross-team unification, it's essential to get everyone working together toward the same goals. First, teams should adopt common terminology and agree on a shared understanding of what constitutes the customer journey. For example, reaching internal agreement on what constitutes a "qualified lead" can prevent discrepancies in how marketing vs. sales manages, tracks, and interacts with this strategically important group.

Second, teams should prioritize creating a unified approach to the customer experience, including delivering consistent messaging and support, no matter which department the customer interacts with.

Third, teams also should adopt a data-driven, team-first mindset, which helps remove personal opinions and personal agendas from the equation and replaces them with shared data and analytics. A data-driven culture depends on all teams having access to the same real-time information and insights.

Challenge #2: Creating a Culture That Embraces Change

Change is inevitable, yet many companies struggle to implement new strategies, systems, and ways of working due to deep-seated resistance. Whether it's skepticism from employees, fear of disrupting existing processes, or simply the comfort of the status quo, overcoming resistance is one of the most critical challenges in driving transformation—especially in RevOps, where alignment across teams is key. Understanding why change is difficult and applying the right strategies can make all the difference between a failed initiative and a seamless evolution.

Understand the Nature of Resistance and Cognitive Inertia. Resistance to change is both a psychological and organizational challenge. On an individual level, employees often prefer familiar routines and fear the uncertainty that comes with change. This phenomenon, known as cognitive inertia, explains why people tend to stick with existing processes even when a better alternative is available.[197]

For Brennan Petar, the meteoric move from sales to RevOps leader to CEO of Papara required a quick, adaptive focus on his existing and expanding skill set.

"It was overwhelming to be honest, because as a seller, you're often given a clear task or direction of how to do something," he admitted on LinkedIn.[198] "As a RevOps leader you have to invent the process and structure for others to follow that same path. I found taking baby steps along the way and then looking back, was the best path for me. Identifying the most pressing problem to solve today, and then continuing to march forward while aligning to the overall strategies, much like scaffolding supports a building as you place one brick at a time."

At the organizational level, businesses develop ingrained workflows and structures that create resistance to new ways of working. These rigid systems can make change feel disruptive rather than innovative.

RevOps initiatives, in particular, often face resistance because they require different teams, each with their own established ways of operating, to align under a unified strategy. Some employees may see RevOps as unnecessary bureaucracy, while others fear it will create more complexity rather than simplify processes.

Most employees react to this type of change by retreating to a "We've always done it this way" mindset, which is often said to be the most dangerous phrase in business.[199] When employees and leaders alike feel that there's no reason to change something because it is already working, it prevents businesses from adapting to new market realities and embracing more efficient ways of working.

Overcome Resistance to Change. To effectively manage and reduce resistance to change, organizations must shift the perception of change from being a threat to being an opportunity. One of the most effective ways to do this is through strategic framing—positioning change as a necessary and beneficial evolution rather than an imposed disruption. Leadership should communicate the positive impact of the change, emphasizing how it will lead to greater efficiency, improved collaboration, and business growth.

When employees see that change isn't just about disruption but about making their jobs easier and more impactful, they are more likely to embrace it.

Aligning leadership buy-in with frontline adoption is also crucial. Many change initiatives fail because leadership is disconnected from the reality of how change impacts day-to-day work. To prevent this, leadership must actively participate in the change process rather than just mandate it. Employees need to see that executives and managers are not only advocating for the new approach but are also involved in making it successful. A Forbes study highlights that companies with strong leadership involvement in change management see much higher adoption rates and long-term success.[200]

Creating a narrative is another powerful tool in overcoming resistance. Instead of presenting change as an abstract concept, leaders should use real-world examples and case studies to show how similar changes have driven success in other organizations. To gain support for change, Gustavo Razzetti in *Forbes* recommends leaders should use narratives to connect employees' work to the company's goals and explain the reasons for change, helping them understand the importance of their role and encouraging their support.[201]

Build a Change-Resilient Organization. Creating a culture where change is not only accepted but actively embraced requires a long-term approach. One of the most effective ways to build a change-resilient organization is to embed adaptability into the company culture. This means fostering an environment where continuous improvement is the norm and employees are encouraged to challenge outdated processes.

Research from Prosci, a change management group, shows organizations that cultivate a mindset of flexibility and experimentation are more likely to thrive in rapidly changing industries.[202]

Continuous learning and upskilling play a crucial role in making employees more comfortable with change. When people feel equipped with the skills and knowledge to navigate new systems and processes, they are far less likely to resist them. A report from Whatfix highlights that lack of training and inadequate communication are two of the biggest reasons employees resist change.[203]

"Continuous learning is critical in RevOps, whether it's Python, SQL, or AI, staying adaptable is what truly drives success," said Matt Volm, CEO and cofounder of RevOps Co-op.

Recognizing and rewarding change agents within the organization can also make a significant impact. Michigan State University found that recognizing change agents helps reinforce a culture of continuous improvement.[204] Employees who champion new initiatives and help others navigate transitions should be acknowledged and incentivized. When organizations celebrate and reward early adopters, they create a ripple effect where more employees feel motivated to embrace change.

Challenge #3: Data Visibility and Access—Who Should Own It, See It, and Have It

Data drives decision-making, aligns teams, and ensures that sales, marketing, and customer success are working from the same playbook. Organizations lose an average of $15 million annually due to poor data quality, according to Gartner research.[205] Managing data effectively is easier said than done. Who owns it? Who should have access to it? How do you balance making data available with keeping it secure?

These questions aren't just theoretical. A lack of visibility leads to bad decisions, misaligned teams, and missed opportunities. On the flip side, too much access without governance can create chaos, inconsistencies, and security risks. Let's break down why data visibility and access is a significant challenge in RevOps—and how companies can get it right.

The Data Dilemma in RevOps. One of the biggest roadblocks to a successful RevOps strategy is fragmented and siloed data. Each department often operates in its own system, with its own reports, and its own version of the data. This creates a nightmare scenario where no one is sure which data is accurate, leading to conflicting numbers and slow decision-making.

Just like silos can bring progress and collaboration to a standstill in RevOps, data silos can do the same thing. Oracle found that data silos make it harder for teams to collaborate and plan effectively, forcing employees to piece together incomplete information.[206] The result is slow deal cycles, misaligned sales and marketing efforts, and lost revenue.

Then there's the balancing act between data accessibility and security. While you want teams to have the information they need to do their jobs, unrestricted access can lead to security risks, data leaks, and compliance issues. A 2019 study from Varonis found that 53 percent of companies have over 1,000 sensitive files open to every employee.[207] This is a massive liability.

And let's not forget the problem of too much (or too little) data. Flooding teams with excessive, unstructured data makes it impossible to extract meaningful insights, while not giving them enough leaves them flying blind. According to Gartner, 91 percent of organizations have trouble using their data effectively, often due to overwhelming complexity or poor governance.[208]

In many organizations, data integrity remains a persistent challenge. With conflicting versions of reality (like marketing math, sales math, and investor math) CROs and CFOs often approach data with skepticism. "No wonder they don't trust the numbers," said Saket Kapoor, a prominent figure in RevOps. "This is where RevOps truly shines. They unify the data. They create that single source of truth that everyone can trust. Instead of debating whether the data is accurate, you can actually use it to make decisions and run the business. That's where I believe RevOps has the most value." So how do you fix these issues? It starts with defining who owns the data and how it's managed.

Who Owns RevOps Data? One of the biggest debates in RevOps is who should own the data. There's no one-size-fits-all answer, but in most organizations, it comes down to three main models:

1. **IT Ownership:** Traditionally, IT has owned data management, ensuring security, compliance, and governance. While this guarantees structure, it often creates bottlenecks, as business teams struggle to access the data they need in real time.

2. **RevOps Ownership:** Increasingly, companies are shifting data ownership to RevOps, since this function sits at the intersection of sales, marketing, and customer success. This approach aligns data management with business goals, ensuring teams get the insights they need without unnecessary roadblocks.

3. **Business Unit Ownership:** Some organizations allow each department to manage its own data. While this provides autonomy, it often reinforces silos and leads to inconsistencies.

According to the Revenue Operations Alliance, high-performing organizations are moving toward a centralized but accessible model, where RevOps owns the data framework, while individual teams have role-based access to the data they need.[209] This approach ensures one source of truth while providing flexibility across teams.

Enable Data-Driven Decision-Making. Having access to data isn't enough—you need a system that makes it usable. That means centralizing data, ensuring teams can access it without bottlenecks, and setting up clear governance so the right people have the right access.

A single source of truth (SSOT) is key. Companies that consolidate their data into one trusted system see massive improvements in efficiency and decision-making. McKinsey Global Institute found that data-driven organizations are nineteen times more likely to be profitable.[210] Additionally, they are twenty-three times more likely to acquire customers and six times more likely to retain them.

While a single source of truth is the standard to aspire to, it's not necessarily feasible to achieve in the real world. Inevitably, different business units will opt to analyze and transform their data using workflows and tools that are disconnected from the single source of truth. Prasad Varahabhatla, Senior Director of GTM Transformation and Master Data Operations at Philips, shared with Amy during a podcast conversation that the solution to overcoming the single-source-of-truth challenge is twofold: First, businesses should expect and demand that once data has been transformed, it gets put back into the data flow. "We have to be pragmatic about it," Prasad says. "Do not lose sight of the fact that even if the process is outside, [the focus needs to be on] how do you get the data that's generated out of the process inside again, and keep the flow going?" Second, businesses should implement controls, including validation rules and other types of guardrails that govern data management practices, Prasad advises.[211]

Another crucial element is role-based access—giving people only the data they need, when they need it. This prevents bottlenecks, reduces security risks, and ensures compliance with regulations like GDPR and CCPA.

Finally, companies need a scalable data framework that grows with them. This means:

- Integrating data across systems, so sales, marketing, and customer success all pull from the same dataset
- Establishing governance policies to keep data clean and accurate
- Conducting regular audits to prevent data drift and ensure ongoing reliability

Without this foundation, RevOps teams end up spending more time chasing down data than using it to drive strategy. When done right, a well-managed data framework will align teams, accelerate growth, and unlock new revenue opportunities without the chaos of fragmented or inaccessible data.

Challenge #4: RevOps at Scale—Adapting Processes as the Company Grows

Scaling a business is one of the most exciting and challenging parts of growth, especially as part of the RevOps team. If you scale too fast, you risk inefficiency, burnout, and costly mistakes. If you scale too slowly, you may miss opportunities and lose ground to competitors. Striking the right balance requires vision, timing, and a disciplined approach to operations.

Ryan knows this journey well. He took Simplus, a company specializing in Salesforce consulting and digital transformation, from a start-up to a globally recognized enterprise, ultimately selling it to Infosys for $250 million. But Simplus's growth wasn't linear and predictable; Ryan found himself constantly needing to adapt RevOps processes to successfully navigate growth and figure out how and when to pivot.

When launching a company, your goal shouldn't be to sell your product or service to every household in America on day one. Instead, you need to find the right pace of growth—one that aligns with your market, resources, and vision. It's important to set a clear, multistep plan for scaling, rather than chasing every opportunity that comes along.

In the early days of Simplus, there were plenty of chances to expand too quickly, but Ryan and his team were disciplined about focusing on the right opportunity—as opposed to just any opportunity. Instead of jumping into multiple service offerings at once, they built a strong reputation in Salesforce Quote-to-Cash (QTC) consulting before expanding into broader digital transformation services. This incremental scaling approach allowed them to build a solid foundation, refine their processes, and grow without overextending.

Timing is everything in business, and a strong vision ensures you recognize the right moments to expand—or exit. Ryan's business partner had built one of the largest wireless internet service providers in the country. After seventeen years of growth, he had a chance to sell the company at one of the highest multiples in the industry. He knew the business inside and out—he could climb a transmission tower to fix an outage just as easily as he could analyze the competitive landscape. But he also understood the law of diminishing returns. He recognized that while the company had seen rapid growth, it was reaching a plateau. Rather than holding on out of emotional attachment, he sold at the right moment, locking in maximum value.

Ryan applied this same principle at Simplus. He didn't rush to exit the business, nor did he cling to it longer than he should have. Instead, he and the team focused on building a beautiful business that became valuable to many potential acquirers. When the time was right, Infosys acquired Simplus for $250 million, a move that validated years of disciplined growth and strategic planning. Ryan and the team positioned the company so well that, after doing a reverse acquisition at Infosys, global business was doing more than $650 million in annual revenue with a 23 percent profit margin.

Westwood's experience highlights a fundamental truth: Scaling isn't just about growth—it's about structured, intentional growth. RevOps plays a crucial role in making this possible. Whether you're a start-up or an enterprise, your revenue operations must evolve alongside your company. The same RevOps processes that work for a ten-person company will collapse under the weight of a five-hundred-person team. Understanding when and how to scale RevOps is critical to sustaining business growth without losing efficiency or agility.

Challenges of Scaling RevOps. In the early stages, start-ups thrive on agility and informal processes. Communication is straightforward, and decisions are made swiftly. However, as the company expands, these informal structures can lead to chaos. The systems that once supported a small team become inadequate for a larger organization. This transition requires a fundamental shift in how RevOps is structured and managed.

It impacts sales reps' skill set as well. Erik Charles explains during the *Go To Market Podcast* episode "3 Ways to Build a Killer Sales Comp Plan."[212]

"If you're in a large company, you'll want to promote somebody who is above the median. But if you have a choice between two people—one person who brought in a ton of revenue, but another person who has sold every product in the company catalog, I'll take the one who sells every product in the company catalog. They get more performance out of the team they manage than just the number one sales rep who went there just by selling a single product."

Growth doesn't happen overnight; it's a series of milestones. Recognizing these inflection points is crucial. For instance, doubling your customer base or expanding into new markets can strain existing processes. Being proactive and identifying these tipping points allows for timely adjustments in RevOps strategies.

Rapid growth often leads to quick fixes—temporary solutions that address immediate needs but aren't sustainable long-term. This accumulation of "technical debt" can result in convoluted processes and outdated systems. A study by McKinsey highlights that companies can spend up to 20 percent of their technology budget addressing issues related to technical debt, diverting resources from innovation and growth.[213]

Design Scalable RevOps Frameworks. Scalability requires flexibility. Investing in systems that can grow with your company is essential. Cloud-based RevOps platforms, for example, offer scalability without the need for significant infrastructure changes. These systems allow for modular expansions, accommodating new functionalities as needed.

Manual RevOps processes can become a bottleneck as operations scale. Automation streamlines repetitive tasks, reducing errors and freeing up human resources for strategic activities. AI further enhances efficiency by providing predictive analytics and personalized customer experiences. According to Gartner, 75 percent of B2B sales organizations will be augmenting traditional sales playbooks with AI-based guided selling solutions.[214]

As operations grow, so does the need for specialized roles within the RevOps team. Defining clear responsibilities and fostering continuous learning are vital. Regular training sessions and workshops can keep the team updated on the latest tools and methodologies, ensuring they are equipped to handle evolving challenges.

Common Pitfalls in Scaling RevOps. As organizations expand, there's a tendency to introduce complex procedures in an attempt to manage increased workloads. However, unnecessary complexity can prevent efficiency and lead to confusion among team members. A report by SEOReseller highlights that premature scaling without streamlined processes can cause agencies to lose control over internal and external aspects of the business.[215]

Regularly checking on your workflows is key to keeping things simple and avoiding unnecessary complexity. This means getting rid of redundant steps and making sure processes stay as streamlined as possible. Also, using scalable infrastructure and tech can help with growth and expansion without adding more complications.

As teams grow, maintaining clear and consistent communication becomes increasingly challenging. Fragmented communication can lead to misunderstandings, duplicated efforts, and misaligned objectives. A survey highlighted by JoinTheCollective.com revealed that 70 percent of small businesses struggle with scaling operations due to inadequate processes and inefficiencies, often exacerbated by poor communication.[216]

Establishing clear communication channels, regular updates, and ensuring that all team members are aligned with the company's vision and strategy are crucial steps in mitigating these issues. Utilizing collaborative tools and platforms can also enhance transparency and foster better teamwork.

Another pitfall when scaling RevOps—which we've explored in depth in other sections—is not maintaining data quality. We cannot stress how important data quality is when your organization is growing.

Seven Challenging Business Scenarios—and their RevOps Solutions

The business world is filled with a range of challenging business scenarios that can stress and stretch companies to their breaking point. Fortunately, when companies embrace RevOps, RevOps approaches and principles can become a key strategy for working through these scenarios—and emerging stronger on the other side. Below are seven common, real-world business challenges and how RevOps can provide a solution.

1. **Mergers and Acquisitions**

The Situation: A current customer gets acquired by a company that's already in your pipeline.

RevOps Solution:

- Conduct what-if scenario planning to assess potential impacts.
- Update sales and customer success (CS) account ownership and quota targets accordingly.
- Ensure sales and CS teams are aligned so they can respond to the customer's needs immediately.

2. **A Target Account Goes Out of Business**

The Situation: A company in your target list shuts down, leaving a gap in your projected revenue.

RevOps Solution:

- Factor the loss into your GTM plan and adjust revenue forecasts.
- Identify alternative ways to meet your original targets, such as shifting resources to higher-potential accounts.
- Provide quota relief to account owners affected by the loss to keep performance metrics realistic.

3. **Competitive Pressure**

The Situation: A competitor makes a major product update that suddenly puts your offering at a disadvantage.

RevOps Solution:

- Have sales, marketing, and CS teams gather intelligence on how the market is reacting.
- Work with strategy and product teams to adjust messaging, positioning, or product road map in response.

- Equip your sales team with updated battle cards and competitive differentiators to win deals.

4. New Market Opportunity (White Space)

The Situation: A new buyer need emerges due to shifts in government regulations or industry changes.
RevOps Solution:

- Analyze capacity across sales, marketing, and CS to determine how best to capitalize on the opportunity.
- Decide whether to reallocate existing resources or build out new teams to target the white space.
- Implement territory and quota adjustments to align with the new growth area.

5. Scaling Sales Teams After Funding

The Situation: Your company secures new funding, and your sales team is growing from 10 reps to 50. That means restructuring sales territories—fast.
RevOps Solution:

- The strategy team re-carves territories, ensuring logical distribution of accounts and potential.
- Some territories are marked as "to-be-hired" (TBH) for future reps.
- Sales managers begin hiring while assigning temporary coverage to TBH territories to avoid pipeline disruption.

6. GTM Segmentation and Customer Upgrades

The Situation: Your business has separate paid and freemium accounts. When a freemium customer exceeds usage limits, they should move to the paid segment—but delays in processing these transitions are creating revenue leakage.

RevOps Solution:

- CS teams monitor account usage in real time instead of waiting until the next review cycle.
- When an account exceeds the freemium limits, an account manager is assigned immediately, ensuring a smooth upgrade process.
- Automating segmentation transitions prevents accounts from falling through the cracks.

7. **Hiring, Promotions, and Employee Turnover**

The Situation: Resignations and promotions impact coverage within your sales and CS teams, leading to gaps in the customer journey.

RevOps Solution:

- Use coordinated planning across sales and CS to create teaming arrangements that ensure customer support doesn't skip a beat.
- Implement effective dating for start and end dates in your CRM to automate coverage transitions.
- Build a process where new hires inherit pipeline and accounts seamlessly, avoiding disruption to customer relationships.

Conclusion

In this chapter, we explored the importance of unifying revenue teams, breaking down silos to create a shared vision. We examined how companies resist change and how RevOps leaders can frame it as an opportunity. We tackled the challenge of data visibility, showing why ownership and access must be carefully managed. And we discussed how to scale RevOps effectively, ensuring that processes grow alongside the business without creating bottlenecks.

Final Thoughts: The Future of RevOps

The term RevOps may not roll off the tongues of the C-suite the same way that CRM or SaaS does. But that paradigm is shifting—fast. That's because RevOps is getting results for businesses.

RevOps helps businesses continuously fine-tune their GTM execution, ensuring they don't get stuck in outdated planning cycles. Gone are the days of rigid twelve- to eighteen-month GTM plans that can't keep up with change. The most successful companies plan and execute in shorter cycles, adapting every quarter—or even faster—to stay on track with revenue goals. When planning and execution are integrated, revenue teams can respond to shifts in the market without missing a beat. Thus, RevOps has become the glue that holds Go-to-Market teams together and the engine that powers revenue growth.

In the coming years, RevOps is poised to undergo a significant transformation, driven by technological advancements and evolving business strategies. A central force in this evolution will be the integration of artificial intelligence (AI) and automation into RevOps frameworks. AI will enhance decision-making processes, streamline operations, and provide deeper insights into customer behaviors. Not only will AI-driven tools automate routine RevOps tasks so teams can focus on strategic initiatives, but AI will be at the heart of enabling more informed RevOps decision-making and efficient operations.

The organizational structure of RevOps also will evolve. Businesses are increasingly recognizing the need for cross-functional teams that break down traditional silos between sales, marketing, and customer success departments. This integrated approach fosters better collaboration and ensures a unified strategy toward revenue generation. Eliminating data silos and encouraging cross-departmental collaboration will naturally make organizations more agile and responsive to market changes.

Data and analytics, meanwhile, will continue to be the backbone of effective RevOps. The emphasis is shifting toward real-time data analysis, enabling companies to make swift, informed decisions. This real-time insight will be crucial for identifying market trends and adjusting strategies promptly. Focusing on real-time metrics will enhance decision-making, allowing teams to respond proactively to emerging challenges and opportunities.

Moreover, customer experience will remain a focal point in the future of RevOps. Modern buyers are more informed and engaged than ever, which will necessitate a customer-centric RevOps approach across all touchpoints. RevOps teams are expected to leverage AI and data analytics to personalize interactions, anticipate customer needs, and enhance overall satisfaction.

The role of RevOps professionals is also set to expand. There will be a growing demand for individuals skilled in data analysis, AI integration, and strategic planning. These professionals will be instrumental in navigating the complexities of modern revenue operations, ensuring that businesses remain competitive in a rapidly changing landscape. According to RevOpsCareers.com, emerging roles such as AI Operations Specialists and Revenue Intelligence Managers are on the rise, reflecting the industry's shift toward integrated revenue systems and predictive analytics.[217]

As RevOps continues to gain traction, the demand for purpose-built RevOps solutions and tools is expected to surge. Companies are realizing that legacy CRM systems and disconnected sales and marketing platforms can no longer support the complexities of modern revenue operations. Instead, businesses will turn to specialized RevOps platforms that provide automation, real-time data synchronization, and AI-driven insights to optimize GTM execution. A growing number of RevOps-specific tools will emerge, focusing on territory management, quota setting, pipeline visibility, and cross-functional alignment.

One such solution that we're building to lead the way is Fullcast, which helps companies automate and operationalize RevOps at scale by integrating territory planning, routing, and policy enforcement into a single, unified system. As the RevOps function matures, tools like Fullcast will become essential for businesses looking to stay agile, data-driven, and strategically aligned in the future.

***

If you've made it this far, congratulations—you've reached the end. You now have a deep understanding of what RevOps is, why it matters, and how it can transform the way companies go to market. This book has walked through the principles, strategies, and real-world applications that make RevOps a critical function for any organization looking to scale, adapt, and thrive. Moreover, this book has underscored the role that AI, automation, and real-time intelligence will play in making RevOps even more valuable. The companies that embrace RevOps will be the ones that stay ahead of the competition, no matter what the market throws their way.

We leave you with one final takeaway—our most essential parting message: RevOps isn't just a framework—it's an approach that ensures your business is always ready for what's next.

The future of revenue growth belongs to those who build scalable, adaptable RevOps functions. Whether you're refining your approach or just getting started, one thing is certain—RevOps is no longer optional.

RevOps is the advantage that will define the next era of business success.

Endnotes

1   Indianapolis Motor Speedway historical account, https://www
    .indianapolismotorspeedway.com/news-multimedia/news/2020/04/29
    /nascar-wood-brothers-fueled-jim-clark-indy-500-win-1965.

2   Wood Brothers Racing historical account, https://www
    .woodbrothersracing.com/news/classic-memories/2010/06/29/wood
    -brothers-appearance-1965-indy-winning-lotus-goodwood-festival-speed.

3   "Fastest F1 pit stop: McLaren has set the world record with
    this speedy stop," October 15, 2023, *USA Today*. https://www
    .usatoday.com/story/sports/motor/formula1/2023/10/15
    /fastest-f1-pit-stop-formula-one/71155604007.

4   Salesforce Configure Price Quote, https://www.salesforce.com/sales/cpq
    /what-is-salesforce-cpq.

5   Jacob Soll, 2014, *The Reckoning: Financial Accountability and the Rise and
    Fall of Nations*. New York: Basic Books.

6   Jim Ulvog, 2017, "How much wealth was in the Roman treasury in 49
    B.C.? How about annual tax revenue under Augustus?" Ancient Finances,
    https://ancientfinances.com/2017/06/01/how-much-wealth-was-in-the
    -roman-treasury-in-49-b-c-how-about-annual-tax-revenue-under-
    augustus.

7   Georgette Green, 2024, "Ford Implements the Moving Assembly Line." Library of Congress. https://guides.loc.gov/this-month-in -business-history/October/Ford - :~:text=Henry Ford%27s Model T automobile,reduced to just 93 minutes.

8   The Henry Ford historical account, https://www.thehenryford.org /collections-and-research/digital-collections/artifact/255638.

9   The Henry Ford historical account, https://www.thehenryford .org/explore/blog/advertising-the-model-t/#:~:text=Almost%20 immediately%20the%20Ford%20Model,Model%20Ts%20had%20 been%20produced.

10   Max Weber, 2019, *Economy and Society: A New Translation* (Keith Tribe, ed.). Cambridge, MA: Harvard University Press.

11   Tom Oliver, 2024, "Your silent assassin: How bureaucracy kills your business," Inquirer.net, https://business.inquirer.net/485709 /your-silent-assassin-how-bureaucracy-kills-your-business.

12   Yves Doz, 2017, "The Strategic Decisions That Caused Nokia's Failure," NSEAD Business School. https://knowledge.insead.edu/strategy /strategic-decisions-caused-nokias-failure.

13   Olga Traskova, "Navigating the Dance of Evolving RevOps Leadership Skills," *Go To Market Podcast*, hosted by Dr. Amy Cook, Spotify, April 2025, https://open.spotify.com/episode /20tpboQAhzaQkUUO1eWXQk?si=f28f57b51e9a4cf8.

14   Evan Liang, "The Rise of Revenue Operations," LeanData, September 15, 2020. https://www.leandata.com/blog/the-rise-of-revenue-operations/.

15   Captivate Talent, "2025 RevOps Trends and Predictions: What Leaders Need to Know," December 11, 2024, https://www.captivatetalent.com/ blog/revops-trends.

16   LeanData and Sales Hacker, The State of Revenue Operations 2019: A Survey of 2,462 B2B Sales and Marketing Professionals, Sunnyvale, CA: LeanData, 2019. https://www.leandata.com/resources /state-of-revenue-operations-2019/.

17   Forrester Consulting, The Rise of RevOps, commissioned by Salesforce, 2021, https://www.salesforce.com/resources/research-reports /rise-of-revops-forrester-consulting/.

18   Nancy Maluso, "Emerging-Company Sales Leaders: Shape-Shift Or Face Failure," Forrester, January 11, 2021, https://www.forrester.com/blogs /emerging-company-sales-leaders-shape-shift-or-face-failure/.

19   Christi Lopez, LinkedIn profile, LinkedIn, accessed April 21, 2025, https://www.linkedin.com/in/christirlopez/.

20   LinkedIn, "LinkedIn Jobs on the Rise 2024: The 25 Fastest-Growing Roles in the U.S.," LinkedIn News, January 17, 2024, https://www .linkedin.com/pulse/linkedin-jobs-rise-2024-25-fastest-growing-roles-us -linkedin-news-dxmie/.

21   Mike Ciulla, "RevOps is Having a Moment, But Does Anyone Really Know What It Is or How It Should Be Structured?" RevOps Co-op, April 1, 2024, https://www.revopscoop.com/post/revops-is-having-a-moment -but-does-anyone-really-know-what-it-is-or-how-it-should-be-structured.

22   Captivate Talent, "2025 RevOps Trends and Predictions: What Leaders Need to Know," December 11, 2024, https://www.captivatetalent.com /blog/revops-trends.

23   Salesforce, "Sales Teams Using AI 1.3x More Likely to See Revenue Increase," Salesforce News, July 25, 2024, https://www.salesforce.com /news/stories/sales-ai-statistics-2024/.

24   Oscar Armas-Luy, "Turning Forecasting Odds in Your Favor," *Go To Market Podcast*, hosted by Dr. Amy Cook, Spotify, November 2024, https://open.spotify.com/episode/2wux6pZmZDdi5GaC4U8JcL.

25   Noah Marks, "Scaling with Purpose: How RevOps Aligns Teams for Growth," *Go To Market Podcast*, hosted by Dr. Amy Cook, Spotify, December 2024, https://open.spotify.com/episode /4igxAAXDk61SNu5WXN1xiA.

26   Margarita Garg, "GTM and Customer Experience: The Key to Success," LinkedIn, October 18, 2024, https://www.linkedin.com/posts/mgarg _gtm-gtm-customerexperience-activity-7189121621985566720 -k1F7?utm_source=share&utm_medium=member_desktop &rcm=ACoAABj991YBrU1rGyLMGOgqNOE24uH9z3gxhhQ.

27   Heidrick & Struggles, "Chief Revenue Officers and Chief Finance Officers: Optimize Their Relationship for Organizational Success," 2024, https://www.heidrick.com/en/pages/corporate-officers/ cros-and-cfos-optimize-their-relationship-for-organizational-success.

28   Revenue Operations Alliance, "State of Revenue Operations Report 2024," accessed April 21, 2025, https://www.revenueoperationsalliance .com/state-of-revenue-operations-report-2024/.

29   John Lafleur, "The Deck We Used to Raise Our $150M Series-B," Airbyte, January 12, 2022, https://airbyte.com/blog /the-deck-we-used-to-raise-our-150m-series-b.

30   Olivia Lucero, "3 Ways RevOps Teams Can Drive Growth—Lessons From ZoomInfo + HubSpot," Forma.ai, October 30, 2023, https://www.forma.ai/resources/article/3-ways-revops-teams-can-drive-growth-lessons-from-zoominfo-hubspot.

31   Nick Rico, "Nick Rico's Profile," Sharebird, accessed April 21, 2025, https://sharebird.com/profile/nick-rico.

32   Gartner, "B2B Buying: How Top CSOs and CMOs Optimize the Journey," accessed April 21, 2025, https://www.gartner.com/en/sales/insights/b2b-buying-journey.

33   Gartner, "Gartner Says Less Than 50% of Sales Leaders and Sellers Have High Confidence in Forecasting Accuracy," February 12, 2020, https://www.gartner.com/en/newsroom/press-releases/2020-02-12-gartner-says-less-than-50--of-sales-leaders-and-selle.

34   Phil Harrell, "2021 In Review: A Recap of the Shifts That Every Sales Leader Should Know About," Forrester, December 10, 2021, https://www.forrester.com/blogs/2021-in-review-a-recap-of-the-shifts-that-every-sales-leader-should-know-about/.

35   Statista, "Data Growth Worldwide 2010–2028," accessed April 21, 2025, https://www.statista.com/statistics/871513/worldwide-data-created/.

36   Hannah Mayer, Lareina Yee, Michael Chui, and Roger Roberts, "Superagency in the Workplace: Empowering People to Unlock AI's Full Potential," McKinsey & Company, January 28, 2025, https://www.mckinsey.com/capabilities/mckinsey-digital/our-insights/superagency-in-the-workplace-empowering-people-to-unlock-ais-full-potential-at-work.

37   *The AI Journal*, "85% of Organizations Identify Poor Data Quality as the Primary Barrier to AI Success in 2025!" LinkedIn, December 3, 2024, https://www.linkedin.com/pulse/85-organizations-identify-poor-data-quality-primary-barrier-uwgcf/.

38   Louis Poulin, "Fix Revenue Flow by Transforming Silos into Streams," Fullcast, February 19, 2025, https://www.fullcast.com/content/louis-poulin-fix-revenue-flow-by-transforming-silos-into-streams/.

39   Louis Poulin, "Fixing Revenue Flow by Transforming Silos into Streams," Fullcast, February 19, 2025, https://open.spotify.com/episode/50Lu9JVYpW9pPkyUrNr5FD?si=7ea1b83338124eab&nd=1&dlsi=a292a25cdc9c49af.

40   BoostUp Labs, "How to Reduce Forecast Bias and Increase Accuracy," BoostUp.ai, February 14, 2025, https://www.boostup.ai/blog/forecast-bias.

41   Monte Carlo, "The Annual State of Data Quality Survey," Monte Carlo Data, last modified May 2, 2023, https://www.montecarlodata.com /blog-data-quality-survey.

42   Prasad Varahabhatla, "Mastering RevOps From Data Integrity to Personal Growth," *Go To Market Podcast*, hosted by Dr. Amy Cook, Spotify, February 19, 2025, https://open.spotify.com/episode /65RPaaaWav371kd4f6XjMa?si=f8130a80e07b495b.

43   Louis Poulin, "Fixing Revenue Flow by Transforming Silos into Streams," Fullcast, February 19, 2025, https://open.spotify.com /episode/50Lu9JVYpW9pPkyUrNr5FD?si=7ea1b83338124eab&nd=1 &dlsi=a292a25cdc9c49af.

44   Demand Metric, "Customer Engagement Playbook," SlideShare, October 12, 2017, https://www.slideshare.net/slideshow/customer -engagement-playbook-80750045/80750045.

45   PYMNTS, "62% of Platform Businesses See Real-Time Data as Key to Growth," PYMNTS.com, October 30, 2024, https://www.pymnts.com /data/2024/62percent-of-platform-businesses-see-real-time-data-as-key -to-growth/.

46   Biswajeet Mahapatra, "CIOs: Get Tech Sprawl Under Control," Forrester, September 17, 2024, https://www.forrester.com/blogs/cios-get-tech -sprawl-under-control/.

47   Saket Kapoor, "The Three Pillars of Successful RevOps Leadership," *Go To Market Podcast*, hosted by Dr. Amy Cook, Spotify, February 19, 2025, https://open.spotify.com/episode/6Bbu92hheyw9oVGYBqmjp0 ?si=72ac193e619d4117.

48   CDP.com, "Customer Data Maturity Study Reveals Importance of Centralized Customer Data Management," October 30, 2024, https:// cdp.com/articles/customer-data-maturity-study-reveals -importance-of-centralized-customer-data-management/.

49   Katerina Ostrovsky, "From Plans to Revenue: How RevOps Drives the Behaviors Needed to Hit Targets," *Go To Market Podcast*, hosted by Dr. Amy Cook, Spotify, February 19, 2025, https://open.spotify.com/ episode/4mjCEN1TWR16KSkvPR8zhS ?si=237d9ffc85ea467f.

50   Marc Benioff, "How to Create Alignment Within Your Company," Salesforce, December 11, 2024, https://www.salesforce.com/blog /how-to-create-alignment-within-your-company/.

51   Dan Thompson, "Revenue Operations Interview: Brandon Bussey at
      Lucid," Kluster, December 11, 2024, https://www.kluster.com/blog
      /interview-sales-operations-lucidchart/.

52   Terry Flaherty, "The Revenue Process Alignment Series, Part 4: An
      Opportunity-Centric Revenue Process Is All About Context," Forrester,
      April 14, 2022, https://www.forrester.com/blogs/the-revenue-process
      -alignment-series-part-4-an-opportunity-centric-revenue-process-is-all
      -about-context/.

53   Andris A. Zoltners, Prabhakant Sinha, and Sally E. Lorimer,
      "Why Sales Teams Should Reexamine Territory Design," *Harvard
      Business Review*, August 7, 2015, https://hbr.org/2015/08/why
      -sales-teams-should-reexamine-territory-design.

54   Fullcast, The Ultimate Guide to Territory Balancing, https://www.fullcast
      .com/ebooks/the-ultimate-guide-to-territory-balancing/.

55   Fullcast, The Ultimate Guide to Territory Balancing, https://www.fullcast
      .com/ebooks/the-ultimate-guide-to-territory-balancing/.

56   Ryan Westwood. Creating a Utah Entrepreneur | Ryan Westwood,
      Fullcast. Silicon Slopes, April 2025. YouTube video.
      https://www.youtube.com/watch?list=TLGGIinkw1n1
      -3cyNDAxMjAyNQ&v=Z_uKwEfsE4c.

57   Seth Marrs, "Your Company's Quota Attainment Is Probably Around
      50%, and That's Not a Bad Thing," Forrester, March 14, 2023, https
      ://www.forrester.com/blogs/your-companys-quota-attainment-is
      -probably-around-50-and-thats-not-a-bad-thing/.

58   Marc Maloy. LinkedIn profile. LinkedIn, accessed April 21, 2025,
      https://www.linkedin.com/in/marcmaloy.

59   Gartner, "Gartner Says Less Than 50% of Sales Leaders and Sellers,"
      Gartner Newsroom, February 12, 2020, https://www.gartner.com/en
      /newsroom/press-releases/2020-02-12-gartner-says-less-than-50--of-sales
      -leaders-and-selle.

60   Fullcast, "Fireside Chat: Capacity Planning and Managing Coverage
      Assignments," July 14, 2020, https://www.fullcast.com/content
      /fireside-chat-capacity-planning-and-managing-coverage-assignments/.

61   CaptivateIQ, "Incentive-Based Pay Impacts Performance,"
      CaptivateIQ Blog, April 24, 2024, https://www.captivateiq.com/blog
      /incentive-based-pay-impacts-performance.

62   Gartner, "Sales Compensation Planning," February 12, 2020,
      https://www.gartner.com/en/sales/insights/sales-compensation-planning.

63 Steve Settle, "Grand Slam RevOps Begins With Team Alignment," *Go To Market Podcast*, hosted by Dr. Amy Cook, Spotify, accessed April 21, 2025, https://open.spotify.com/episode/4KWAfYNsu4DfunWRAvqY2q.

64 BrainyQuote, "Joe Montana Quotes," accessed April 21, 2025, https://www.brainyquote.com/authors/joe-montana-quotes.

65 Cody Guymon, "RevOps on the Rise—Shaping the Future from the Executive Team," *Go To Market Podcast*, hosted by Dr. Amy Cook, Fullcast, accessed April 21, 2025, https://www.fullcast.com/podcasts/cody-guymon-revops-on-the-rise-shaping-the-future-from-the-executive-team/.

66 Whitney Merrill. 2025. Final Frontier—RevOps Ebook. Fullcast, accessed April 21, 2025. https://19965450.fs1.hubspotusercontent-na1.net/hubfs/19965450/eBooks/Final%20Frontier%20-%20RevOps%20Ebook.pdf.

67 Chris Berkley, "40 Go-to-Market and Product Marketing Stats for 2024," Ignition Blog, accessed April 21, 2025, https://www.haveignition.com/blog/product-marketing-stats.

68 Tyler Morrow, "Winning Together: Tyler Morrow's Secrets to Motivating Your RevOps Team," *Go to Market Podcast*, hosted by Dr. Amy Cook, Fullcast, accessed December 11, 2024, https://www.fullcast.com/podcasts/secrets-to-motivating-your-revops-team/.

69 Louis Poulin, "Fix Revenue Flow by Transforming Silos into Streams," Fullcast, accessed April 21, 2025, https://www.fullcast.com/content/louis-poulin-fix-revenue-flow-by-transforming-silos-into-streams/.

70 Steve Settle, "Grand Slam RevOps Begins With Team Alignment," *Go To Market Podcast*, hosted by Dr. Amy Cook, Spotify, accessed April 21, 2025, https://open.spotify.com/episode/4KWAfYNsu4DfunWRAvqY2q.

71 Stewart Bond, "Driving Business Value from Data in the Face of Fragmentation and Complexity," *IDC InfoBrief*, Informatica, 2021, accessed April 21, 2025, https://www.informatica.com/lp/driving-business-value-from-data-in-the-face-of-fragmentation-and-complexity_4241.html.

72 CDP.com, "Customer Data Maturity Study Reveals Importance of Centralized Customer Data Management," accessed April 21, 2025, https://cdp.com/articles/customer-data-maturity-study-reveals-importance-of-centralized-customer-data-management/.

73 Sean Lane and Laura Adint, *The Revenue Operations Manual*, https://www.revenueoperationsmanual.com/.

74　Edge Delta, "What Percentage of Data Is Unstructured? 3 Must-Know Statistics," last modified March 6, 2024, accessed April 21, 2025, https://edgedelta.com/company/blog/what-percentage-of-data-is-unstructured.

75　Julia Limitone, "Data Is the New Currency, Hewlett Packard Enterprise President Says," Fox Business, January 24, 2019, accessed April 21, 2025, https://www.foxbusiness.com/business-leaders/data-is-the-new-currency-hewlett-packard-enterprise-president-says.

76　G2, "Discrete vs. Continuous Data: What's the Difference," September 13, 2024, accessed April 21, 2025, https://www.g2.com/articles/discrete-vs-continuous-data.

77　G2, "Discrete vs. Continuous Data: What's the Difference," September 13, 2024, accessed April 21, 2025, https://www.g2.com/articles/discrete-vs-continuous-data.

78　HubSpot, "What Is First-Party Data (+ Second-Party and Third-Party Data)?," HubSpot Blog, updated November 15, 2024, accessed April 21, 2025, https://blog.hubspot.com/service/first-party-data.

79　HubSpot, "What Is First-Party Data (+ Second-Party and Third-Party Data)?," HubSpot Blog, updated November 15, 2024, accessed April 21, 2025, https://blog.hubspot.com/service/first-party-data.

80　Katerina Ostrovsky, "From Plans to Revenue: How RevOps Drives the Behaviors Needed to Hit Targets," *Go To Market Podcast*, hosted by Dr. Amy Cook, Spotify, accessed April 21, 2025, https://open.spotify.com/episode/4mjCEN1TWR16KSkvPR8zhS.

81　Patrick Gibson, "Types of Data Analysis," Chartio, accessed April 21, 2025, https://chartio.com/learn/data-analytics/types-of-data-analysis/.

82　Jakub Lewkowicz, "While Most Companies Focus on Data, Only About 16% Are 'Data-Driven,'" *SD Times*, January 8, 2024, accessed April 21, 2025, https://sdtimes.com/data/while-most-companies-focus-on-data-only-about-16-are-data-driven/.

83　Prasad Varahabhatla, "Mastering RevOps: From Data Integrity to Personal Growth," *Go To Market Podcast*, hosted by Dr. Amy Cook, Spotify, accessed April 21, 2025, https://open.spotify.com/episode/65RPaaaWav371kd4f6XjMa.

84　Salesforce, State of Marketing: 9th Edition, 2024, accessed April 21, 2025, https://www.salesforce.com/form/marketing/state-of-marketing-9/.

85　SAS, "Predictive Analytics: What It Is and Why It Matters," SAS Insights, accessed April 21, 2025, https://www.sas.com/en_us/insights/analytics/predictive-analytics.html.

86   Charlie Cowan, "Predictive Analytics: Revenue Operations Explained," CharlieCowan.ai, November 4, 2023, accessed April 21, 2025, https://charliecowan.ai/revops-articles/predictive-analytics-revenue-operations-explained.

87   Josh Howarth, "39+ Data Analytics Statistics (2024)," Exploding Topics, last updated August 16, 2024, accessed April 21, 2025, https://explodingtopics.com/blog/data-analytics-stats.

88   Winning by Design, The Bowtie: A Proposed Standard, May 2024, accessed April 21, 2025, https://winningbydesign.com/wp-content/uploads/2024/05/The-Bowtie-A-Proposed-Standard.pdf.

89   Rob Levey, "From Rolodex to AI: The Evolution of Revenue Operations," *Go To Market Podcast*, hosted by Dr. Amy Cook, Spotify, accessed April 21, 2025, https://open.spotify.com/episode/0NvCLui3W4LjNtZ6Fzg3LX.

90   Rachel Krall, LinkedIn, October 2024, accessed April 21, 2025, https://www.linkedin.com/posts/rachelkrall_earlier-this-month-i-had-the-opportunity-activity-7252679800622874625-iQ6-.

91   Prasad Varahabhatla, "Mastering RevOps: From Data Integrity to Personal Growth," *Go To Market Podcast*, hosted by Dr. Amy Cook, Fullcast, accessed April 21, 2025, https://www.fullcast.com/podcasts/prasad-varahabhatla-mastering-revops-from-data-integrity-to-personal-growth/.

92   Alexa Grabell, "Demystifying the AI Sales Landscape," Pocus, January 21, 2025, accessed April 21, 2025, https://www.pocus.com/blog/demystifying-the-ai-sales-landscape.

93   Andrew Sims, "Accurately tracking marketing campaign attribution can be tricky . . .," LinkedIn, September 2024, accessed April 21, 2025, https://www.linkedin.com/posts/andrewsimssfdc_growth-marketingattribution-data-activity-7237791111505670144-VkkW/.

94   MX, Top Trends to Grow Deposits and Engagement in 2025, webinar, presented by Jane Barratt and James Dotter, January 23, 2025, accessed April 21, 2025, https://www.mx.com/webinars/top-trends-grow-desposits-engagement-2025/.

95   Workato, 2024 Work Automation and AI Index Report, 2024, accessed April 21, 2025, https://www.workato.com/work-automation-index.

96   Miami Local, "AI in Revenue Operations at ZoomInfo—Tessa Whittaker," *Miami Local*, February 17, 2025, accessed April 21, 2025, https://miamilocal.com/ai-revenue-operations-zoominfo-tessa-whittaker/.

97   Ella Harrison, "What Is a RevOps Framework? A Complete Guide to
      Driving Scalable Growth," Revenue Operations Alliance, December 9,
      2024, accessed April 21, 2025, https://www.revenueoperationsalliance
      .com/what-is-a-revops-framework-a-complete-guide-to-driving-scalable
      -growth/.

98   Michael Mapes. "Driving Agility Through Structure: How
      Business Standards Can Help Innovation." *Forbes*, May 24, 2022,
      accessed April 21, 2025. https://www.forbes.com/councils
      /forbesbusinesscouncil/2022/05/24/driving-agility-through-structure
      -how-business-standards-can-help-innovation/.

99   Antoine Fort, RevOps: Key Trends to Dominate in 2025, webinar,
      Qobra, January 30, 2025, accessed April 21, 2025, https://www.qobra.co
      /webinars-podcasts/revops-trends-2025.

100   Tumisang Bogwasi, "Examples of RevOps in Practice," Fine Media,
      October 31, 2023, accessed April 21, 2025, https://www.finemediabw
      .com/blog/examples-of-revops.

101   Anthony Cardillo, "How Many Companies Use AI? (New Data),"
      Exploding Topics, March 4, 2025, accessed April 21, 2025, https
      ://explodingtopics.com/blog/companies-using-ai.

102   6sense, "A Guide to Revenue Operations KPIs," accessed April 21, 2025,
      https://6sense.com/glossary/revenue-operations-kpis/.

103   Sneha Aravind et al., "Growing User Base and Revenue through
      Data Workflow Features: A Case Study," *International Journal
      of Communication Networks and Information Security* 16, no. S1
      (September 2024): 16, accessed April 21, 2025, https://www.researchgate
      .net/publication/387239073_Growing_User_Base_and_Revenue
      _through_Data_Workflow_Features_A_Case_Study.

104   Nicole Replogle, "How 8 RevOps Professionals Use AI and Automation,"
      Zapier, December 10, 2024, accessed April 21, 2025, https://zapier.com
      /blog/revops-ai-automation/.

105   Jason Bramble, "How AI Is Revolutionizing Revenue Operations
      Automation," Revcarto, September 13, 2024, accessed April 21, 2025,
      https://www.revcarto.com/blog/how-ai-is-revolutionizing
      -revenue-operations-automation.

106   Stav Levi, "Revolutionizing RevOps: How AI is Transforming Revenue
      Operations," Alta, April 15, 2025, accessed April 21, 2025, https://www
      .altahq.com/post/revolutionizing-revops-how-ai-is-transforming-revenue
      -operations.

107 Rebecca Stewart, "Using Generative AI in Your Revenue Operations Strategy," Revenue Operations Alliance, July 18, 2023, accessed April 21, 2025, https://www.revenueoperationsalliance.com /using-generative-ai-in-your-revenue-operations-strategy/.

108 John Rivers, "5 Steps for an Effective Revenue Enablement Strategy," Seismic, August 8, 2024, accessed April 21, 2025, https://seismic.com /blog/how-to-create-an-effective-revenue-enablement-strategy/.

109 Rebecca Stewart, "Utilizing the 4 Pillars of Business Analytics in RevOps," Revenue Operations Alliance, September 25, 2024, accessed April 21, 2025, https://www.revenueoperationsalliance.com/4-pillars-of -business-analytics-in-revops/.

110 Qlik, "8 Predictive Analytics Examples, 12 Use Cases," accessed April 21, 2025, https://www.qlik.com/us/predictive-analytics/predictive -analytics-examples.

111 Charlie Cowan, "Predictive Analytics: Revenue Operations Explained," CharlieCowan.ai, November 4, 2023, accessed April 21, 2025, https://charliecowan.ai/revops-articles/predictive-analytics-revenue -operations-explained.

112 Allabaksh Shaik et al., "Design and Analysis of Low Power Single Exact Adder Dual Approximate Adder," *International Journal of Scientific Research in Science and Technology* (*IJSRST*) 11, no. 2 (March–April 2024): 313–320, accessed April 21, 2025, https://srrjournals.com/ijsrst /sites/default/files/IJSRST-2024-0039.pdf.

113 Thomas C. Redman, "Bad Data Costs the U.S. $3 Trillion Per Year," SAP Community, September 1, 2023, accessed April 21, 2025, https ://community.sap.com/t5/technology-blogs-by-sap/bad-data-costs -the-u-s-3-trillion-per-year/ba-p/13575387.

114 Steen Rasmussen, "The Cost of Data, Part 1: Sorry, but Your Data Is Too Good," *Medium*, January 17, 2024, accessed April 21, 2025, https ://medium.com/@me_68087/ the-cost-of-data-part-1-sorry-but-your-data-is-too-good-8346d13ef21c.

115 Wavestone, 2024 Data and AI Leadership Executive Survey, January 2024, accessed April 21, 2025, https://static1.squarespace.com /static/62adf3ca029a6808a6c5be30/t/66635b1a6aeebf2548742 37b/1717787418584/DataAI-ExecutiveLeadershipSurveyFinalAsset.pdf.

116 Ganes Kesari, "Building a Data-Driven Culture: Four Key Elements," *MIT Sloan Management Review*, January 23, 2025,

accessed April 21, 2025, https://sloanreview.mit.edu/article
/building-a-data-driven-culture-four-key-elements/.

117   Gulf Bank, "Gulf Bank Launches Second Edition of 'Data Ambassadors'
Program," January 23, 2023, accessed April 21, 2025, https
://www.e-gulfbank.com/en/about-us/media/press-releases/2023/01
/gulf-bank-launches-second-edition-of-data-ambassadors-program/.

118   Ganes Kesari, "Building a Data-Driven Culture: Four Key
Elements," *MIT Sloan Management Review*, January 23, 2025,
accessed April 21, 2025, https://sloanreview.mit.edu/article
/building-a-data-driven-culture-four-key-elements/.

119   Gartner, "Revenue Operations: The What, Best Practices & RevOps
Guide," accessed April 21, 2025, https://www.gartner.com/en
/sales/topics/revenue-operations.

120   Joe Barron. "8 RevOps Best Practices for Driving Revenue Growth."
Cognism, March 18, 2025, accessed April 21, 2025. https://www
.cognism.com/blog/revops-best-practices.

121   Feras Abdel, "You Know They Aren't Right and You Run Them Anyway,"
Outreach, August 10, 2021, accessed April 21, 2025, https://www
.outreach.io/resources/blog/data-accuracy-lead-reporting.

122   Fullcast, "Fireside Chat: Survivorship Bias in RevOps Data,"
April 15, 2022, accessed April 21, 2025, https://www.fullcast.com
/content/fireside-chat-survivorship-bias-in-revops-data/.

123   Fred Reichheld, *Loyalty Rules! How Today's Leaders Build Lasting
Relationships*, chap. 1, "Timeless Principles," Bain & Company, 2001,
accessed April 21, 2025, https://www.bain.com/contentassets
/29f74ec417fa4e36a1d7d7e7479badc5/loyalty_rules_chapter_one.pdf.

124   Tableau, "A Guide to Data-Driven Decision Making: What It Is, Its
Importance, & How to Implement It," accessed April 21, 2025, https://
www.tableau.com/learn/articles/data-driven-decision-making.

125   Rebecca Stewart, "Utilizing the 4 Pillars of Business Analytics in
RevOps," Revenue Operations Alliance, September 25, 2024, accessed
April 21, 2025, https://www.revenueoperationsalliance.com/4-pillars
-of-business-analytics-in-revops/.

126   Ramesh Panuganty, "Challenges and Benefits of Data-Driven Decision
Making," MachEye, accessed April 21, 2025, https://www.macheye.com
/blog/challenges-and-benefits-of-data-driven-decision-making/.

127   Fullcast, "4 Tips to Steer Your Career Path from VP of RevOps
to COO," December 10, 2024, accessed April 21, 2025,

https://www.fullcast.com/content/4-tips-to-steer-your-career-path
-from-vp-of-revops-to-coo/.

128 Rebecca Stewart, "13 Key Statistics from Our State of Revenue
Operations Report 2023," Revenue Operations Alliance, November 15,
2023, accessed April 21, 2025, https://www.revenueoperationsalliance
.com/key-statistics-from-our-state-of-revenue-operations-report/.

129 CaptivateIQ, "5 Revenue Forecasting Models & Methods for
Accurate Projections," February 25, 2025, accessed April 21, 2025,
https://www.captivateiq.com/blog/revenue-forecasting.

130 Barton C. Hacker and James M. Grimwood, On the Shoulders of
Titans: A History of Project Gemini, NASA SP-4203 (Washington, D.C.:
NASA, 1977), accessed April 21, 2025, https://www.nasa.gov
/wp-content/uploads/2023/03/sp-4203.pdf.

131 Stephen Diorio, "What Is Revenue Operations and How Does It Create
Value?" *Forbes*, July 14, 2021, accessed April 21, 2025, https://www
.forbes.com/sites/stephendiorio/2021/07/14/what-is-revenue
-operations-and-how-does-it-create-value/.

132 Anthony McPartlin, "RevOps Strategies Are Missing an Operating
Model," Forrester, November 29, 2023, accessed April 21, 2025,
https://www.forrester.com/blogs/rev-ops-strategies-are-missing-an
-operating-model/.

133 Mari Manglaras, "Mastering RevOps Before It Was RevOps," *Go To
Market Podcast*, hosted by Dr. Amy Cook, Fullcast, November 2024,
accessed April 21, 2025, https://www.fullcast.com/podcasts/mari
-manglaras-podcast-interview-mastering-revops-before-it-was-revops/.

134 Ben Mohlie, "RevOps Maturity Model," Hyperscayle, November 2,
2023, accessed April 21, 2025, https://hyperscayle.com/insights
/revops-maturity-model.

135 Rebecca Stewart, "How to Map the Customer Journey for Revenue
Operations Success," Revenue Operations Alliance, January 23, 2024,
accessed April 21, 2025, https://www.revenueoperationsalliance.com
/how-to-map-the-customer-journey-for-revenue-operations-success/.

136 Gartner, "AI in Sales: How Generative AI Will Change Selling," accessed
April 21, 2025, https://www.gartner.com/en/sales/topics/sales-ai.

137 Matt Haller, "Sales Ops Leaders: Interview with Matt Haller,"
Fullcast, accessed April 21, 2025, https://www.fullcast.com/content
/sales-ops-leaders-interview-with-matt-haller/.

138   Fullcast, "4 Must-Know RevOps Trends for 2024," accessed April 21, 2025, https://www.fullcast.com/content/4-must-know-revops-trends-for-2024/.

139   Manoj Garg. LinkedIn, April 21, 2025. https://www.linkedin.com/posts/mgarg_gtm-gtm-customerexperience-activity-7189121621985566720-k1F7.

140   Six & Flow, "What Is a RevOps Maturity Model?" October 24, 2023, accessed April 21, 2025, https://www.sixandflow.com/marketing-blog/what-is-a-revops-maturity-model.

141   Balaji Krish, "Balaji Krish: How to Align Strategy, Operations, and Tactics for GTM Success," *Go To Market Podcast*, hosted by Dr. Amy Cook, Spotify, January 15, 2025, accessed April 21, 2025, https://open.spotify.com/episode/0v5iipZTsNAIN5HS59qsNE.

142   Nani Shaffer, "The Rise of RevOps (And What It Means for B2B Marketing)," *Forbes*, June 7, 2023, accessed April 21, 2025, https://www.forbes.com/councils/forbescommunicationscouncil/2023/06/07/the-rise-of-revops-and-what-it-means-for-b2b-marketing/.

143   ExactBuyer, "Maximizing Revenue Operations for B2C Businesses," ExactBuyer Blog, accessed April 21, 2025, https://blog.exactbuyer.com/post/maximizing-revenue-operations-for-B2C-businesses.

144   Kierstin Payne, "Why Revenue Operations Works for Manufacturing," GO2 Partners, November 21, 2022, accessed April 21, 2025, https://www.go2partners.com/blog/why-revenue-operations-works-for-manufacturing.

145   revVana, "What Is Revenue Operations (RevOps) and Why Is It Important?" September 13, 2024, accessed April 21, 2025, https://revvana.com/resources/blog/what-is-revenue-operations-revops-and-why-is-it-important/.

146   Venkat Viswanathan, "Why RevOps Matters to Customers and How Creating the Right Tech Stack Can Drive Revenue Growth," *Forbes*, June 26, 2023, accessed April 21, 2025, https://www.forbes.com/councils/forbestechcouncil/2023/06/26/why-revops-matters-to-customers-and-how-creating-the-right-tech-stack-can-drive-revenue-growth/.

147   LinkedIn Talent Solutions. 2015. The Ultimate List of Hiring Statistics, accessed April 21, 2025. https://business.linkedin.com/content/dam/business/talent-solutions/global/en_us/c/pdfs/Ultimate-List-of-Hiring-Stats-v02.04.pdf.

148 Lynchburg Regional SHRM, "Essential Elements of Employee Retention," Lynchburg Regional SHRM Blog, October 29, 2017, accessed April 21, 2025, https://lrshrm.shrm.org/blog/2017/10 /essential-elements-employee-retention.

149 LinkedIn Talent Solutions. 2015. The Ultimate List of Hiring Statistics, accessed April 21, 2025. https://business.linkedin.com/content/dam /business/talent-solutions/global/en_us/c/pdfs/Ultimate-List-of-Hiring -Stats-v02.04.pdf.

150 DSMN8, "60+ Employer Branding Statistics You Need To Know," DSMN8 Blog, August 23, 2024, accessed April 21, 2025, https://dsmn8 .com/blog/employer-branding-statistics/.

151 Gary Zurnamer, "25 Employer Brand Statistics To Know in 2025: Updated," Vouchfor Blog, December 1, 2023, accessed April 21, 2025, https://vouchfor.com/blog/employer-brand-statistics.

152 Lis Anderson, "Employer Branding Strategy: How to Recruit and Retain Top Talent," *Forbes*, January 24, 2024, accessed April 21, 2025, https://www.forbes.com/councils/forbesagencycouncil/2024/01/24 /employer-branding-strategy-how-to-recruit-and-retain-top-talent/.

153 Lindsay Bicknell, "2019 CXO Of The Year Honorees," *Utah Business*, June 6, 2019, accessed April 21, 2025, https://www.utahbusiness.com /archive/2019/06/06/2019-cxo-of-the-year/.

154 Tyler Morrow. "Winning Together: The Dynamic Partnership of Sales and RevOps." *Go To Market Podcast*, hosted by Dr. Amy Cook, Spotify, April 21, 2025. Accessed April 21, 2025. https://open.spotify.com /episode/7IWlfwHK80IDFfcL8AZVsK.

155 Fullcast, Mastering RevOps Careers: Insights from Practitioners, accessed April 21, 2025, https://www.fullcast.com/ebooks/mastering-revops -careers-insights-from-practitioners/.

156 Fullcast, Mastering RevOps Careers: Insights from Practitioners, accessed April 21, 2025, https://www.fullcast.com/ebooks/mastering-revops -careers-insights-from-practitioners/.

157 Fullcast, Mastering RevOps Careers: Insights from Practitioners, accessed April 21, 2025, https://www.fullcast.com/ebooks/mastering-revops -careers-insights-from-practitioners/.

158 Wandee Lee, "The Role of AI in Revolutionizing Revenue Operations," Handoffs.com, January 10, 2024, accessed April 21, 2025, https://www .handoffs.com/post/ai-in-revenue-operations.

159   Hans-Georg Wolff and Klaus Moser, "Effects of Networking on Career Success: A Longitudinal Study," *Journal of Applied Psychology* 94, no. 1 (2009): 196–206, accessed April 21, 2025, https://homepages.se.edu /cvonbergen/files/2013/01/Effects-of-Networking-on-Career-Success_A -Longitudinal-Study.pdf.

160   Fullcast, Mastering RevOps Careers: Insights from Practitioners, accessed April 21, 2025, https://www.fullcast.com/ebooks/mastering-revops -careers-insights-from-practitioners/.

161   Amy Cook, "Whitney Merrill's Guide to Stellar Growth," Fullcast, February 11, 2025, accessed April 21, 2025, https://www.fullcast.com /content/whitney-merrills-guide-to-stellar-growth/.

162   Kyril Kotashev, "Startup Failure Rate: How Many Startups Fail and Why in 2024?" Failory, January 9, 2024. Accessed April 21, 2025. https ://www.failory.com/blog/startup-failure-rate.

163   Leland McFarland, "Startup Statistics—The Numbers You Need to Know," Small Business Trends, October 21, 2024, accessed April 21, 2025, https://smallbiztrends.com/2019/03/startup-statistics-small -business.html.

164   Steve Bernstein, "Case Example: Accelerating Growth by Listening to Customers," Waypoint Group, October 17, 2019, accessed April 21, 2025, https://waypointgroup.org/case-example-accelerating -growth-by-listening-to-customers/.

165   Investopedia, "Kaizen: Understanding the Japanese Business Philosophy," accessed April 21, 2025, https://www.investopedia.com/terms/k /kaizen.asp.

166   Toyota Motor Corporation, "Toyota Production System," Toyota Global, accessed April 21, 2025, https://global.toyota/en/company/vision-and -philosophy/production-system/.

167   Masaaki Imai, "What Is KAIZEN™?" Kaizen Institute, accessed April 21, 2025, https://kaizen.com/what-is-kaizen/.

168   Forbes India. "World's Biggest Car Companies," March 26, 2025. Accessed April 21, 2025. https://www.forbesindia.com/article /explainers/worlds-biggest-car-companies/92341/1.

169   CMO Huddles Hub, "Bonus Huddle: What B2B CMOs Need to Know with Mike McKinnon," YouTube video, posted August 23, 2023, https ://www.youtube.com/watch?v=KzDlxgJDOrg.

170   Heidi K. Gardner, "When Senior Managers Won't Collaborate," *Harvard Business Review*, March 2015, accessed April 21, 2025, https ://hbr.org/2015/03/when-senior-managers-wont-collaborate.

171 Amy C. Edmondson, Sujin Jang, and Tiziana Casciaro, "Cross-Silo Leadership," *Harvard Business Review*, May–June 2019, accessed April 21, 2025, https://hbr.org/2019/05/cross-silo-leadership.

172 Vanessa Fuhrmans, "Worker Salary Performance Pay Bonuses," *Wall Street Journal*, September 30, 2024, accessed April 21, 2025, https://www.wsj.com/lifestyle/careers/worker-salary-performance-pay-bonuses-6f916a69.

173 LinkedIn Sales Solutions, "B2B Prospecting Tools Help Marketing Make a Sales Impact," accessed April 21, 2025, https ://business.linkedin.com/sales-solutions/role/marketing.

174 Stephen J. Bigelow, "What Is a Project Post-Mortem?" TechTarget, March 2024, accessed April 21, 2025, https://www.techtarget .com/searchcio/definition/project-post-mortem.

175 McKinsey & Company, "The Impact of Agility: How to Shape Your Organization to Compete," accessed April 21, 2025, https://www .mckinsey.com/capabilities/people-and-organizational-performance /our-insights/the-impact-of-agility-how-to-shape-your-organization -to-compete.

176 McKinsey & Company, "Enterprise Agility," accessed April 21, 2025, https://www.mckinsey.com/capabilities/people-and-organizational -performance/how-we-help-clients/enterprise-agility.

177 McKinsey & Company, "Enterprise Agility," accessed April 21, 2025, https://www.mckinsey.com/capabilities/people-and-organizational -performance/how-we-help-clients/enterprise-agility.

178 Freek Vermeulen, "Businesses and the Icarus Paradox," *Harvard Business Review*, March 4, 2009, accessed April 21, 2025, https://hbr .org/2009/03/businesses-and-the-icarus-para.

179 Olaf Storbeck, Patricia Nilsson, and Guy Chazan, "Is Germany's Business Model Broken?" *Financial Times*, March 2025, https://www.ft.com /content/6c345cf9-8493-4429-baa4-2128abdd0337.

180 Jared Robin, "Why Founders Need to Rethink Community-Building—And How RevGenius Did It," *Go To Market Podcast*, hosted by Dr. Amy Cook, Spotify, accessed April 21, 2025, https://open.spotify.com/episode/6XHsDPrzj7w8CiZXGDVOFb ?si=b1d801e641ea4497.

181 Tori Miller Liu, "The 2025 Information Management Tech Stack," AIIM Blog, October 15, 2024, https://info.aiim.org/aiim-blog /the-2025-information-management-tech-stack.

182   InsightSquared, "Sales Tech Stack Consolidation Report," 2022, https://www.insightsquared.com/resources/sales-tech-stack-consolidation-report/.

183   Arpit Srivastava, "When Your Tech Stack Outgrows: Signs and Strategies for Scalability," Growth Natives, August 1, 2023, updated March 4, 2025, https://growthnatives.com/blogs/marketing/when-your-tech-stack-outgrows-signs-and-strategies-for-scalability/.

184   Revenue Enablement Institute, Markets in Motion Report, 2022, https://www.revenueenablement.com/download-the-markets-in-motion-report/.

185   Revenue Enablement Institute, The Revenue Operating System, accessed April 21, 2025, https://www.revenueenablement.com/product/the-revenue-operating-system/.

186   Amy Cook, "How RevOps Drives the Behaviors Needed to Hit Targets," *Go to Market Podcast*, Fullcast, accessed April 21, 2025, https://www.fullcast.com/podcasts/how-revops-drives-the-behaviors-needed-to-hit-targets/.

187   Raffaele Filieri, Francesco Luigi Milone, Emilio Paolucci, and Elisabetta Raguseo, "A Big Data Analysis of COVID-19 Impacts on Airbnbs' Bookings Behavior Applying Construal Level and Signaling Theories," *International Journal of Hospitality Management* 111 (March 2023): 103461, https://doi.org/10.1016/j.ijhm.2023.103461.

188   Brian Chesky, "A Message from Co-Founder and CEO Brian Chesky," Airbnb Newsroom, May 5, 2020, https://news.airbnb.com/a-message-from-co-founder-and-ceo-brian-chesky/.

189   Doyinsola Oladipo, "Airbnb CEO Says Company Focused on Boosting Long-Term Stays," *Reuters*, September 19, 2024, https://www.reuters.com/technology/airbnb-ceo-says-company-focused-boosting-long-term-stays-2024-09-19/.

190   Airbnb, "What 12 Individuals Learned After One Year of Living Anywhere on Airbnb," Airbnb Newsroom, August 18, 2022, https://news.airbnb.com/what-12-individuals-learned-after-one-year-of-living-anywhere-on-airbnb/.

191   Laura Hayes. LinkedIn profile. LinkedIn, accessed April 21, 2025, https://www.linkedin.com/in/laurahayes000/.

192   Sara Colton, "Driving Communication Between Revenue Teams," Kluster, April 21, 2025, https://www.kluster.com/blog/driving-communication-between-revenue-teams-sara-colton.

193 Common Denominator. "Meet a LiveIntenter: Lauren Zion, VP of Revenue Operations," July 3, 2017. https://commondenominator.email /meet-a-liveintenter-lauren-zion-vp-of-revenue-operations/.

194 Anna Talerico, "I Achieved the Holy Grail of Sales and Marketing Alignment . . . or So I Thought," Aberdeen, June 7, 2016, https://www .aberdeen.com/cmo-essentials/i-achieved-the-holy-grail-of-sales-and -marketing-alignmentor-so-i-thought/.

195 HubSpot, "Why Your B2B Company Should Explore a Revenue Operations Strategy," HubSpot Blog, April 8, 2021, https://blog.hubspot .com/sales/revenue-operations.

196 Nicole Farina, "When Things Come Full Circle," LinkedIn, January 2024, https://www.linkedin.com/posts/nicole-farina-54740231_when -things-come-full-circle-the-ansys-activity-7159155811682828288-nE-A.

197 Piyush Sagar Mishra, "Cognitive Inertia at Workplace," *Medium*, February 17, 2018, https://medium.com/@psmishra/cognitive-inertia -at-workplace-7c0862529a77.

198 Brennan Petar. LinkedIn profile. LinkedIn, accessed April 21, 2025, https://www.linkedin.com/in/brennanpetar/.

199 Ben Zimmerman, "The Most Dangerous Phrase in Business: 'We've Always Done It This Way,'" *Forbes*, January 28, 2019, https://www.forbes .com/councils/forbeslacouncil/2019/01/28/the-most-dangerous-phrase -in-business-weve-always-done-it-this-way/.

200 Vered Kogan, "Three Tips For Managing Resistance To Change," *Forbes*, June 15, 2020, https://www.forbes.com/councils/forbescoachescouncil /2020/06/15/three-tips-for-managing-resistance-to-change/.

201 Gustavo Razzetti, "Stop Fighting Resistance To Change: Do This Instead," *Forbes*, July 5, 2024, https://www.forbes.com/councils /forbeshumanresourcescouncil/2024/07/05/stop-fighting-resistance-to -change-do-this-instead/.

202 Debbie McCarthy, "Psychology of Change: Building Change-Ready Organizations," Prosci, February 1, 2024, https://www.prosci.com/blog /psychology-change-management.

203 Levi Olmstead, "Resistance to Change: 7 Causes & How to Overcome Them," Whatfix, November 5, 2022, https://whatfix.com/blog/causes-of -resistance-to-change/.

204 Michigan State University Online, "How to Overcome Resistance to Organizational Change," November 22, 2021, https://www .michiganstateuniversityonline.com/resources/leadership/executing -smooth-and-permanent-change/.

205 Gartner, "How to Create a Business Case for Data Quality Improvement," accessed April 21, 2025, https://www.gartner.com/smarterwithgartner/ how-to-create-a-business-case-for-data-quality-improvement.

206 Oracle, "What Are Data Silos?" accessed April 21, 2025, https://www.oracle.com/database/data-silos/.

207 Varonis, 2019 Global Data Risk Report, accessed April 21, 2025, https ://info.varonis.com/hubfs/Varonis%202019%20Global%20Data%20 Risk%20Report.pdf.

208 Gartner, "Gartner Survey Shows Organizations Are Slow to Advance in Data and Analytics," Gartner Newsroom, February 5, 2018, accessed April 21, 2025, https://www.gartner.com/en/newsroom/press -releases/2018-02-05-gartner-survey-shows-organizations-are-slow-to -advance-in-data-and-analytics.

209 Rebecca Stewart, "Database Governance vs. Database Management for RevOps," Revenue Operations Alliance, February 27, 2024, accessed April 21, 2025, https://www.revenueoperationsalliance.com /database-governance-vs-database-management-for-revops/.

210 McKinsey & Company, "Using Customer Analytics to Boost Corporate Performance," January 2014, accessed April 21, 2025, https://www.mckinsey.com/~/media/McKinsey/Business%20Functions /Marketing%20and%20Sales/Our%20Insights/Five%20facts%20 How%20customer%20analytics%20boosts%20corporate%20 performance/Datamatics.pdf.

211 Prasad Varahabhatla, "Mastering RevOps: From Data Integrity to Personal Growth," Fullcast, February 27, 2024, accessed April 21, 2025, https://www.fullcast.com/content/prasad-varahabhatla-mastering-revops -from-data-integrity-to-personal-growth/.

212 Erik Charles, "Erik Charles: 3 Ways to Build a Killer Sales Comp Plan," *Go to Market Podcast*, hosted by Dr. Amy Cook, Spotify, February 12, 2024, accessed April 21, 2025, https://open.spotify .com/episode/0TZKTlzboIpxpWIc6cmIqH.

213 Vishal Dalal, Krish Krishnakanthan, Björn Münstermann, and Rob Patenge, "Tech Debt: Reclaiming Tech Equity," McKinsey & Company, October 2020, accessed April 21, 2025, https://www.mckinsey.com /~/media/McKinsey/Business%20Functions/McKinsey%20Digital /Our%20Insights/Tech%20debt%20Reclaiming%20tech%20equity /Tech-debt-Reclaiming-tech-equity.pdf.

214 Gartner, "Gartner Predicts 75% of B2B Sales Organizations Will Augment Traditional Sales Playbooks With AI-Guided Selling Solutions by 2025," Gartner Newsroom, March 10, 2021, accessed April 21, 2025, https://www.gartner.com/en/newsroom/press-releases/gartner-predicts -75--of-b2b-sales-organizations-will-augment-tra.

215 David Kauzlaric, "11 Major Challenges of Scaling Operations Explained," SEOReseller, December 6, 2019, accessed April 21, 2025, https://www .seoreseller.com/blog/11-major-challenges-of-scaling-operations -explained/.

216 Join The Collective, "Overcoming Common Challenges in Scaling Operations," January 24, 2024, accessed April 21, 2025, https://www .jointhecollective.com/article/overcoming-common -challenges-in-scaling-operations/.

217 RevOps Careers, "Top RevOps Career Opportunities and Job Market Trends in 2025," February 17, 2025, accessed April 21, 2025, https ://revopscareers.com/blog/top-revops-career-opportunities -and-job-market-trends-in-2025/.

Index

About the Authors

Ryan Westwood

Ryan Westwood is a tech entrepreneur who has successfully exited three companies. Ryan cofounded Simplus, which he grew from $0 to more than $400M. Ryan is currently the CEO of Fullcast, which recently raised a $35M seed round. He has served as a public and private company board director. He has been both Ernst & Young Entrepreneur of the Year and *Utah Business* CEO of the Year.

Amy Osmond Cook, PhD

Amy Osmond Cook, PhD, is a marketing, revenue operations, and communications executive, recognized for her innovative strategies in technology and healthcare marketing.

She is the cofounder and Chief Marketing Officer of Fullcast and has a proven track record helping high-growth companies move from series A through acquisition (Simplus, 2020; PathologyWatch, 2023; Onboard, 2024). Amy founded and led Stage Marketing as

CEO for fifteen years, building it into a leading full-funnel marketing firm before it was acquired by Ampleo in 2024. Amy was recognized by *Utah Business* as a 2024 Business Leader of the Year.

Amy has taught business, writing, and communication courses intermittently for twenty-five years as adjunct faculty at Arizona State University, Brigham Young University, and the University of Utah.

With a PhD in Communication from the University of Utah, Amy has authored numerous articles and served as a prominent voice in business and healthcare communities. Her passion for empowering others is evident in her work and community involvement. She and her husband Jeff have five awesome children.

Bala Balabaskaran

Bala Balabaskaran is a seasoned technologist and entrepreneur with over two decades of experience building scalable enterprise platforms. He has been at the forefront of shaping and operationalizing Revenue Operations—first as Vice President of Go-to-Market Technology and Operations at Salesforce, and now as cofounder and CTO of Fullcast, a category-defining platform that enables organizations to manage their entire revenue engine from *plan to pay*.

At Salesforce, Bala led the rapid automation of internal Go-to-Market systems, aligning technology with sales, support, and service teams. He oversaw the company's annual planning cycle and managed the sales operations function during a period of hypergrowth and ongoing M&A, driving operational agility across the organization.

Driven by the belief that tight alignment between strategy and execution is critical to scaling revenue, Bala cofounded Fullcast in 2016. Since then, he has helped organizations turn complex revenue processes into streamlined, connected systems. His work bridges strategic planning with daily execution, enabling RevOps teams to operate with speed, precision, and confidence.

Bala's technical foundation spans leadership roles in both product engineering and technology operations, having built globally deployed platforms at Microsoft and architected mission-critical infrastructure at HP. He holds multiple patents in software innovation and is widely recognized for building systems that scale from startup agility to enterprise-grade complexity.

Acknowledgments

Amy

Writing this book has been an extraordinary experience. I am grateful to have collaborated with so many professionals providing their incredible expertise in many facets of the book's production.

Thank you to the original research team, especially Spencer Ricks, MA, and Jacob Bingham, MS, who played a crucial role in the research design, data collection and analysis, and in-depth interviews. Thank you for providing a solid foundation for the findings and framework of this book.

Thank you to our esteemed advisors who have provided thought leadership and many practical insights as we have strived to provide an authoritative guide to Revenue Operations. I am especially grateful to Louis Poulin, Whitney Merrill, Erik Charles, Rob Levey, Jared Barol, and others who worked with us on in-depth interviews and whiteboarding sessions to inform specific chapters of this book. The value that you and our other advisors provide to our industry and community cannot be overstated.

A big thanks to Skyhorse Publishing and Simon & Schuster for the publishing and distribution of this book. I am especially grateful to our editor Michael Campbell for his consistent guidance and amazing editorial skills.

I'm grateful for my Fullcast colleagues. Thank you especially to Ryan and Bala, my cofounders and coauthors, who are people I respect and admire both personally and professionally. Special shoutout to our other awesome cofounders, Isaac and Lance, our fantastic executive team, and the crackerjack inside sales and marketing teams I have the privilege of working with every day.

Finally, thank you to my incredible family and friends who have supported me throughout this journey. Jeff, thank you for being a wonderful partner and for making me laugh every day. Thank you, Jacob, Maia, Lizzy, Jenny, and Hailey, for your support, patience and grit as I learned to juggle business calls and carpool rides. I love you with all my heart.

Ryan

I am incredibly fortunate to have been born in America and to have grown up on a farm in the 1980s surrounded by the love of my parents and grandparents, who always prioritized my wellbeing. From the age of eight, I knew I wanted to be an entrepreneur, and starting my career early has been one of the greatest blessings in my life.

My journey would not have been possible without the unwavering support of my wife, who believed in my dreams.

I've been blessed to work alongside incredible cofounders and executives, with a special mention to my brother Isaac Westwood, whose partnership has been invaluable. Our collaboration has been a cornerstone of my success.

A heartfelt thank you goes to Bala and Amy, without whom this book would not have come to fruition. Working with you both has been an amazing experience, and your contributions to writing this book have been nothing short of extraordinary.

To everyone mentioned here, and to the many others who have touched my life in countless ways, I offer my deepest gratitude. Your support has shaped not just this book, but my entire journey.

Bala

To Christ — my redeemer.

To my daughter, Joy — your unconditional love brings meaning to all I do.

To my parents — thank you for your strength, sacrifice, and faith that shaped me.

To my cofounder, Dharmesh — thank you for the support over the years and collaboration on many of the ideas shared in this book.

To Amy and Ryan — thank you for your partnership in bringing this book to life.